DATE DUE

Economy and Society During the French Regime, to 1759

Readings in
Canadian Social History
Volume 1

Edited by
Michael S. Cross
and Gregory S. Kealey

McClelland and Stewart

McClelland and Stewart Limited
The Canadian Publishers
25 Hollinger Road
Toronto, Ontario
M4B 3G2

Canadian Cataloguing in Publication Data

Main entry under title:
Economy and society during the French regime, to 1759

(Readings in Canadian social history; v. 1)
ISBN 0-7710-2455-X

1. Canada – Economic conditions – To 1867 – Addresses,
essays, lectures.* 2. Canada – Social conditions –
To 1867 – Addresses, essays, lectures.* I. Cross,
Michael S., 1938–   III. Kealey, Gregory S., 1948–
III. Series.

FC305.E36	971.01	C82-095232-X
F1030.E36		

Printed and bound in Canada

Contents

Abbreviations / *iv*

General Introduction — The Series / *5*

Introduction to Volume 1 / *9*

I Economic Overview / *15*

Richard Colebrook Harris, The Habitants' Use of the Land / *17*

II Social Structure / *42*

Marcel Trudel, The Beginnings of a Society: Montreal, 1642-1663 / *44*

Fernand Ouellet, Seigneurial Property and Social Groups in the St. Lawrence River Valley, 1663-1760 / *68*

III The Working Class / *86*

Peter N. Moogk, In the Darkness of a Basement: Craftsmen's Associations in Early French Canada / *88*

IV Violence and Protest / *120*

Terence Crowley, "Thunder Gusts": Popular Disturbances in Early French Canada / *122*

V Social Control / *152*

Bruce G. Trigger, The Deadly Harvest: Jesuit Missionaries among the Huron / *154*

VI Native Peoples / *183*

Calvin Martin, The European Impact on the Culture of a Northeastern Algonquian Tribe: An Ecological Interpretation / *185*

Abbreviations

AN   Archives Nationales, France
AQ   Archives du Québec
BRH   *Bulletin des Recherches historiques*
CHR   *Canadian Historical Review*
IOI   Pierre-Georges Roy, *Inventaire des ordonnances des intendants de la Nouvelle-France*, 4 vols. (Beauceville, 1919)
JDCS   *Jugements et déliberations du Conseil souverain de la Nouvelle-France, 1663-1716*, 2 vols. (Quebéc, 1895-91)
OCGI   Pierre-Georges Roy, éd., *Ordonnances, commissions, etc., etc., des gouverneurs et intendants de la Nouvelle-France, 1639-1706*, 2 vols. (Beauceville, 1924)
PAC   Public Archives of Canada, Ottawa
RAPQ   *Rapport de l'Archiviste de la Province de Québec*

General Introduction
– The Series

The emergence of social history has been perhaps the most significant development of the last fifteen years in Canadian historical writing. Historians young and old have brought new approaches and new perspectives to Canada's past, revealing areas previously overlooked and offering new interpretations of old areas. The result has been what historian Ramsay Cook has called the discipline's "golden age." This five-volume series of readers in social history is intended to make the fruits of that "golden age" readily available to teachers, students, and general readers.

Modern social history is an approach rather than a specific subject matter. Where once social history was seen as what was left over after political and economic history was written, social history now is a "global" discipline, which can embrace politics and economics as well as the history of social groups or charitable institutions. The ideal of social history is to write the history of society, to study all of the ways in which people, groups of people, and classes of people interact to produce a society and to create social change. Such a global picture may never be drawn but its goal of an integrated history underlies recent study in Canada. The social historian, then, may write about a small subject over a limited period of time. However, that historian must be conscious of the links to the larger reality; of how local politics, say, indicate the relations of social classes, how they react with ideological assumptions of provincial politicians, how they affect local social customs.

It is a new field and that means its effort has been scattered. Canadian social history has embraced everything from the study of women's groups to computer analysis of population changes to the history of disease. It also has been marked by some sharp differences of opinion. The editors of this series, as practitioners and partisans, make no claim to objectivity in assessing these differences. Broadly, some historians treat social history as an extension of previous historical writing and share its assumptions about the general sweep of Canadian development: its liberal-democratic character; its fluid class structure; its peaceful and orderly growth. Others, however, break from that interpretation and argue for a different picture: a more rigid and influential class structure; a greater degree of conflict and violence; an emphasis on the working class. Which interpretation will prevail remains to be seen. The essays chosen for the series attempt to present as many viewpoints as possible, but the overall structure clearly reflects the judgement of the editors, which favours the second approach, the "working class" approach.

Rather than being structured along the traditional political divisions, the volumes in the series have been organized around dates which seemed most appropriate to social history:

    I New France to the Conquest, 1760

   II Pre-Industrial Canada, from the Conquest to the end of the imperial economic system, 1760 to 1849

 III Canada's Age of Industry, from the coming of the railway to the full flowering of industrialism, 1849 to 1896

 IV The Consolidation of Capitalism, from the beginnings of economic monopoly to the Great Crash, 1896 to 1929

  V The Emergence of the Welfare State, from the origins of large-scale state intervention to the present, 1930 to 1981.

Again, the internal divisions of the volumes have been chosen to illustrate basic themes that represent building blocks in social history. Not all themes could be included and some historians might argue with the particular choices made here. We would suggest several rationales for the selection: these themes seem important to us; the volume of writing and research on them, completed and underway, suggests that many others find them important; and they have proven useful in teaching social history.

Different periods and the availability of good literature require some variance from volume to volume. The general structure, however, is consistent. Each volume begins with an essay on the major economic developments of the period, for we work from the assumption that changing economic forms underlie most social changes. The second theme is that of social structure and social institutions, of the classes and groups of Canadian society and the way in which they interact. This theme will embrace subject matter as diverse as politics, religion, and landholding patterns.

Certain groups have emerged to centre stage historically in recent years. One is workers, the third theme in each volume. Workers and their work have been perhaps the area of richest development in historical writing in the last decade; social history has made its most profound impact in reshaping historical knowledge in this area. The fourth theme is one in which social history has had a similarly important influence, if only because interest in it is so recent. That is violence and protest, now receiving close attention from historians, sociologists, and criminologists. Violence and protest involved many Canadians and touched the lives of many more, and therefore are significant in their own right. However, they also provide a sharply defined picture of the structures and values of the society in which they occurred. The things people consider important enough to fight and protest about give us some indication of the values of particular groups. The attitudes of the leadership of society emerge in the fifth theme, social control. This theme studies the checks placed on violence and protest and inappropriate behaviour, as well as the institutions created to mould appropriate behaviour.

Along with workers, the other group to receive due attention from social history is women. No area, perhaps, was so neglected for so long as the study of women, outside of occasional writing on the suffrage movement. Recently, however, there has been a flood of literature, not just on feminism and women's organizations, but on women's productive and reproductive work. In a field devoted to creation of an integrated picture of society, this is a welcome and exciting development. Some of the trends in women's history, and some of the major achievements, are illustrated in these volumes.

The structure adopted here is offered as a useful one which will open to teachers and to students an exciting area of Canadian studies. It makes no claim to comprehensiveness; it is very much a starting point for that study. The additional readings suggested will help to move beyond that starting point and to introduce the controversies which cannot be reflected adequately in the small number of essays reprinted here. These volumes, however, do serve as a report on some approaches we have found helpful to students of social history and on some of the best literature available in this new field. More, they are collected on the premise that the investigation of social change in Canadian history, the ideas exposed and the questions raised, may allow students to understand more fully the nature of the Canadian society in which they live.

M.S. Cross
G.S. Kealey
Halifax and
St. John's,
July, 1981

Introduction
to Volume 1

New France often has seemed a place apart, the very antithesis of our world. The land of the voyageurs, the Jesuit martyrs, the nobility symbolized by dashing Count Frontenac, it was an intrusion of the mediaeval past into a new world of progress. That it failed, then, was less surprising than that it lasted so long. This picture of New France and its appendage, Acadia, has begun to fade as closer examination reveals a country which was certainly unique, as all countries are, but equally "normal" in its development; it grew with its own logic. This volume presents some of the results of this re-examination.

New France was born out of commercial ambition, for Champlain was an agent for the fur and mineral seekers when he planted colonies at Port Royal in 1605 and Quebec in 1608. Commerce would remain the rationale of New France, a large part of its purpose in the eyes of the mother country. That made it typical of colonies, for Canada would exist as a staple-producing plantation, sending furs and timber and wheat to France and then to England until the mid-nineteenth century. That was not all of New France. To most of her people it was a home and a farm, and the vagaries of international trade and empires were relatively unimportant.

The imperial authority did have a decisive role in the life of New France, however. Competition with the Dutch and the English for furs and the transfer to the colonies of European quarrels meant that New France was perpetually at war. This shaped the colony in many ways. The presence of large numbers of soldiers gave a military cast to its life and added the sophistication and aristocratic views of the officer class. The military also injected large sums of money into the economy and became as important an economic factor as the fur trade. A further stimulus came with the construction of the great fortress at Louisbourg, on a remote tip of what is now Cape Breton Island, beginning in 1720. The fabulous expenditures on the fortress, which amazed and horrified French officialdom, brought prosperity to New France. All of these advantages of the war machine were balanced by the insecurities under which the *Canadiens* were forced to live. The war that knew no end made the colony subject to invasion, as it was when the Kirke brothers captured Quebec, and took Champlain prisoner, in 1629, as it was in 1690 when Frontenac faced down an invading force from the English colonies, as it was when Louisbourg fell in 1745 and again in 1758. And as it was in 1759 when the British attacked the St. Lawrence heartland and took Quebec and, the following year, Montreal.

Despite the military threat the lower classes of New France undoubtedly enjoyed a better material existence than they could have hoped for in old France. It was symbolic of their improvement and their ambitions that they thought of themselves not as peasants, as they would have in Europe, but as *habitants*. Land was readily available and the feudal dues were low. The towns and Louisbourg provided markets for any agricultural surplus. And they had the outlet of the fur trade which provided ready employment for hundreds of young men. The fur trade also represented travel and adventure. Where French peasants were tied to the land, the Canadian *habitants* had a whole continent to wander. Life often was better for the town workers, as well, since the government attempted to attract skilled labour to the colony by making it much faster and easier for men to achieve the status of master artisans than was true at home.

The working class of non-agricultural workers was small in New France, at least as conventionally calculated. However, there was a huge proletariat both inside and outside the colony, that is, the Indians. They were progressively integrated into the economy but kept outside both physically and socially. They were the labourers who manufactured the colony's most valuable product, the beaver pelt. Controlled by the French monopoly on trade goods and often by force of arms, they progressively were stripped of their independence and reduced from merchants, of sorts, to simple workers. As such their economic value to the French was enormous. However, they gave much more. Indian technology, clothing, and food helped the whites to learn quickly how to survive in a severe climate. The natives were the shock troops in the colonial wars and in the continuing struggle with the Iroquois. All the Indians paid a heavy price for their alliances with the French. They suffered heavy losses in war. They disrupted their lifestyles, neglecting agriculture and traditional hunting to pursue the beaver. They were physically debilitated by the twin European curses of disease and alcohol. The Huron, in 1649, paid the ultimate price as their nation was destroyed by the Iroquois. Finally, with grim inevitability, faced with the technologically superior and constitutionally more aggressive whites, the Indians lost their land and their freedom.

The central institution of New France was the New World variant of feudalism, the seigneurial system. As Cole Harris makes clear in the first essay in this volume, the institution changed drastically when transported to Canada. The basics remained. A seigneur was granted a substantial plot of land, which he in turn let to peasants or *censitaires*, as they were known in Canada. In return they agreed to pay certain dues to the seigneur, grind grain at his mill for a fee, and pay other dues and taxes. The short supply of tenants in New France and the government's desire to attract population by easing the conditions for *censitaires* meant that dues were much less onerous than in France. Another major difference from the Old World was in the topography of farm lots. The desire of all to have access to the river, either the St. Lawrence or the Richelieu, created the familiar Quebec strip farms, long narrow lots extending miles back from the river front. Out of that grew certain characteristics of French Canadians. Contact with neighbours could be maintained along the river, without concentrating into villages. This failure to establish villages meant a social life very different from rural France. It meant that it was more difficult for government to exert control over the population. And the strip farms, in the long run, would prove less efficient and would contribute to future agricultural problems in Quebec.

These factors helped create the social structure discussed in the essays by Trudel and Ouellet. While historians still debate how open this society was, how independent the people were, there is no argument that it was far more liberal than the parent French society. The differences were often highly visible. Some

Canadiens aped Indian fashions, with elaborate costumes, tobacco smoking, and freer manners. Horses, unattainable luxuries for French peasants, were symbols of independence in Canada. Critics complained that *habitants* wasted their resources buying these playthings instead of practical oxen or sheep. That, however, missed the spirit of men who no longer were peasants.

New France was never a colony of settlement in the same sense as the British colonies along the Atlantic seaboard. Yet it had some of the characteristics of an established country, among them the three flourishing towns of Quebec, Montreal, and Trois-Rivières and, in Acadia, the fourth large urban centre around the fortress of Louisbourg. Small in absolute terms, the urban population nevertheless represented a larger percentage of the total population than in most western countries. The skilled workers, whose organizations are described by Peter Moogk, were therefore an unusually significant factor in the colony. So, too, were the voyageurs. By the nature of their wandering life and the understandable lack of written records, it is impossible to develop more than a general picture of the social history of the fur traders. Their influences on New France cannot be doubted, however. It was through them, in large measure, that Indian technology was transmitted to the French, all of those artifacts and skills which allowed the European to function in the Canadian climate. They pushed the colony into its reckless expansion west and into conflict with its neighbours. And, with nearly every family having one or more members involved in the trade, their attitudes and lifestyles – unique to this new world – must have infected most habitants.

Few countries have lived so intimately with violence as New France. In 1609 Champlain fired on a party of Iroquois and began the ceaseless war of the next century and a half. It needs little analysis to establish that war profoundly affects a society and that constant war must have done much to shape society in New France. That violence should have spilled over into civil life is quite natural, as Terence Crowley shows in his essay on popular disturbances. The ragtag army, badly paid and fed, treated with brutality by its officers and often with contempt by civilians, was an obvious source of domestic disorder. So, too, were the people themselves in times of economic distress or food shortage. It is perhaps a measure of the success of New France that there was not more violence. The economy was able to satisfy most needs most of the time, so that the endemic protest over economic conditions which marked old France was not a factor in Canada. The political and judicial systems were flexible enough to absorb discontent. The result was that, if anything, New France was less prone to domestic disorder than its successor, nineteenth-century Quebec.

Attempts to establish French dominance over the culture of the Indians are the subject of Bruce Trigger's essay on the Jesuits and the Hurons. Social control, to prevent deviant behaviour and to instill the values of society in the population, is practised in all nations. In New France, as in Huronia, the Church was one of the most important institutions of social control. Under François de Laval-Montmorency, Bishop Laval after 1674, the Church militant attempted to control the moral behaviour of the people and to bend the government to its will. By the end of his episcopacy in 1688 it was clear that Laval had failed to impose a stern Christian morality on the colony. To the end, however, the Catholic Church was an important check on the licence of a frontier society. Government, likewise, was a factor in checking the excesses of such a society. French law crossed the Atlantic with the settlers and assured that the controls of civilization reached out into the wilderness. The elaborate royal government and the military establishment also served as agents of social control, creating a fine balance between France and America in the style of the colony and, probably, in the minds of the people.

The final section, in Calvin Martin's "ecological" study, is concerned with the most pervasive influence on the life of New France, the native peoples. The French made contact with natives from the beginning, from Cartier's first voyage in the early sixteenth century. They made contact with a great variety of Indians: the warlike farmers, the Iroquois; the primitive, wandering Montagnais; the lords of the plains, the Cree; the stubborn and intelligent hunters, the Micmac. These and many more suggest that there was no single pattern of relationship, for the native peoples were as diverse as the European nations. Nor is it enough to feel humanitarian sorrow at what was done to them. It is clear that Indians were conscious actors in the drama. For example, the history of the colony might have been different if Champlain had not been forced to take sides in Indian politics and to do so without adequate knowledge of the implications. He was drawn into war against the Iroquois, the most efficient and implacable war machine on the continent. Joining into the quarrels of its neighbours with the Iroquois doomed New France to suffer a continuing onslaught which bled away its strength. Obviously it is true that the force of white civilization and over-rapid changes it demanded eventually wrecked most native cultures. However, as with the origins of the wars after 1609, the Indians were not passive victims and they influenced the French perhaps nearly as much as the French influenced them.

New France was a world distant in time from our own and distant in many of its social forms. Although vast in geographical terms, as it spilled its traders across North America, it was small in population, limited in economic activity. That makes it a particularly useful area for historical study. In these narrower social and economic perimeters it is easier to measure the impact of various factors. It is easier, in fact, to see how a society is constructed and what contributes to its evolution. Perhaps we even can see how, from the strange plantings of that dim and distant past, our present began its growth.

I
Economic Overview

The economy of New France usually is seen to be synonymous with the fur trade. The trade accounted for the colony's too-rapid expansion across the continent, fur companies supplied the government before direct royal rule was established in 1663, and competition for furs helped keep New France in almost continuous war with England and her colonies. Its importance makes the fur trade an underlying theme in many of the essays in this book and its general outlines are the subject of H.A. Innis's influential book, *The Fur Trade in Canada* (Toronto, 1962), an excerpt from which is found in volume 2 of this series.

The fur trade, however, enriched only outsiders. For the bulk of the population the most important economic activity was agriculture. Cole Harris's description of the organizational form for agriculture, the seigneurial system, is comprehensive; here we reproduce some of his treatment of its direct impact on the life of the people. It was a unique system as it developed, nearly as different from French feudalism as it was from the freehold agriculture of the English colonies. The seigneurial system survived the Conquest and persisted until it finally was abolished in 1854 and replaced by individual, freehold tenure of land.

Harris employs certain French terms throughout. The basic linear measure was the *arpent*, 192 feet. Eighty-four *arpents* made a league of about three miles. A square *arpent* represented five-sixths of an acre. Grain was measured in *minots* of 1.05 bushels. The *roture* was the land grant made to a *habitant*.

FURTHER READING:
More on the fur trade is found in E.E. Rich, *Montreal and the Fur Trade* (Montreal, 1964). For a survey of agriculture, see H.M. Thomas, "Agricultural Policy in New France," *Agricultural History*, IX (1935), 41-60, and E.R. Adair, "The French-Canadian Seigneury," *Canadian Historical Review* [*CHR*], XXXV, 2 (1954), 187-207. International trade is discussed in Dale Miquelon, "Havy and Lefebvre of Quebec: A Case Study of Metropolitan Participation in Canadian Trade, 1730-60," *CHR*, LVI, 1 (1975) 1-24, while an important theoretical discussion of the economy is L.R. MacDonald's "France and New France: The Internal Contradictions," *CHR*, LII, 2 (1971), 121-43.

Works in French include Louise Dechêne's much acclaimed *Habitants et marchands de Montréal au XVIIe siècle* (Montréal, 1974); Jean Hamelin, *Economie et Société en Nouvelle-France* (Québec, 1960); and Marcel Trudel, *Les Débuts du régime seigneurial* (Montréal, 1974).

Richard Colebrook Harris is a geographer at the University of British Columbia.

The Habitants'
Use of the Land

by Richard Colebrook Harris

Because many aspects of the seigneurial geography of early Canada reflected less the influence of the seigneurs and seigneuries than that of the *censitaires* and their *rotures*, it is necessary to examine some of the patterns which developed within seigneuries. The point of departure for this large-scale geography of the seigneurial system is the *roture*, the concession of land which a *censitaire* received from his seigneur. Most of the cleared land in the colony was on *rotures*, most of the colony's agricultural produce came from them, and most of the people in the colony lived on them. The size and shape of *rotures*, the location of them within a seigneury, and the number held by individual *censitaires* – considerations of much relevance to an understanding of the economic as well as of the seigneurial geography of the colony – are discussed in this essay.

Except where *rotures* abutted on a shoreline they were bounded by straight lines, and these lines almost invariably formed approximate rectangles. Probably the oldest extant *roture* contract was the concession in 1637 by Robert Giffard, seigneur of Beauport, of 300 square *arpents* to Noel Langlois. This *roture*, which was to front on the St. Lawrence and extend into the interior between two parallel lines, was roughly rectangular.[1] In

Reprinted from Richard Colebrook Harris, *The Seigneurial System in Early Canada: A Geographical Study* (Madison: University of Wisconsin Press, Québec: les Presses de l'Université Laval, 1968), 117, 119-21, 146, 149-51, 153-5, 157-68. Reprinted by permission of the author and the publisher.

the next decade, all concessions for which record has been preserved were for parcels of land with the river-front dimension a small fraction of the depth. In most cases the ratio was approximately 1:10, although ratios of nearly 1:100 were known.

As fields were extremely irregular in shape throughout much of France, the straight line boundary and characteristic proportion of field breadth to length of 1:10 were not automatically introduced to Canada as part of the settlers' French heritage. To be sure, the open field of the early Middle Ages was divided into long, thin strips, and later, during the period of agricultural prosperity and expansion throughout the last half of the twelfth and thirteenth centuries, street or dike villages (*Waldhufendör-fer, terroir en arête de poisson*) with elongated farms extending at right angles from them appeared in the Netherlands, in Germany, and in northwestern France. In North America sections of the New England proprietary townships were subdivided in long, thin strips, and the strip farm appeared in areas of French settlement in Illinois, Wisconsin, and Louisiana. Whether the Canadian strip farm was copied from those in Europe or in New England (the latter connection is extremely unlikely) or developed independently in a Canadian context is unknown. Certainly there is a connection between the strip farm and an organized approach to agricultural settlement, whether organization was provided by the lord or overseer of a mediaeval manor, by the director of a colonization scheme in East Germany in the thirteenth century, by the proprietors of a New England township, or by seigneurs and royal officials in Canada. In each case, individuals were not completely free to select and to demarcate their own agricultural land; when they were, a hodge-podge of field shapes such as that in colonial Virginia was the result.

Whatever the importance of these considerations, the elongated rectangle with its long axis at right angles to the river and with a width-to-length ratio of approximately 1:10 offered many advantages which help to explain why the rectangular strip appeared so quickly and was modified so little in Canada. These are summarized in the following list.

1. A strip pattern gave frontage on a major transportation artery, whether river or road, to a maximum number of *rotures*. A *censitaire* living along the St. Lawrence was on the colony's main street and was connected to the town markets or to the furs of the interior. When access to the river was complicated by par-

ticularly steep banks or by marshes along the shore, settlement lagged until a road was built away from the river, and then the line of attachment became the road. When all the river front had been conceded, *rotures* lined the roads for the same reason as they had lined the river front. Sometimes the road marked the boundary between ranges; sometimes it cut through the middle of a range; but in either case the ribbon-like *rotures* gave all *censitaires* direct access to it.

2. The rectangle with a low ratio of width to length permitted families to live on their own farms but close to their neighbours. If the rectangle were two *arpents* in width, a *censitaire* could have neighbours on either side almost within a hundred yards, and he could enjoy the convenience and comradeship of close neighbours without a daily trek to his land.

3. The rectangular shape permitted rapid and cheap surveying. A seigneur could divide his seigneury into *rotures* in an afternoon by walking along the shore and driving a stake every so many paces. A chain established the shore dimension precisely. If a *censitaire* had acquired a *roture* adjacent to a previously surveyed concession, and if the back line for the range had been determined, he needed to survey only one straight line to know exactly what land he held. No system could have been easier to employ.

4. The strip pattern, as applied to riverside locations, permitted maximum access to the river for fishing. Throughout the French regime fish taken from the St. Lawrence were an important source of food, and in the years of initial settlement or of poor harvests, life would have been even leaner without them. The narrowness of the *rotures* placed this food source at as many doorsteps as possible.

5. Because the strips cut across the grain of the land, they often included a variety of soil types and vegetation associations. Some concessions began in the natural grassland along the shore of the river, ended a mile or more away and several hundred feet higher in the rocks of the Shield, and in between crossed several slopes and terraces with different soils and plant associations. Not many *rotures* included such a range, but where they did the variety may have commended the strip to its holders; on the other hand, if they wanted a little more of the pasture along the shore and less of the rocks behind, it may have been annoying.

Against these advantages was the fact that a ribbon of land a hundred yards wide and a mile deep was often an awkward unit to farm. The cows might have been pastured in a field a mile or more from the house and the pigs let loose in a woodlot even farther away. A milking might have involved a two-mile walk, an attempt to round up the pigs, even more. Yet most farmers were closer to their livestock than if they walked to their farm every day from a compact agricultural village, and with numerous progeny they should not have lacked for cow- or swineherds. Although service roads on strip farms were longer and took up a larger percentage of the farm area than if the *roture* had been more nearly square, land was seldom scarce during the French regime. If the standard *roture* had been square, the river front would have been quickly conceded, settlement would have been forced away from the river, and an elaborate network of roads would have been required. *Censitaires* would have lived in compact agricultural villages or in isolated farmsteads rather than in the straggling linear villages which became common. Canada would have been a different colony, and probably one that was less well adapted to the valley. It is arguable that strip farms in contemporary Quebec are inefficient anachronisms, but in early Canada probably no other shape would have provided so much net advantage.

Whether or not *rotures* were developed by the original grantees, some land was cleared sooner or later in most of them. Trees were felled and burned or were girdled and left to blow over. In 1636 a Jesuit reported that a man could clear two *arpents* of trees, if not of stumps, in a year,[2] but it is apparent that the rate and amount of clearing varied enormously in different parts of the colony, and even within individual seigneuries. Except in Île Dupas et Chicot, where the farms were small, and in the parish of Sainte-Famille, where the farms were relatively large, there were wide variations in the amount of cleared land per *roture* in each of the seigneuries. Even more striking are the differences in the amount of cleared land per *roture* in different seigneuries. Three decades before the conquest approximately 75 per cent of the *rotures* in the parish of Sainte-Famille contained more than sixty arpents of arable and pasture, whereas in Notre Dame des Anges, La Prairie de la Magdeleine, and Saint-Sulpice, most clearings were patches of twenty-five *arpents* or less. In Beaupré and on the Île de Montréal, the majority of *rotures* contained thirty to sixty *arpents* of cleared land, while in Île Dupas et Chicot the largest clearing on a *roture* was less than twenty *arpents*.

Farms tended to be largest near Quebec and Montreal, where, by 1739, the land had been settled for several generations. As *rotures* near the towns were beginning to be divided by this date, the rapid extension of clearing rather than the appearance of small, submarginal farms appears to have been the first corollary of the subdivision of *rotures*. However, even in the areas of extensive clearing, few *habitants* owned more than 100 *arpents* of arable and pasture. The high price of farm labour, the small market in the colony and abroad for its agricultural products, the absence of primogeniture at the *en censive* level, the checks on sales inherent in the *coutume*, and, near the towns, the growing population pressure which made it steadily more difficult for the ambitious *habitant* to buy additional *rotures* – all militated against these larger farms. In many seigneuries, even a few of those near the towns, no farms were larger than forty or fifty *arpents*, while probably no *habitant* during the French regime ever controlled as much as 200 *arpents* of cleared land.

The amount of cleared land per family was generally smallest in the Government of Trois-Rivières and well below Quebec, both areas in which settlement was relatively recent in 1739. Recency of settlement is undoubtedly the principal explanation of the small farms in Île Dupas et Chicot and of the many farms of a similar size in Saint-Sulpice where, in 1731, settlement along the Assomption River was beginning. On the other hand, in 1739 almost all the settlement along the Richelieu below Chambly was less than fifteen years old, while that along the Chaudière was scarcely five. Settlers were apparently optimistic about the agricultural potential of land in these southward projections of settlement which occupied areas of generally fertile soils and which were connected by road to points on the south shore near Montreal or Quebec. There was apparently less optimism about the future of agriculture and hence less clearing in the Government of Trois-Rivières, where even after the completion in the late 1730's of a through road from Quebec to Montreal, markets for agricultural produce were remote; and along the lower St. Lawrence, where the handicaps of a cool summer and short growing season were added to the problems of marketing.

The small amount of cleared land per family in some of the seigneuries near Quebec and Montreal can be explained neither by recency of settlement nor by problems of marketing. La Prairie de la Magdeleine, the Jesuits' seigneury opposite Montreal, had been settled in the 1670's, but clearings were still small and patchy sixty years later. The difficulty of draining the low, flat land in the seigneury may account for these small farms, but the fact remains that few *habitants* in the seigneury can have sold agricultural produce in the nearby Montreal market. As La Prairie de la Magdeleine lay across the busy fur route from the upper St. Lawrence and Ottawa Rivers to the Richelieu River, Lake Champlain, and Albany, it is a fair guess that the fur trade, rather than agriculture, was the principal interest of most of its population. In Portneuf, fishing is known to have been the first occupation of many *habitants*, as may have been the case in De Maure, a seigneury controlled in 1739 by the Sisters of the Hôtel-Dieu in Quebec and operated in part as a haven for indigent families. The low ratios of arable and pasture per family in the seigneuries immediately north of Quebec reflect the small *rotures*, most of them no larger than forty square *arpents*, which were originally conceded there. An error in the census data may account for the low ratio in Bellechasse, on the south shore opposite the eastern tip of the Île d'Orléans.

Although an average figure for the amount of cleared land per family in Canada during the later years of the French regime is only misleading, it can be said that in those areas near the towns where agriculture was the prime economic activity, most farms contained more than thirty and less than 100 *arpents* of cleared land. Elsewhere farms were generally much smaller, a reflection of recency of settlement, or relatively low assessments of the agricultural potential of the areas, and, in some cases, of conflicting economic interests.

THE FARM OPERATION

The *habitant* in Canada, like most farmers in North America in the seventeenth and early eighteenth centuries, was not abreast of many agricultural practices common in the Europe of his day. No attempts were made in Canada to improve stock by selective breeding, and in the long run the quality of stock in the colony undoubtedly deteriorated. Crop rotation was unknown during the early years when high seed-to-yield ratios – commonly 1:10, and sometimes even 1:25 – were obtained from virgin soils.

Later, although there were occasional reports of crop rotation, probably neither the three-course rotation (wheat or rye followed by barley, oats, or peas, and then by a year of fallow) which was common in northern France, nor the two-course rotation (wheat followed by one or two years of fallow) which was more characteristic of the Midi, became standard practice in Canada. Moreover, there were many reports that the *habitants* did not know what it was to fertilize their land,[3] although there are indications here and there in the documents that manure was occasionally put on the land and that fodder crops were sometimes plowed under.[4] With such slight care soils were soon overworked; reports of soil exhaustion appeared in the 1660's and continued throughout the French regime. Probably *habitants* in Canada planted grains or pulse in a field until the seed-to-yield ratio dropped to approximately 1:3, and then either neglected the field or converted it to meadow. Peter Kalm noted that most Canadian meadows had once been cultivated land,[5] and presumably they were destined to be cultivated again when the soil had regained some of its original fertility.

The abandonment in North America of several fundamental techniques of European agriculture stemmed less from the facts that many of the immigrants had been urban poor in Europe and that, at the level of individual farmers, contacts with Europe ended when the Atlantic was crossed, than from the discovery that land was as plentiful in North America as it was scarce in Europe. In France a peasant with eight or ten *arpents* of land could feed his family and his livestock and produce a modest surplus for sale only if he tended his land carefully. To neglect manuring or to shift a rotation from three to two courses was to court disaster. If an advance in technique resulted in the short run in improved living standards, in the long run it usually led to a smaller farm, and when this contraction took place the peasant could not abandon the innovation.[6] North American agriculture, on the other hand, quickly became extensive. It mattered relatively little if soils in one field were worn out as long as there was empty land nearby. Because agricultural production per man almost certainly rose in North America the change was not necessarily atavistic, but rather a change from one agricultural system to another which lasted as long as land remained plentiful.

Whatever the size of the *habitant's* farm or the methods by which he worked it, wheat was almost invariably his staple crop.

Grains and pulse (peas were a field crop in Canada) were planted on at least nine-tenths of the planted arable in the colony and wheat on approximately three-quarters of it. There was a slight tendency to diversify agricultural production in the eighteenth century, but the percentage of wheat in the total grain and pulse harvest was only a few points lower in 1739 than it had been forty and more years before. Some of this crop was winter wheat, although most was planted in late April or early May soon after the snow left the ground.[7] In either case the harvest came in the first weeks of September, and the level of prosperity in Canada usually varied directly with its size.

In 1739 most of the wheat grown in the colony was produced within a thirty-mile radius of Montreal or Quebec, principally because the population was low and settlement relatively recent farther from the two principal towns. Wheat production per family was between 80 and 130 *minots* in most census units, although there was a concentration of higher yields per family immediately north and east of the Île de Montréal in an area of generally fertile soils close to the Montreal market and a concentration of lower yields per family around Lake Saint-Pierre and in a few seigneuries near Quebec. Yields per *arpent* and seed-to-yield ratios are more difficult to calculate because they must be based on precise estimates which are not available in the documents of the amount of seed sown per *arpent* and of the percentage of cleared land planted in wheat each year. In France in the late Middle Ages approximately two bushels of wheat were sown per acre (1.55 minots per *arpent*);[8] and for want of any other, this figure may be assumed in Canada. The fraction of cleared land in Canada which was planted in wheat varied from place to place, but an average of three-eighths is suggested by the many reports that approximately half of the cleared land (excluding natural prairie) was planted in any given year[9] and by the census totals for the principal crops which indicate that approximately three-quarters of this half was planted in wheat. If the total wheat crop in 1739 is divided by three-eighths of the cleared *arpents* in that year, an average yield per *arpent* of 9.08 bushels is obtained. This figure divided by 1.55 gives an average seed-to-yield ratio of 1:5.8. . . .

It is certain that yields per acre and seed-to-yield ratios in Canada during the French regime compare very unfavourably with contemporary standards and probably were little if any better than those in mediaeval Europe, when seed-to-yield ratios of

1:3 to 1:4 were characteristic.[10] That early Canadian ratios were not still lower is a reflection less of the quality of agricultural techniques than of the fact that some of the arable was fertile virgin land on which seed-to-yield ratios may have been as high as 1:24.

Almost every *habitant* raised peas, oats, and barley. Peas were always a dietary staple, and in the eighteenth century a surplus was exported almost every year to the French West Indies and occasionally to France. Oats were raised for feed, as was the small quantity of barley grown on most farms, although whenever the wheat harvest failed, barley bread appeared on many tables. Some *habitants* planted a little rye. Corn, the mainstay of agriculture in the Indian villages in the colony, was not popular with the *habitants*, who apparently were little more fond of it than of potatoes, with which they were familiar, but which they would not grow.[11] By 1739 many *habitants* in almost every seigneury raised some flax. On the other hand, hemp, which had been in vogue during the first decades of the century when the king had intermittently subsidized its production, had all but disappeared.

Almost every farmhouse had a kitchen garden nearby. Onions, cabbage, lettuce, several varieties of beans, carrots, cucumbers, red beets, common radish and horseradish, parsnips, thyme, and marjoram were all grown in Canada, and probably any *habitant* had planted most of them in his kitchen garden at one time or another. Pumpkins and melons could be raised during the longer summers near Montreal and were common there. Usually there was a patch of tobacco in a corner of the garden. Most adults smoked, as often did boys of ten or twelve years of age.[12] The prosperous in the towns could afford Virginian tobacco; the *habitants* smoked a coarser leaf which they had grown, or which had come from those areas of sandy soils in the Government of Trois-Rivières, where in the eighteenth century some specialization in tobacco production had developed.

Most *habitants* had several fruit trees somewhere on their *rotures*. Apple trees were most common, and much of the crop was converted into a cider which was reported to be the equal of that in Normandy.[13] Plum trees thrived everywhere in the colony. Pears could be grown near Montreal but farther downstream the winters were too severe, as they were everywhere for peaches and apricots.[14] Cherry trees may have been grown here and there, and a few vineyards were planted on sunny southern exposures near Montreal.[15]

Of the approximate half of their cleared land which the *habitants* did not plant in any one year, some was plowed fallow, but most was meadow and pasture. Although there were commons in many seigneuries, and although *habitants* often turned their cattle, sheep, and particularly their swine out to graze in the forests behind their farms, the need to put up a lot of hay to tide livestock over a long winter, and to provide a pasture from which they could not stray into neighbouring fields, led *habitants* to supplement these meadows and pastures with their own. Initially natural meadow along the river was used for both hay and grazing, but when it became insufficient a sizable field in another part of the farm was allocated for these purposes. Other than Peter Kalm's remarks that grass and white clover were planted in the meadows, and that he considered them better than those in the English colonies,[16] there is little information about the quality and carrying capacity of the Canadian meadows.

From the earliest years of the colony, cattle were its most important livestock. In the 1660's most *habitants* owned two or three cows and perhaps an ox, and by the eighteenth century there were five or six cows and one or two oxen on most well-established farms, while the most prosperous *habitants* owned as many as eighteen or twenty head. Cattle were raised primarily for domestic use and provided milk, butter, cheese, and meat for the *habitant's* table and power for his farm operation. There were small surpluses on many farms, and milk, butter, cheese, and occasionally a cow or an ox found their way to the town markets. Most of the cattle in the colony were concentrated near the towns, although this concentration was not as marked as in the case of wheat because livestock could be walked to market. Consequently the average number of cattle per family was not necessarily highest near the towns. In the Government of Quebec the ratios were highest toward the westward margin of the government, and in Beaupré, on the Île d'Orléans, and well below Quebec along the south shore; in the Government of Montreal similar ratios were on the mainland north and south of the Île de Montréal and for some miles to the east toward Lake Saint-Pierre. Areas in which there was a good deal of low, wet land, such as Baie Saint-Paul and Rivière du Sud in the Government of Quebec, or Saint-Sulpice and La Prairie de la Magdeleine in the Government of Montreal, in which wheat production per family was low, were not anomalous in terms of numbers of cattle.

The first horses came to Canada during Talon's intendancy,[17] and before long they were being bought from the New Englanders in such numbers that the Intendant Champigny complained about the money which was draining to the English in return for unneeded horses.[18] But the *habitants* loved hard, fast rides, and at first they kept horses for this pleasure more than for work. Pedestrians were soon protected by an ordinance which fined a rider ten *livres* plus costs for each man he knocked down, and churchgoers were ordered to walk their horses when within ten *arpents* of the church to prevent tangles of carriages or sleighs in the churchyard. As the number of horses increased, some officials became concerned that horses were consuming feed which could be better used for cattle, and for this reason Jacques Raudot ordered in 1709 that no *habitant* was to keep more than two horses and a foal. Because horses had become work animals, Raudot could not ban them altogether. In 1710 he forbade *habitants* to borrow their neighbours' horses for midnight gallops because the horses had to rest after the labour of the day.[19] Later the same year he admitted to the minister in France that horses were needed in Canada for the many farm tasks which they performed more efficiently than oxen.[20] Nevertheless, officials were worried that there was too much riding. The *habitants* were becoming *efféminés*; they were forgetting how to snowshoe and were losing the advantage in winter warfare which they had always held over the English.[21] Probably, however, few *habitants* needed or could maintain more than two horses and a foal, and certainly after the excitement of their arrival had worn off, these horses saw much more service as draft animals on the farm than they did for pleasure riding.

Some sheep were sent to Canada in the first years of royal government, but twenty years later Governor Denonville reported that few *habitants* kept even two or three.[22] Sheep had to be sheltered and fed throughout the winter, and as long as feed was scarce the *habitants* saved whatever they had for their cattle. In 1705 Raudot explained to the minister that the *habitants* did not keep more sheep for this reason, but he pointed out that six sheep ate no more than one cow and were certainly more profitable.[23] Before long many *habitants* had decided as much, and the sheep population rose steadily. In 1739 there were sheep in all developed seigneuries in the colony, although they were not as inevitably present on Canadian farms as either cattle or swine. Areas in which the ratios of wheat and cattle per family were high, such as the south shore near Montreal, contained notably few sheep. On the other hand, in several seigneuries, particularly a number along the south shore in the Government of Quebec, there was some specialization in sheep, although it is uncertain whether the relatively high figures for sheep in these seigneuries reflect several large or many small flocks. Certainly in some parts of the colony few *habitants* owned any sheep; in other areas many *habitants* may have owned four or five, and a few may have had flocks of twenty or thirty.

Because pigs were usually turned out in the forest behind a man's farm or in the streets of one of the towns at night, travellers in Canada seldom saw them. The censuses indicate, however, that pigs were common in all parts of the colony, and that in the eighteenth century most *habitants* had three or four. The only clue in the census of 1739 that there was any specialization in pigs is in the figures for the seigneury of Deschambault, in the Government of Quebec.

Almost all *habitants* kept some poultry. Poultry were not counted in any of the censuses, but the single fact that *rentes* were often paid in part in capons is proof that there were chickens on almost all farms. Turkeys, ducks, and geese were not uncommon.

With the possible exception of the pigs, livestock were quartered indoors from mid-December to late March or early April. In a few cases *habitants* had all-purpose barns in which they kept both hay and livestock, but much more frequently they built three separate structures: a barn in which grain was threshed and hay stored, a stable for cattle *(étable),* and another for horses *(écurie).* Robert-Lionel Séguin has described these buildings carefully,[24] and there is no need to repeat his description here, except to point out that although construction materials were usually planks or squared logs and thatch, they were often purchased by the *habitant*, who frequently hired a carpenter to put up the buildings. Community barn-raisings were rare until the nineteenth century.[25] During the French regime an average barn was approximately thirty feet long and twenty feet wide, and construction costs may have been as much as three to four hundred *livres* in years when money was relatively valuable.[26] The stables were smaller buildings which cost substantially less.

After the few tools which had been shipped from France were broken or lost, the *habitant* made most of his own.[27] He fashioned rakes, picks, and forks entirely from wood but had to buy a saw, an axe, and the blades for his sickle, scythe, and hooking bill *(serape)* which he used to harvest peas. A forge was established in Montreal in 1674 to manufacture these blades, and soon there were blacksmiths and forges scattered through rural Canada. Plows, which were in common use by the 1670's, usually had an iron cutting edge, and the heavy wheel in front of the Canadian plow was often made by a wheelwright. In the eighteenth century a winnowing screen *(crible)* replaced the simpler basket and had to be purchased. Other tools were usually made by the *habitant*, and by the North American standards of the day they were not unduly crude.

Although the labour on the great majority of farms in Canada toward the end of the French regime was supplied entirely by the *habitant* and his family, many *habitants*, perhaps 10 or 15 per cent of them, employed additional help.[28] A few took *engagés* who, like the indentured servants in Virginia, were bound to several years of service in return for their Atlantic passage. Others, although these *habitants* were never very common, owned Negro or Indian slaves.[29] Much more frequently the *habitant* agreed to provide food, clothing, and shelter for the young son or daughter of a neighbour in return for several years of service from the child. A girl would usually stay in the *habitant's* family until she married, a boy until he was old enough to establish his own farm, and to this end the *habitant* with whom he had lived usually agreed to give him a cow when he left.[30] Nor were day labourers or hired hands uncommon, especially toward the end of the French regime when an increasing population reduced the value of labour to the point where a man could be hired for an average yearly wage of approximately 150 *livres*.[31] A prosperous *habitant* was likely to have one or two girls from the neighbourhood living with the family and working about the house with his wife, a boy who performed some household chores and assisted with planting and harvesting, and one or two hired hands.

It is clear from the above pages that there was a wide range in the income which different *habitants* received from their land. At one extreme some *habitants* owned a hundred or more *arpents* of cleared land and hired one or two farm hands; at the other, they lived on a very few cleared *arpents* and, if agriculture was their only livelihood, walked a narrow line between a meagre living and starvation. It may be possible to suggest the amount of cleared land the *habitant* needed before he could begin to market a surplus and the income he might have obtained from a large farm.

Consider a farm of fifteen cleared *arpents*. Approximately three-eighths of the land (between five and six *arpents*) were planted in wheat. Two *arpents* were devoted to grains grown primarily as feed for livestock, to peas, and to a kitchen garden. Most of the remaining land was in meadow, for the live-stock – the horse, the ox, the two or three cows, and one or two pigs – had to be tided over a long winter. Assuming an average yield of nine *minots* per *arpent*, the farm produced approximately fifty *minots* of wheat. Of this, one-sixth was reserved for the next year's seed, one-fourteenth went to pay milling charges, one twenty-sixth went to the Church, and two or three *minots* may have been used to pay the *cens et rentes*. Approximately thirty-four *minots* were left for domestic consumption and sale. An average *habitant* had six people to feed, counting himself, his wife, and four children, and if each of them consumed 400 pounds of flour a year, or just over a pound a day,* then the thirty-four *minots* would be consumed on the farm. The few eggs, the small quantity of milk, and the vegetables from the kitchen garden were probably consumed by the family as well, although Peter Kalm remarked that the poorer people were content with meals of dried bread and water, and took "all other provisions such as butter, cheese, meat, poultry, eggs, etc., to town to get money for them . . . to buy clothes and brandy for themselves and finery for their women."[32] Even if this were true, the sales from such a farm must have been small and intermittent.

Although there were farms of this size in most parts of the col-

---

* An exact figure for the average flour consumption per person in Canada during the French regime cannot be calculated; but the estimate seems conservative in view of the fact that bread was as much the staple of Canadian diet as wheat was the staple of the colony's agriculture. In other bread-eating societies (pre-revolutionary Russia, for example) average flour consumption has been at least this high. Labourers in Canada were occasionally allocated two pounds of flour per day, but the consumption would have been higher than the average for men, women, and children.

ony, their size was not static unless their owners were more interested in fishing, lumbering, or the fur trade than they were in agriculture. Otherwise land clearing proceeded steadily. When the farm reached thirty *arpents* of cleared land, roughly a hundred *minots* of wheat were produced on it, some sixty of which were available for domestic consumption or sale. There were probably one or two horses and as many oxen, five or six cows, three or four pigs, and perhaps a small flock of sheep on such a farm. A fraction of the farm produce – ten or fifteen *minots* of wheat, a pig or a calf, some butter, and perhaps some fruit and vegetables – was sold almost every year. In good years there may have been an income from sales of 200-300 *livres* (assuming average wheat prices); in other years there would be no sales at all.

Those few *habitants* who owned as much as a hundred *arpents* of cleared land were distinctly more prosperous. Such a farm produced just over 300 *minots* of wheat, more than 200 of which remained after the several charges and reserves. There may have been ten or fifteen cows, three or four oxen, three or four horses, half a dozen swine, and perhaps ten sheep. The farm produced a marketable surplus of at least 100 *minots* of grain, a calf or two, as many lambs, a pig, some dairy products, and some fruit and vegetables. The average yearly income from the farm may have been 500 *livres* (again assuming average wheat prices), and it is not difficult to imagine years when the income might have approached 1,000 *livres*. If the owner of the farm was not wealthy, by the standards of the day he was comfortable. Perhaps the *habitants* desired no more and, unlike some of the Puritans, relaxed their labours when they had reached this standard. Be that as it may, there were hurdles in Canada which made it extremely difficult for the *habitant* to farm enough land to become wealthy, however hard he worked or however shrewdly he bargained.

Inevitably the *habitant* began with an uncleared *roture* or, at most, with a farm of average size, for the inheritance system at the *en censive* level ensured that larger holdings should be subdivided. He could, of course, purchase additional land and hire men to farm it. However, labour was always expensive, as was cleared land (its price reflected the labour costs for clearing), and the only justification for these expenditures was a buoyant market for agricultural produce. Herein lay the overriding dilemma of Canadian agriculture. The lower St. Lawrence did not produce an agricultural staple for which there was a French market. Throughout the seventeenth century the only market for the surplus from Canadian farms was the sixth of the population who lived in Quebec, Trois-Rivières, and Montreal, and although by the end of the French regime this market had expanded to 16,000 people, many townsmen still raised most of their own food. In the eighteenth century Canadian wheat, peas, pork, and beef were shipped to Louisbourg or to the French West Indies, but this trade was never large, and in some years it was interrupted altogether. The few seigneurs who, with more capital and better credit than the *habitants*, attempted to establish large, commercial farms bankrupted themselves unless they had an assured market in the members of a religious order.[33] An industrious *habitant* might build up a farm of approximately a hundred cleared *arpents*; he might employ one or two hired hands and live comfortably; but he could hardly become wealthy by either French or colonial British standards.

NON-FARMING OCCUPATIONS

A number of *habitants* were artisans who supplemented their income by doing odd jobs for their neighbours. Blacksmiths, carpenters, wheelwrights, harness-makers, and masons were scattered through rural Canada. These men were usually farmers who practised their trades on the side, and although the ordinary *habitant* was a jack-of-all-trades, he would seek out their special skills from time to time.

Most *habitants* were woodcutters, and many were fishermen. In the early years a man had to clear his land before he could farm it, and later he needed wood for buildings, fences, and fuel. By the beginning of the eighteenth century, wood was scarce in some of the oldest seigneuries, so that for the first time in Canada standing timber had some value.[34] Many *habitants* near Quebec and Montreal began to supplement their incomes by regular sales of firewood,[35] and throughout the eighteenth century there were a very few *habitants* who owned and operated small, water-powered sawmills (mentioned from time to time in the *aveux et dénombrements*) as adjuncts to their principal occupation of farming.

All *habitants* who held *rotures* on the river fished now and then. In the 1650's eels were reported to be so abundant that during September and October two men could take 5,000 or

6,000 each night.[36] If such quantities were not constant, nevertheless eels were caught throughout the French regime. Between Montreal and Quebec *habitants* also fished for salmon, catfish, bar, chad, carp, sturgeon, and many other species.[37] Below Quebec, herring, cod, and porpoises were important. Most *habitants* built fish traps of reeds or branches in shallow water close to the shore,[38] a few fished with lines from canoes or rowboats, and in winter they took large quantities of fish in nets stretched under the ice.[39] Some *habitants* applied for *rotures* only to acquire fishing sites, and every spring others left the banks of the St. Lawrence for the cod fishery in the Gulf or to take up permanent residence in one of the sedentary fishing stations which merchants from Quebec or the mother country had established around the Gaspé shore.

It was the fur trade rather than the fishery which drew the largest number of *habitants* away from the agricultural fringes along the lower St. Lawrence. A season in the woods was an adventure which might be profitable, and throughout the French regime the lure of furs along the upper Ottawa and around the Grand Lac beyond attracted many of Canada's most vigorous youths. From the official point of view, these *coureurs de bois* were an endless headache. They enormously complicated the policing of the fur trade: the value of monopoly privileges in the trade was often seriously reduced by illegal competition, royal taxes were avoided, and a large volume of furs was regularly siphoned off to the English along the Hudson River, who paid more for beaver than any merchants in Quebec.[40] Because many able-bodied men were absent from Canada, the forest was cleared more slowly, and women and children as well as farms were neglected. Several officials reported that with many husbands away the morals of Canadian women had deteriorated almost as far as those of the *coureurs de bois* who changed Indian girls every week.[41]

All officials disapproved of the *coureurs de bois*, but to stop them was another matter. Many ordinances forbade *habitants* to leave their farms without permission. Even a man hunting in the woods could be breaking the law unless he had a pass, and the officials had discovered that hunting passes were likely foils for activities in the fur trade.[42] Fines of as much as 1,500 to 2,000 *livres* were listed for a first offence, the stocks or a whipping for a second, and Frontenac ordered the death penalty for a third offence.[43] At least one man was hanged. These measures, stern as they were, had almost no effect. Canada was a straggling colony spread out for two hundred miles along the St. Lawrence; the wilderness was at almost every back door, the river at the front. The routes out of Canada could not be policed, and the vast majority of the *habitants* who left for the fur country did so with impunity.

In 1679 the Intendant Duchesneau reported that the *coureurs de bois* earned little enough,[44] and a few years later Champigny described their life as one of *"une misère extraordinaire."*[45] If these comments were accurate – and because similar observations were made repeatedly there must have been some truth in them – the attraction of the fur trade for so many *habitants* is not easily explained. Perhaps immigrants who had not been farmers in France accustomed themselves slowly to the routine of a farm. Perhaps the complete independence a man found in the forest, not to mention the charms of willing Indian girls, was compensation enough for many discomforts. Perhaps the fur trade was simply an adventure. But certainly the fur trade was the principal source of most of such wealth as there was in Canada, and if little of it filtered down to the *coureurs de bois*, they could at least hope that it would. Farming presented no better prospects than a full larder and a few luxuries from France; the fur trade appeared to offer more, and the *habitants* were neither the first nor the last in North America to be enticed into the wilderness by this hope.

The attractions of the fur trade were clearest in the seventeenth century when almost no markets existed outside Canada for Canadian agricultural produce, and it was then that officialdom was most exasperated by the *coureurs de bois*. Half or more of the able-bodied men in the colony before 1700 may have spent at least one season along the upper Ottawa. In the eighteenth century, as markets for agricultural produce expanded and the price of furs declined, the fur trade diminished in relative importance. Men still left the lower St. Lawrence for the fur country, perhaps in greater numbers than during the seventeenth century, but they were a much smaller percentage of the Canadian population.[46]

THE HABITANT'S STANDARD OF LIVING

With a farm of thirty cleared *arpents* or more and perhaps some additional revenue from non-farming occupations, the *habitant* and his family were able to live comfortably. To be sure, winter was frequently a time of privation and occasionally in the early years a time of scurvy and death. Although acute shortages could occur whenever shipments of salt did not arrive, or a thaw ruined the meat which had been frozen for the winter, or drought reduced the harvest, these periods of hardship were exceptional in the eighteenth century. "Il n'y en a pas un seul qui ne mange pas de bon pain de froment," wrote the king's engineer Gideon de Catalogne in 1712.[47] Curds were eaten by young and old.[48] Beef, pork, and later mutton were also standard fare for at least part of the year, although it was not true, as Peter Kalm remarked, that "excepting the soup, the salads, and the desserts, all their dishes consist of meat variously prepared."[49] Eggs, poultry, and fish appeared regularly on the *habitant's* table. Vegetables of many varieties, particularly cabbages and onions, were eaten in season. "The common people in Canada," said Peter Kalm, "may be smelled when one passes by them on account of their frequent use of onions."[50] Apples, plums, and pears were plentiful in the fall. The forest yielded berries and nuts as well as some game.[51] A few *habitants* could afford French wines; many more drank Canadian beer or cider, or Canadian bouillon, a decoction brewed from spruce tips which was used from time to time in the fur trade.[52] The *habitants* were usually described as tall, strong, and vigorous, attributes which were as much the reflection of diet as of an invigorating climate and an out-of-doors existence.

In the seventeenth century, the *habitants'* clothes were usually made of material imported from France rather than of furs or skins.[53] Several governors and intendants urged the king's ministers to send hemp and flax seed and many more sheep to Canada, because Canadians were forced to buy French cloth and thread at exorbitant prices.[54] By the beginning of the eighteenth century some *habitants* were making "quelques mauvaises étoffes," and when French officials complained that this manufacture was detrimental to French interests, the Intendant Jacques Raudot retorted that "la moitié des habitants seroient sans chemises" if weaving in Canada were forbidden.[55] Domestic weaving was principally hampered by a shortage of wool or flax. When Madame de Repentigny attempted to establish a small weaving industry in 1709, she experimented with nettles, bark, buffalo hair, and even with the fluff from cottonwood flowers.[56] Clothing in those days can hardly have been elegant. Most *habitants* had one much-patched outfit made of imported cloth, some wore skins or furs, and a few wore cloth which had been woven in Canada. In summer, children were usually very scantily clad, even virtually naked.[57] Later in the eighteenth century when sheep and flax became common, much more cloth was made in Canada. There were spinning wheels in most farmhouses, while a loom, which was much more expensive, was usually shared by several neighbours.[58] The *habitant* bought only some bright cloth and a bonnet for his wife, and perhaps an outfit for himself which he wore to mass or to any other event which required some display.

Most of the first farmhouses in Canada were built of posts driven in the ground (*poteaux en terre*) to make a palisade-like structure which was chinked with clay and eventually covered with boards.[59] The roof was thatch or bark, and the floor was dirt. Very soon, however, farmhouses began to be built of roughly squared logs laid horizontally to meet at rebated corners. Some farmhouses of this French *pièce sur pièce* construction were covered with planks and others were plastered. Inside, floor and ceiling were usually planks. Toward the end of the seventeenth and throughout the eighteenth century, many farmhouses were built of beams and stone (*en colombage*), a type of architecture which resembled Tudor in construction if seldom in finish or elegance. Other houses were made entirely of stone. Their walls were two feet thick, windows were deeply inset and usually covered with paper or parchment,[60] floor and ceiling were planks, and the roof was thatch or boards. Whatever the construction, these farmhouses were rarely more than thirty-five to forty feet long and twenty-five to thirty feet wide. There was always an attic above the ground floor and often a cellar below.

Inside the farmhouse there were usually one or two bedrooms and a kitchen which opened into a dining and sitting room. The *habitant*, his wife, and the baby had a bedroom to themselves. The other children slept in two large beds in the other bedroom or upstairs in the attic, which on a cold winter night was the warmest part of the house. There was at least one large stone or clay fireplace and bake oven and, by the eighteenth century, often a heavy iron stove as well.[61] The *habitant* had purchased the stove, a few pots and pans, and some cutlery, but he made almost all the furniture himself.

In clearing and cultivating his land, in putting up a house, barn, and stable, in making tools and furniture, in fishing and fur trading, the *habitant* was both resourceful and industrious. There can be little doubt that his standard of living was substantially higher than that of most peasants in France, or that it compared favourably with living standards in rural New England. Indeed, however different they may have thought themselves to be, the *habitant* in Canada and the farmer in eighteenth century New England had much in common. At one level similarities can be found in the facts that they were both small-scale, independent farmers, that with the exception of wheat they raised much the same crops, that they manured their land and rotated their crops equally little, that their buildings were similar in size and comforts if distinct in architecture, that in the older areas they faced increasing population pressures on the land and the contraction of farms. At another level there was a common zest for profit. If the conclusions from the study of one frontier township in mid-eighteenth-century Connecticut can be taken as representative, pioneer farmers in eighteenth-century New England appear to have been inveterate speculators who were involved both on and off the farm in an "almost frantic pursuit of a wide variety of projects or schemes."[62] Much the same can be said of the *habitant*, who was often trading land and developing a farm, who was involved in one way or another with the fur trade, who was fishing and occasionally cutting timber. The comparison of the *habitant* and the New England farmer can be pushed too far, but it cannot be too strongly emphasized that the *habitant* in Canada during the French regime was anything but a member of a docile and unenterprising peasantry. If he was not rich the explanation lies less in a lack of drive than in the absence of a large, accessible market for his agricultural produce, and in a legal system which stressed the common good over individual initiative.

Throughout the seventeenth century and into the eighteenth, the *habitant's* way of life was in a state of flux. Land changed hands rapidly: farming held little more attraction than fishing, and often a good deal less than the fur trade. A man was a farmer one year, a trader the next, and often a fisherman on the side. He moved freely within the colony, often selling a *roture* in one area to take up land in another, and he left the colony just as easily, although participation in the fur trade was almost as active along the lower St. Lawrence as in the Ottawa country. Denonville complained that every house in Canada had become a cabaret, and implied that their owners were selling alcohol to

Indians who came to the colony;[63] and some officials denounced the immorality and lawlessness of the *habitants* almost as frequently as they attacked the *coureurs de bois*. Later in the eighteenth century, to be sure, most *habitants* settled into an agricultural routine. A moderately prosperous rural society was emerging, and as land became scarce in older areas near the towns, an attachment to the family land was developing. By this time the fur trade had spread far into the interior, and probably most of its practitioners had forsaken an agricultural life for good. If two social groups were emerging,[64] it is nonetheless clear that the *habitants* remained a vigorous, independent people who differed in occupation but probably little in temperament from the *coureurs de bois*.

NOTES

1. Concession par Robert Giffard à Noel Langlois, 29 June 1637, Lespinasse, notary, in Archives Judiciare de Québec, Pièce détachée.
2. R.G. Thwaites, ed., *The Jesuit Relations and Allied Documents* (Cleveland, 1897), IX, 154-5. In one year twenty men could clear thirty *arpents* suitable for plowing.
3. See, for example, PAC, MG 1, Serie C 11 A, Archives des Colonies, Paris, Correspondence Générale, Canada, VII, De Meulles au Ministre, 28 September 1685.
4. Robert-Lionel Séguin, *L'Equipement de la ferme canadienne au XVIIe et XVIIIe siècles* (Montréal, 1959), 40.
5. A.B. Benson, ed., *The America of 1750: Peter Kalm's Travels in North America* (New York, 1937), II, 458.
6. B.A. Slicher Van Bath, *The Agrarian History of Western Europe, A.D. 500-1850* (London, 1963), 18-23.
7. PAC, MG 1, Serie C 11 A, XXX, Vaudreuil et Raudot au Ministre, 14 November 1708, 3; Séguin, *L'Equipement de la ferme*, 40-2; Nicholas-Gaspard Boucault, "Etat présent du Canada (1754)," in *RAPQ* (1920-21), 20.
8. Slicher Van Bath, *Agrarian History*, 18.
9. See, for example, *RAPQ* (1933-34), M. de la Pause, Rapport sur la population et sur la culture des terres, 1759, 211-12.
10. Slicher Van Bath, *Agrarian History*, 18.
11. Benson, *America of 1750*, II, 438.
12. *Ibid.*, II, 510.
13. *RAPQ* (1920-21), Boucault, "Etat présent," 20.
14. Benson, *America of 1750*, II, 508-9. The engineer Gideon de Catalogne reported peach trees in Canada in 1712, but there can-

not have been many. See PAC, MG 1, Serie C 11 A, XXXIII, Catalogne, Mémoire sur Canada, 7 November 1712, 299. Catalogne's report is printed in full in William B. Munro, ed., *Documents Relating to the Seigniorial Tenure in Canada* (Toronto, 1908), 94-151.

15. Catalogne wrote of cherry trees, but there are few other references to them. The best description of the vineyards is again from Peter Kalm: Benson, *America of 1750*, II, 514.
16. *Ibid.*, II, 458.
17. When Pierre Boucher wrote his description of Canada in 1664 there were still no horses in the colony: Pierre Boucher, *Histoire véritable et naturelle des moeurs et productions du pays de la Nouvelle-France*, ed. by C. Coffin (Montréal, 1882), 137; in English, *Canada in the Seventeenth Century*, ed. by E.L. Montizambert (Montreal, 1873), 70.
18. PAC, MG 1, Serie C 11 A, XVII, Champigny au Ministre, 26 May 1699, 87.
19. These regulations were imposed by a series of ordinances. See *OCGI*, I, 239-40 (Ordonnances contre ceux qui courent à cheval dans les grands chemins, 10 November 1706); II, 54-5 (Ordonnance pour les carioles et chevaux dans les grands chemins, 21 January 1708); III, 74-6 (Ordonnance qui défend aux habitants du gouvernement de Montréal d'avoir chez-eux plus de deux cheveaux et un poulain, 13 June 1709); IV, 4-5 (Ordonnance qui défend aux habitants de prendre les cheveaux des autres, 29 October 1710).
20. PAC, MG 1, Serie C 11 A, XXXI, Vaudreuil et Raudot au Ministre, 2 November 1710, 22.
21. *Ibid.*, Memoire de Vaudreuil à Pontchartrain, 88; *ibid.*, XXXIII, Vaudreuil et Begon au Ministre, 12 November 1712, 32.
22. *Ibid.*, VII, Denonville au Ministre, 13 November 1685, 59. Denonville urged the minister to agree to an ordinance requiring every *habitant* to keep two or three sheep.
23. *Ibid.*, XXII, Raudot au Ministre, 19 November 1705, 288.
24. Séguin, *Les granges du Québec* (Ottawa, 1963), 1-30.
25. *Ibid.*, 113.
26. *Ibid.*, 12.
27. Séguin, *L'Equipement de la ferme*, 9-34; Séguin, "Nos premiers instrument aratoires sont-ils de bois ou de fer?" *Revue d'histoire de l'Amérique française*, XVII, 4 (1964), 531-6.
28. The census taken by the English from 1762 to 1765 lists additional help and these listings suggest the percentage indicated: *RAPQ* (1925-26), 1-143.
29. Marcel Trudel, *L'Esclavage au Canada Français* (Québec, 1960), 156.
30. *OCGI*, I, 311-12 (Ordonnance de l'Intendant, 17 March 1707).

31. Benson, *America of 1750*, II, 411.

32. *Ibid.*, II, 479.

33. J.-N. Fauteux, *Essai sur l'industrie au Canada sous le régime français* (Québec, 1927), II, ch. 4.

34. *OCGI*, I, 183-4 (Les habitants de l'île de Montréal au sujet de la réserve que les seigneurs ont fait dans les concessions pour le bois de chauffage, 2 July 1706).

35. PAC, MG 1, C 11 A, XXXIII, Catalogne, Mémoire, 1712, 277-368; Munro, *Documents*, 138, 140.

36. *Rélations des Jésuites*, XL, 214, cited in Fauteux, *Essai sur l'industrie*, II, 500-1.

37. Boucher, *Histoire*, 19, 44-7; Boucault, "Etat présent," *RAPQ* (1920-21), 14-15.

38. Benson, *America in 1750*, II, 423-4, 494.

39. Boucault, "Etat présent," *RAPQ* (1920-21), 14-15.

40. Jean Lunn, "The Illegal Fur Trade out of New France," Canadian Historical Association *Report* (1939), 61-76.

41. See, for example, the following descriptions of the ills wrought by the *coureurs de bois:* PAC, MG 1, C 11 A, V, Duchesneau au Ministre, 10 November 1679, 52-3; *ibid.*, VII, Denonville au Ministre, 13 November 1685, 42-6; *ibid.*, XI, Mémoire instructif sur le Canada joint à la lettre de M. de Champigny, intendant, 10 May 1691, 468.

42. *Ibid.*, IV, Ordonnance qui défend la chasse hors l'étendue des terres défrichées, 12 May 1678, 276-87.

43. *Ibid.*, Mémoire de Frontenac au Ministre, 170-3.

44. *Ibid.*, V, Duchesneau au Ministre, 10 November 1679, 52-3.

45. *Ibid.*, XI, Mémoire instructif . . ., 468.

46. It may be impossible to determine the number of *habitants* who were attracted to a life, or even to a season, in the forest, but the question of the influence of the fur trade on the development of agricultural Canada, which H.A. Innis (*The Fur Trade in Canada* [Toronto, 1930]) introduced, and W.J. Eccles (*Frontenac: The Courtier Governor* [Toronto, 1959]) has expanded on, still needs a great deal of work. Certainly, the fur trade required a lot of manpower, almost all of which had to come from Canada.

47. PAC, MG 1, C 11 A, XXXIII, Catalogne, Mémoire, 1712, 299.

48. *Ibid.*, XXIV, Raudot au Ministre, 2 November 1706, 90.

49. Benson, *America in 1750*, II, 511.

50. *Ibid.*, II, 510.

51. *OCGI*, I, 433-4 (Ordonnance qui défend à tous les habitants d'aller sur les terres des autres enlever les fruits, 4 August 1707).

52. Boucher, *Histoire*, 71-2; Fauteux, *Essai sur l'industrie*, II, 379-80.

53. Talon established a tannery in the 1660's and, unlike his other industries, it did not collapse when he departed. By the 1680's there were tanneries in Montreal and Quebec: PAC, MG 1, C 11 A, VII,

Denonville au Ministre, 13 November 1685, 54; Fauteux, *Essai sur l'industrie*, II, 405-48.

54. See, for example, PAC, MG 1, C 11 A, VIII, Champigny au Ministre, 16 November 1686, 338.

55. *Ibid.*, XXIV, Raudot au Ministre, 2 November 1706, 87.

56. *Ibid.*, XXII, Mme. de Repentigny au Ministre, 13 October 1705, 348-52.

57. *Ibid.*, VIII, Denonville au Ministre, 8 May 1686, 22.

58. The tools used for carding, spinning, and weaving are best described by Séguin, *L'Equipement de la ferme*, 93-9. The best discussion of the weaving industry during the French regime is in Fauteux, *Essai sur l'industrie*, II, 444-82.

59. On architecture in the colony, see particularly Nora Dawson, *La Vie traditionnelle à Saint-Pierre* (Québec, 1960), 23-9; Gerard Morisset, *L'Architecture en Nouvelle-France* (Québec, 1949).

60. Benson, *America in 1750*, II, 460.

61. *Ibid.* These stoves had been made at the iron works near Trois-Rivières.

62. C.S. Grant, *Democracy in the Connecticut Frontier Town of Kent* (New York, 1961), 29.

63. PAC, MG 1, C 11 A, XI, Mémoire concernant le Canada par Denonville, January, 1690, 319.

64. R.M. Saunders, "The Emergence of the Coureurs de Bois as a Social Type," Canadian Historical Association *Report* (1939), 22-3.

II
Social Structure

All western societies have broad similarities. Pre-industrial
societies shared divisions into aristocracies, bourgeoisies, artisan
classes, labouring classes, peasantries. New France's founding
and growth created certain peculiarities, however, with a powerful military presence and the importance of the fur trade. The
exact nature of the peculiarities has been a matter of debate.
Cole Harris in his work on the seigneurial system has seen the
aristocratic seigneurs as weak and, in fact, not really aristocratic, being drawn from all ranks of society. That fits with a
popular image of the people of New France as an independent
lot, unchecked by authority and therefore much freer than their
counterparts in France. Often it has been suggested that the fur
trade produced this independence, for when men readily could
escape into the woods, they could not be controlled effectively at
home.

The other side is represented by Fernand Ouellet in his essay
below. He, along with W.J. Eccles and Sigmund Diamond, sees
a more traditional and aristocratic society. Equally important is
to understand the elements of the whole society and Marcel
Trudel's article offers a picture of that society at a particular
point in time, just before the establishment of royal government
in 1663. The final goal of this section is to present a sampling of
the work of perhaps the most important French-Canadian historians of our time. Marcel Trudel, an astonishingly prolific
writer, is undoubtedly the greatest influence on this generation
of Quebec historians. Fernand Ouellet made his reputation

writing on a later period, from the Conquest to 1850, and established the standards for a new economic and social history based on statistical analysis. More recently he has begun to apply those techniques to New France.

FURTHER READING:
Details on the population are given in Bertrand Desjardins *et al.*, "Automatic Family Reconstitution: The French-Canadian Seventeenth Century Experience," *Journal of Family History*, II, 2 (1977), 56-76. Excellent and controversial general studies are: Sigmund Diamond, "An Experiment in Feudalism: French Canada in the Seventeenth Century," *William and Mary Quarterly*, third series, XVIII (1961), 3-34; W.J. Eccles, "The Social, Economic, and Political Significance of the Military Establishment in New France," *CHR*, LII, 1 (1971), 1-21. A local study but with general significance is Robert J. Morgan and Terrence D. MacLean, "Social Structure and Life in Louisbourg," *Canada: An Historical Magazine*, I, 4 (1974), 61-75.

In French, Ouellet's "Officiers de milice et structure sociale au Québec (1660-1815)," *Histoire sociale*, XII, 23 (1979), 37-65, and Robert-Lionel Séguin, *L'habitant aux XVIIe et XVIIIe siècle* (Québec, 1964), are useful.

Marcel Trudel and **Fernand Ouellet** are professors of history at Université d'Ottawa.

The Beginnings of a Society: Montreal, 1642-1663

by Marcel Trudel

Because Montreal was geographically isolated and because she wanted independence from the rest of the Laurentian colony, her foundation furnishes us with a rare occasion for studying, in a milieu of almost complete solitude and at the most advanced point toward the interior of the continent, the formation and development of a society. Our study fits between quite precise limits: 1642, which marked the establishment of a small group of Europeans on the Île de Montréal, and 1663, the last year of an independent existence because from 1663 the parent country put into operation a system which henceforth integrated Montreal into the society of the St. Lawrence. Furthermore, the colonists who arrived after the establishment of this new regime rapidly modified the traits which had until then characterized the Montreal colony.

Of this population which lived isolated from the other Laurentian establishments we will here content ourselves to observe certain social customs: the practices of the group in regard to marriage; the time of marriages and births; the prestige of godparenting; nobility and class consciousness; the formation of the merchants' group; the situation of the lower class; the ascension of "the new men."

Translation from the French of Marcel Trudel, "Les débuts d'une société: Montréal, 1642-1663 – Étude de certains comportements sociaux," *Revue d'histoire de l'Amérique française,* XXIII, 2 (1969), 185-206. Reprinted by permission of l'Institut d'histoire de l'Amérique Française.

THE SEARCH FOR A SPOUSE

The business of marriage had been slow to get underway; it did not begin until five years after the foundation of Ville-Marie. For six years marriage there remained altogether an outstanding event in the year; it occurred three times, then twice, then once, then, as in 1653, not at all. From 1654, evidently due to the immigration of the preceding year, marriage became a more frequent ceremony. In total in these twenty-one years, we count seventy-nine marriages contracted in Montreal; we add to that six marriages contracted in Quebec and at Trois-Rivières by Montrealers who subsequently returned home with their spouses. It is thus on these eighty-five marriages that our observations rest.

None of these couples was mixed from the racial standpoint. Although Montreal marked the furthest point of European penetration no one there had yet contracted a marriage between a person of European origin and one of Amerindian origin, although at Trois-Rivières we know of two Frenchmen who in the course of this period were united in marriage to natives (Pierre Boucher and Pierre Couc *dit* Lafleur). This absence of intermarriage at Montreal was not the result of a systematic opposition to racial mixing; it was, we believe, that at Montreal one did not come as close to Amerindians as at Trois-Rivières, where an important colony of Montagnais and Algonquins had established itself right next to the French.

If the Montrealers never went to seek wives in the Amerindian tribes, they rarely went either to seek them in the other French establishments of the St. Lawrence: one counts but six marriages (of eighty-five) contracted by Montrealers outside of their colony in this period of twenty-one years. One would have expected much more since the population of Montreal, long of negligible size, was not able to renew its own human resources. Except for the six who went to seek wives at Trois-Rivières and at Quebec, the Montrealers awaited patiently the coming of the immigrants; and on the other hand no one from Trois-Rivières or from Quebec went to Montreal to appropriate for himself one or another of the all too rare new feminine recruits. This was perhaps due to the sedentariness which was characteristic of the French of the Old Regime, the peasant hardly going to seek marriage outside the district where he lived. This was perhaps also due to the remoteness of Montreal – a couple of days from

Trois-Rivières and three or four from Quebec. In any case this situation seems to us to characterize accurately the distance the Montrealers took care to guard in reference to the other French people of the St. Lawrence.

Thus the Montrealers married among themselves. One might assume that couples united on the basis of affinities of origin – that such-and-such a young man sought out a certain young lady because she came from the same province as he. Our inquiry leads us to conclude the contrary. In fact, of seventy-nine couples (out of eighty-five) for whom we know the provincial origins, there are but fourteen who had originated from the same province; for the rest, these couples came from the provinces that had furnished Montreal with the greatest number of immigrants: Normandy furnished five couples; Anjou, Aunis, the Île-de-France, and Poitou furnished the nine others. The partners of sixty-five couples came from different provincial milieux: that gives evidence of the mixing of the population which was accomplished in a situation as restricted as that of Montreal.

It does not seem that couples sought to form marriages within a close degree of kinship; to be sure we see Jacques Le Ber marry Jeanne Le Moyne on 7 January 1658, and Anne, sister of the latter, marrying, on the following 25 February, Michel Messier, nephew of Jacques Messier and related by marriage to Charles Le Moyne. But neither in these two cases nor in any of the eighty-five Montreal marriages was it necessary to obtain a dispensation for consanguinity.

Were the marriage partners of the same social level? Here we are, in short, reduced to an approximation: the documents are imprecise in this area to the point where it becomes impossible to judge of qualifications which one or another person claimed for himself or his parents. It was, in particular, a practice of the notary Basset to transform *dit* in a name to *de* and to precede the *de* with a *Sieur* (capitalized), even when he had before him a joiner or a mason; likewise, he gave the title *Ecuyer* (Squire) to people for whom ennoblement did not follow until long after. Another difficulty: how to know if one is observing at Montreal the hierarchy which in France classed trades according to a rigorous scale. This is why, somewhat lacking perspective, we have put the trades and professions on the same footing.

Understanding a little better the social strata, of seventy-nine of the eighty-five couples we can show that among seventy-four of them there was social equality between the marriage partners: tradesmen or labourers united with the daughters of tradesmen or of labourers; and the equality could be as exact as in the case of the surgeon (the surgeon being then no more than a man of trade skilled at cutting flesh) who married the daughter of a butcher. At a more elevated level we notice that the merchant Jacques Le Ber married Jeanne Le Moyne, daughter of a hotel-keeper and sister of merchants. These married couples each established themselves at the same social level.

Thus at Montreal endogamy* was the most frequent practice; this general rule, it appears, would apply similarly to the nobles although they were not sufficiently numerous to permit us such a generalization. Of seventy-nine couples we know of only five exceptional cases: two of hypergamy** and three of hypogamy.** Two husbands allied themselves to wives of superior rank: the soldier Pierre Raguideau, son of a sergeant, married the daughter of a middle-class Parisian merchant; Louis Gueretin, a maker of wooden shoes, had for a wife the daughter of a Parisian merchant. But here hypergamy might be no more than fictive if the wife felt herself removed from the more elevated milieu that she had become used to as she developed. Three of the alliances stem from hypogamy and can, at first view, appear to be misalliances: Jean de Saint-Père, noble and notary, in 1651 married Mathurine Godé, daughter of a joiner; Jacques Le Moyne, merchant and son of a hotel-keeper, in 1658 married this same Mathurine Godé, who had become a widow. However, it is necessary to add that Le Moyne had only just gained access to commerce and that the father-in-law carried the title of master joiner. The third misalliance would be that of Gabriel Celle du Clos. If his nobility were real[1] he would have been misallied in marrying Barbe Poisson, a commoner of Perche and widow of a commoner. However, Celle du Clos would hardly have a glittering nobility: he lived on the land like a simple *habitant*, without attempting commerce, and he did not know how to sign his name, no more than did his spouse. Whatever may have happened in these cases, while marriages created a mixture of provincial groups there does not seem to have been before 1663 a mixture of social groups: one married within one's group.

---

* Marriage within one's own group. [editors' note]

** Customs permitting men, in the first case, and women, in the second, to marry above their social rank. [editors' note]

We have been struck by the great age disparity among the partners. Our study on this point rests on seventy-four of the eighty-five couples formed at Montreal, the others having been left aside because the age of one of the partners was missing. The women married young, at an average age of 20.9 years, which is younger by four or five years than certain comparable groups in France. This gave promise of long fertility. Of seventy-four wives for whom we know the age, sixty-nine contracted marriage before the age of thirty-one; six married at the age of twelve; eleven among them were but thirteen or fourteen years old. At twenty-one years of age Catherine Larion was already on her third marriage. Marie Pontonier had yet more experience: married at fourteen, she was liberated by annulment in 1660; she remarried right away and found herself five months afterward without a mate; at her third marriage in 1661, she was but eighteen years old. With the women, if they remarried in some rare cases after the age of thirty, they never married at all past forty-five years old. With the men, without their marrying later (there was a single marriage among the men aged forty-five to fifty), marriage was much less precocious: only two men married at less than twenty-one years of age. Furthermore, the minimum required age for men to marry was fixed at fourteen years. The majority of husbands (sixty-two out of seventy-four) were from twenty-one to thirty-four years old at the time of their marriage.

Very rare, then, were partners of the same age: equality existed between but four of the seventy-four couples. With the others the disparity could be from one year to twenty-seven years. The cases of great disparity are numerous: with thirty-four couples the disparity ranged from ten to twenty years. In addition, Etienne Bouchard was twenty-one years older than his spouse; Blaise Jiullet was twenty-three years older; Lambert Closse comes safely first with a seniority of twenty-seven years. But one also finds some husbands younger than their wives. Of these we know nine cases, of which certain ones are surprising, unless the documentation has led us into error: Laurent Archambault, married at eighteen years, would be eight years younger than his wife; Guillaume Estienne and François Royné were at least ten years younger. These were, on the whole, the men who extended and enlarged the statistics: the average age of male Montrealers at marriage was 29.2 years (which corresponds a little more closely to what one knows of group studies in France) while that of women was only 20.9 years. This disparity of age favouring the man is evidently explained by the obligation of the husband to provide for the needs of the spouse, but the youth of the female immigration also accounts for a part.

NOVEMBER, THE MONTH OF MARRIAGES; AUGUST, THE MONTH OF BIRTHS

Never preceded by engagements, so it seems (engagements were well on the way to disappearing in Europe), but almost always accompanied by a contract, the seventy-nine marriages consecrated right in Montreal did not take place at just any time of year: the Church had its regulations on that to which were added the various requirements of the material world. Advent and Lent were forbidden times, except by dispensation. In fact, in these twenty-one years there never was a marriage in Lent; we count but two during the time of Advent (9 December 1658 and 9 December 1661), a dispensation having been obtained in each case.

If we redivide these seventy-nine marriages according to the chronological order of the calendar year we establish that January accounts for ten; then the frequency of marriage falls back a little in February and March: only two marriages in each of these months; and folk married very little in the course of the spring: three marriages in April, two in May. The coming of summer changed nothing. June had but three marriages, and July is the month of the year when they married the least: in twenty-one years there was only a single marriage in July, and here as during Advent it was a matter of a marriage having become urgent by an all-too-apparent pregnancy. Nuptials picked up in August (five marriages), and then the activity accelerated (thirteen in September and twelve in October) to reach its peak in November: twenty-three marriages. Finally, there was a sharp falling off in December when only three marriages were registered.

It thus seems that rather than conforming to the prohibitions of the Church, marriage was subject to a seasonal movement: no nuptials in the course of spring and the first part of summer. The busiest time of marriage presented itself in autumn: the great voyage having been accomplished, the female recruits for the colony arrived at this point, and, supposing they had been there for some weeks, there might well have been time for one to make their acquaintance. In autumn, too, one probably was paid the balance of the revenues due from the trade in furs. In any case, it was necessary to do things quickly – Advent was not far away.

In the natural progression of things, the monthly distribution of the 165 births of these seventy-nine marriages followed, with the necessary interval of nine months, a similar curve to that of the marriages: July marked the thinnest time for marriages; March of the following year also marked the leanest time for births. November, the peak in marriages, corresponded to the following August, the peak in births.

It is almost the same if we consider all together the 218 births, the offspring of the marriages contracted by Montrealers and by immigrant couples. In distributing these 218 births over the twelve months of the year we see that their number, from nineteen in January, diminishes to reach the low in May (eleven births); it climbs again rapidly until August to mark the highest point of the year (twenty-five births); it dips in September, climbs back a little until November (twenty-four births), to fall again to the level of September. It thus follows that the fruitful procreation, very active in January and February, diminished afterwards in March and more again in the course of the summer (August marking the slimmest time: this was besides the great month for confinements). Fruitful procreation picked up in September to attain in November a peak a little higher than that of February. Here again we are tempted to establish a relation between this periodic movement and the religious calendar: the two peaks of fruitful procreativity are both situated at the end of a long period of penitence: Advent and Lent. It must have been recommended – as was done in the *Rituel* of Mgr. de Saint-Vallier – to married couples that they abstain then from sexual relations.[2]

GODPARENTING

Because of the imprecision of the notation *recens natum*, as they ordinarily described infants in the registers, it is impossible to know if the Montrealers hastened to present the newly born for baptism. We are better informed of the sponsorship. Here this was an honour in great demand, at least in these early years; the more restrictive the milieu, the more godparenting, it seems, held honoured importance. We must, moreover, recall that the first Montrealers had come in an apostolic spirit: to be a godfather or godmother concretized in some way a pious dream. During the first five years, from 1642 to 1647, no one was baptized except Amerindians. Of course, the first year, only four received baptism because they had not had time to prepare longer for the sacrament. The first mystics knew a success in 1643 which far surpassed their hopes: they baptized seventy-eight Amerindians of whom only eight were young children. The year 1644 is almost empty because they had baptized all the available recruits the preceding year, but 1645 marked a comeback: twenty-nine baptisms. A decrease followed, then a new peak in 1651 with thirty-seven baptisms of Amerindians; after that one finds them in the registers only from time to time: the Jesuits perhaps kept separate registers which have not been recovered.

In all cases, the 124 baptisms of Amerindians which were carried out from 1642 to 1647 procured for these apostolic souls many occasions for being the spiritual parents of converted "savages." As thirty-six of these baptisms were made without godfather or godmother, there remain eighty-eight baptisms of Amerindians for whom we have documentation of the sponsorship. For the four baptisms of 1642 the sponsorship was held by but two persons: Chomedey, the first (as he must have been) to serve as godfather and who held the position two other times; and Madame de La Peltrie, godmother of the second baptism. In 1643 for the seventy-eight baptisms of Amerindians, one counts 110 acts of sponsorship, undertaken not by 110 persons but by only thirty-one; and of these thirty-one people who stood as godparents in 1643, there were outstanding ones who took unto themselves the larger part. Thus, thirty-two acts of sponsorship were accomplished by twenty-two lower-class people; seventy-eight acts by only nine persons, but these nine dominant ones constituted the dynamic element in this missionary foundation. In 1645, of ten instances of godparenting only three were reserved to the lower class; in 1646, the eight acts of sponsorship were almost all reserved for the dominant ones, in particular for Jeanne Mance, Madame de La Peltrie, and Madame de Boullongne: one sees appearing only two members of the lower class. In these first five years two-thirds of the acts of sponsorship pertained to the dominant figures: Jeanne Mance acted as godmother thirty-one times; Madame de La Peltrie, twenty-one times; Madame de Boullongne, thirteen times. Among themselves, these three accounted for nearly half of all the acts.

Later this behaviour was going to change, at first because baptisms of Amerindians became less and less numerous (to judge of it solely by the registers); then, because for the baptisms of European infants occurring from 1648 on, familial relations came to introduce different customs. The lower-class folk acted as godfathers and godmothers more and more often, to the point that they ended up by counting for 60 per cent of the 621 acts of sponsorship. It is significant all the same that 24.5 per cent of this godparenting involved the nobility, represented here nevertheless by only fifteen adults.

Although the recruitment of godfathers and godmothers tended to grow with the years, certain persons, duly marked so to speak for the vocation of godparenting, returned regularly to the baptistry. In this devoted course of action it was Jeanne Mance who carried the honours with a percentage of 20.7 (of a total of 353 baptisms where there were godparents, she acted as godmother seventy-three times), thus advancing well beyond her closest contender, Chomedey, who reaped but 12.2 per cent of the acts of godparenting: notwithstanding, a high percentage in the case of Chomedey since this governor had been absent from the country during six of the winters. Madame de La Peltrie and Madame de Boullongne each registered twenty-four certificates of godparenting, but as Madame de La Peltrie had been in Montreal only eighteen months she had accumulated in these eighteen months as much as the other had in nine years!

A fact repeated from time to time in the Church ceremonies was that godfathers and godmothers were not necessarily of the same social level. Certainly, in the cases of Chomedey and Jeanne Mance, the association (which presented itself eighteen times) appeared normal: Chomedey was of the lesser nobility; Jeanne Mance came from a family of lawyers. They were both from the province of Champagne and manifested the same dynamism of authority. Furthermore, social disparity was usual in the baptism of the commoners. One frequently encounters a noble godfather and a commoner godmother. What surprises us more are the commoner godfathers with the noble godmothers: the joiner Nicolas Godé with Madame de La Peltrie; with her again, Pierre Quesnel and the carpenter Gilbert Barbier. In 1656 the same Godé had for fellow-sponsor Madame de Boullongne;

the latter returned to the baptistry in 1659 with the baker Jean Gervaise. Each time, when it was a matter of an infant of the nobility, the social parity seems correct. If we examine the cases of eleven infants of nobles who lived at Montreal in June of 1663, we verify that eight of them had for godfathers and god-mothers representatives of the hierarchy or members of the nobility; the exceptions are the three children of Celle du Clos (whose nobility appears doubtful to us), but two of these children all the same had had, each of them, at least one noble sponsor.

NOBILITY AND GROUP CONSCIOUSNESS

A little colony transplanted from Europe in an isolated place, did the establishment of Montreal reunite and conserve there in a sort of microcosm the traditional framework of the European society? Let us not try to find again here the orders (clergy, nobility, and third estate) such as they existed juridically in France. Pushed here and there in the diverse social strata ac-cording to the hazards of recruitment, the immigrants could assuredly not give a systematic representation of these three orders. Let us see, however, which elements of the French so-ciety are met again at Montreal in June of 1663 and how these elements interacted among themselves.

In this little society which counted 605 persons[3] at the end of June 1663, the clergy had but three representatives: two Sulpi-cians in residence (Soüart and Galinier) and a travelling Jesuit (Chaumonot). In France these simple priests would not have en-joyed any particular dignity in the clerical order; none of them, further, was part of the nobility. As for the feminine religious, there were only as yet the *filles séculières* who devoted themselves to Church work. The most eminent of these secular daughters, as much by virtue of her role as a hospitaler as by her determined participation in the establishing of Montreal, Jeanne Mance, had as her principal function the administration of the *Hôtel-Dieu*. From 1659 we have in this house a little community of four members: the *Congregation de Religieuses hospitalières de Saint Joseph*. They were not yet cloistered; nor, living in secular dress, were they wimpled or veiled.[4] The three female religious from France, directed by a superior who was of the nobility, were more than forty years old, but they recently had

had join them a young recruit from Quebec, Marie Morin, aged only fourteen years. Another secular community, also very recent, the *Filles séculières de la Congrégation de Notre-Dame*, had begun its work of education: they, too, were in the secular state, without vows or regular habits. Whereas the personnel of the *Hôtel-Dieu* had an average age of 42.7 years, the four *Filles de la Congrégation* were on the average not so old: thirty-four years.

Just as the first order (the clergy) had only such representation as was due to chance, likewise there were circumstances in Montreal which reunited a certain number of people of quality: in June of 1663 we count there thirty nobles.[5] If it is true that the d'Ailleboust family was of a slightly elevated nobility, the others, whatever the function that they filled, seem to have issued from the least considerable stratum of the French nobility: Chomedey, Closse, and Dupuy were of that category; the Artis de Sailly family, for example, and above all the Celle du Clos family are difficult to distinguish from the common class.

What was the social behaviour of these nobles? If no land was without a seigneur, it is also true to say that in France there was no noble without land. The title of nobility attached itself to a landholding as to the revenues which were to be drawn from it. Did the Montreal nobles in 1663 correspond to this European situation? The hospitaler is being excluded from these statistics because she was an integral part of a religious community. We find that the most eminent of these nobles (the widow d'Ailleboust and the d'Ailleboust des Muceaux family) possessed Canadian land under seigneurial title; it was the same for the widow Closse of the lesser nobility. Others of the lesser nobility, Celle du Clos and Robutel de Saint-André, had land but only in taxable terms; the others did not yet have land, at least not in Canada: Artus de Sailly, Chomedey de Maisonneuve, Zacharie Dupuy, Catherine Gauchet, Marie Moyen, Madeleine Mullois de La Borde, Perrine Picoté de Belestre, and Agathe de Saint-Père. Counting women and children we thus find eighteen out of thirty nobles who had an agricultural base. This does not suggest that the nobles without land revenues lived less nobly than the others: the military functions proper to the nobility were suited naturally to Chomedey and Dupuy. Louis Artus de Sailly and Claude Robutel de Saint-André were in "merchandising," an occupation which, beginning to be of good reputation in Montreal, augmented the prestige of those who practised it. Artus de Sailly had begun to trade in Martinique, but we do not know where he stood in business before 1663. As regards Robutel de Saint-André, he had already won respect; in 1660 he purchased at a price of 1,000 *livres* the house of Jean Desroches to whom he immediately paid 500 *livres* in merchandise from France; and in 1661 Chomedey conferred on him the right to collect taxes. For the lesser noble Celle du Clos, a taxpayer like Robutel, the notarial minutes do not teach us enough to observe his rank in life.

In the aggregate these nobles were "lettered": of fourteen adults whom we count we can from this point of view judge all of them, and of these fourteen a single one, Celle du Clos, did not know how to sign his name. As half of the adult population in June 1663 did not know the alphabet, we can conclude that the nobles held their rank well in that society.

The nobles enjoyed the consideration that their noble rank conferred upon them. Certainly, in the course of the period we are studying (1642-1663) no noble was elected churchwarden, perhaps because churchwardenship (*marguilliage*) was as yet nothing more than a simple office, a bookkeeper without prestige; furthermore, if in the confirmation ceremony of August 1660 Chomedey and Closse came at the head, being then at the top of the hierarchy, the noble Zacharie Dupuy is placed as if by chance among the commoners, but the lists of confirmation ordinarily do not take social distinctions into account. Otherwise we encounter the nobles in the first class, which was their due. When it came to mastery at arms it was the nobles who occupied the highest posts: Chomedey, Closse, Dupuy, and d'Ailleboust des Muceaux presiding over the military life of the colony. Was it necessary to command the *habitants* who were organized into a militia in February of 1663? The *habitants* were raised by Chomedey and Dupuy, but this militia was subdivided into twenty squads, and each one elected its leader by majority vote: were the militiamen going to seek out the command of the nobles? Of nobles who did not make a career in arms and who consequently were subject to service in the militia, there were but three: Artus de Sailly, Celle du Clos, and Robutel de Saint-André; but then, these three nobles had been elected by the militiamen to direct squads, so that in the militia no noble was subordinate to a commoner. We do not believe that this was due to chance.

Furthermore, the nobles were sought out to serve as witnesses whether at marriages or baptisms. In the marriage records, of 289 recorded witnesses, nobles were nevertheless but a small minority, numbering seventy-seven, that is to say 26.6 per cent. Their contribution is again more considerable in the godparenting of commoner children: ninety out of 203 of these infants, being 44.3 per cent, had at least a godfather or a godmother chosen from the nobles.

With respect to the practice of endogamy among the nobles it was too soon in 1663 to judge it because the information that one can cull is too meagre. Indeed, of fourteen adult nobles we find seven who were unmarried, of whom one was a religious; of the nobles who were married or who remained widowed, five marriages seem to have been of the same social level; a single one was contracted with a partner of an inferior class: Celle du Clos married a commoner at Montreal in 1651; the mother of Agathe de Saint-Père was of the common class and remarried in the common class. Rather then attributing these exceptions to an absence of class consciousness might they not have been simply the result of the scarcity of nobles? This we are inclined to believe when we see Robutel de Saint-André taking advantage of a voyage to France to marry there a daughter of the nobility.

The place where the nobles seem to us to operate in full consciousness of class is at the baptismal fonts. Already, in the span of the Amerindian godchildren from 1642 to 1649, the nobility, represented by certain special individuals, had easily taken the lead: in the years 1642, 1644, 1645, and 1646 the nobles had reserved to themselves nineteen of twenty-six acts of sponsorship; in the totality for the period 1642-1649 they stood as godparents in seventy-five of 123 instances, being 61 per cent. The intervention of nobles again appears more systematic in the godparenting of children of the nobility: of these eleven children, offspring of the nobles of Montreal and who were still living in June 1663, eight had godfather and godmother in the nobility; two children of Celle du Clos had at least a godfather or godmother who was of the nobility; a third child of the same Celle du Clos, the only one in this case, had entirely common godparents, and we notice here as well that the godmother was the widow of a noble.

A GROUP IN FORMATION: THE MERCHANTS

This consciousness of class that we have been trying to perceive among the nobles, even though we have too few cases to consider – can we find it in another stratum of society which corresponds to the third estate in France?

Here, as in France, we encounter the superior part of this stratum, a dynamic element, the merchants. Because Montreal was always directed by men of missionary zeal and because this colony had no right to its own store until 1655, the merchant group had not yet formed except for certain individuals. Outside of Robutel de Saint-André and Artus de Sailly, whom we have mentioned in connection with the nobility and whom we here leave aside, we have in June of 1663 Jean Aubuchon *dit* L'Espérance, Marc-Antoine Galibert *dit* des Colombiers, Jacques Le Ber *dit* Larose, the brothers Charles and Jacques Le Moyne, André Charly, Jean Gervaise, and Jacques Testard, the latter coming just prior to his death.[6] Numbering only eight, they had taken upon themselves qualities of merchants quite recently: Charles Le Moyne in 1657, Le Ber and Jacques Le Moyne in 1658, Charly in 1659, Aubuchon, Galibert, and Testard in 1660, Gervaise in 1662. Prior to the time that the documentation reveals this characteristic to us, they doubtless had been in merchandising, but this could not have been over a long period of time: truly we are in attendance at the birth of a social group. However, because the merchants are a recent creation, the notarial records are not yet numerous enough to enlighten us on their affairs; in the same way, the contractual alliance between Charles Le Moyne and Médard Chouart des Groseilliers in regard to the western fur trade in 1660[7] is of too brief a character. In all cases the archives before 1663 do not at all permit us to follow the evolution of business enterprise, nor, with stronger reason, the progress of these merchants.

We are able at the very most to note certain social behaviours. Of these eight merchants, only one did not know how to sign his name: Charly, who rose to the rank of merchant through the baker's shop. Seven possessed land. Four were closely related (Le Ber, Testard, and the two Le Moynes) in such a way that there already was a nucleus within this little group which could develop into a sort of family power. Just as the nobles ordinarily recruited their godfathers and godmothers from among nobles, we believe we recognize among the merchants this tendency to look within their group or above: of the thirty-six godfathers and godmothers who stood at the baptisms of eighteen children of merchants, fifteen came from merchant families and a sixteenth was a gunsmith, that is to say, almost a merchant. The

other half is largely composed of nobles or persons who had a
certain social prestige, like Jeanne Mance and Marguerite
Bourgeoys. If one sets aside one person of unknown profession,
one can say that the merchants did not seek but two godparents
out of thirty-six from among the lower-class folk.[8] Nevertheless,
these merchants barely stood out from the mass of these same
lesser folk.

We believe we understand that they began to enjoy a certain
prestige. From the formation of the militia in February of 1663,
the militiamen had chosen from among themselves by majority
vote the leaders of the twenty squads. We have seen that the
three non-military nobles each had been designated to command
a squad. Next then, we can ascertain in examining the roll of the
squads that the merchants occupied a privileged position; of the
seven out of eight merchants enlisted, three commanded squads;
three others were placed immediately under the direction of
nobles (although there were but three nobles among the twenty
leaders of squads); the other, the baker Charly, was in a squad
which a merchant directed. Thus no one among the fourteen
lower-class people at the heads of squads had authority over the
merchants.

THE SOCIAL BEHAVIOUR OF THE LOWER CLASS

In France, coming below the merchants in order of dignity, was
a first group composed of labourers, cultivators, or farmers (in
fact, agricultural entrepreneurs), then a second group which
comprised artisans or tradespeople, and finally a last group, that
of manual labourers, domestics, the one and another classed
among the lowliest of the lower class. As immigration was not
the result of a social choice and the lower class of Montreal had
to organize itself with the elements introduced into it by the luck
of circumstance, we cannot expect to see this class reconstruct in
Montreal, at least not in the seventeenth century, the same
hierarchy of groups among the lower class.

We have set up for June 30, 1663, a list of occupations in
Montreal, an inventory which includes 271 men aged fourteen
years and over. Deleting from it the three priests, the four
military officers, and the ten noble or common merchants, we
are left with 254 working lower-class males of fourteen years and
up. What are their occupations? For 129 among them, being

50.8 per cent, we know the trades they practised or what they had declared themselves to be at a given time; basing this on documents the closest possible to June 1663, we obtain the following table:

gunsmiths	4	sailors	2
baker	1	joiners	6
brewer	1	millers	5
collier	1	notary	1
carpenters	13	wooden-shoe maker	1
coppersmith	1	pit sawyers	10
surgeons	6	locksmiths	5
cobblers	2	soldiers	23
cook	1	edge-toolmakers	2
land-clearers	22	tailors	5
gardener	1	tanner	1
labourers	3	cooper	1
masons	11		

Is the trade a person declares the one he habitually practises? Several tradesmen gave various declarations: one, for example, called himself at first a pit sawyer, much later one rediscovers him as a surgeon; we have retained the most recent declaration.[9] As for those who were qualified as "masters," we have not found it useful to distinguish them from the others: it is impossible to verify the authenticity of the title and we discover, furthermore, that such-and-such a labourer thus qualified neither took nor received this title other than in an occasional fashion. In most cases we have been obliged, lacking more recent information, to hold ourselves to the trade declared at the time of the contract for work in France, but since one trade is less remunerative than another would the immigrant not be tempted sometimes to pass himself off for one more skilled than he actually was? And this skill duly inscribed in the work contract, was it actually practised in Montreal? Did the wooden-shoe maker live by his clog-making? Could a population of 605 persons support five tailors? In the trades related to agriculture we discover the same difficulties. In France the labourer came after the merchant, and beneath the skilled tradesmen; there was an agricultural entrepreneur, a well-off peasant. What does one do with our three labourers? Pierre Gadois and Henri Perrin did not have land except for that which was given in common to the people. And what of Pierre Perusseau? He was but a simple *engagé* [indentured servant] whom one finds as a domestic in

1666. These labourers could not have been, on their departure from France, anything but farm workers.

As to the rest, a great number of those to whom the documentation attributes a skill arrange themselves into one or the other of the following two large categories: on one hand the people who served as domestics (which does not necessarily mean that they were attached to the service of a house) or who were bound by a work contract, without one knowing exactly the tasks they filled; and on the other hand, the people characterized as *habitants*. This is why, if one wants to discover all the social groups of the lowest class, it is necessary to redivide the lower class not according to the skills they claim but more often according to the means by which they subsisted: those who subsisted by working for others, and those who subsisted by themselves. One thus obtains, like the proposal put forth by the historian Faillon,[10] a first group formed of employees, domestics, day labourers, and soldiers, all in the service of others. Including with them the members of their families, we evaluate this group in June of 1663 at 255 persons, being 44.7 per cent of the lower class, or 42.2 per cent of the whole population of Montreal. The second group is that of the *habitants*.

This word *habitant* does not yet necessarily have the connotation of "landed": in our inventory of June 1663, of forty male adults who are qualified as *habitants*, there were nine of them who had not yet received land, and a joiner who lived "in town" and who survived by his trade perhaps was given the same title *habitant* as the joiner to whom had been conceded a piece of land. That is, the designation of *habitant* applies to whomever was settled for good in Montreal, as opposed to those who had not yet definitely opted for the country – a distinction that finds official confirmation in a Montreal ordinance of November 4, 1662, by which the soldiers and servants who had cleared at least four *arpents* of land are declared to be *habitants*.[11] This group of *habitants* was somewhat more numerous than the preceding one: to forty adults whom the documentation qualifies as *habitants* it is necessary to add thirty-eight who had the right to the title because they had received a piece of land, and ninety-two others who in 1662 had taken on the work of clearing land should properly be included under the title. If to these 170 persons we add the members of their families, the whole body of *habitants* is found to include 284 persons, composing 49.7 per cent of the commoner population or 46.9 per cent of the total population.

Briefly then, setting aside some common families who were in "merchandising" (a total of thirty-three persons), the lowest class of people is divided nearly equally between people who were settled and people who, not yet being so, worked in the service of others:

Habitants	284
Servants, Domestics, Day labourers, Soldiers	255

Of these two groups of lower-class people only that of the *habitants* seems to us to have some consistency. Indeed, in addition to having the wish to belong to the country and, with that, to run the same risks, the *habitants* had an exclusive privilege which set them clearly apart and above those who were not settled: they alone among the lower class had the right to participate in the fur trade; hence the repeal of the ordinance of November 4, 1662. In obtaining the qualification of *habitant*, which the practising of a trade did, one had access to a privileged group, superior to the rest of the lower class, and the superiority of the *habitants* over the other people of the same social level (a superiority, furthermore, which proceeded from the privilege of the fur trade) again manifests itself when we examine the same incomplete lists of the domestics. That the Sulpicians Soüart and Galinier had at least nineteen domestics should not surprise us since, representing the *Société de Notre-Dame* seigneurial property of the Île de Montréal, they were responsible for the upkeep of the whole domain; likewise, it was normal in this society for the nobles and the merchants to be provided with domestic servants. But what surprises us is that lower-class folk such as Jean Leduc, Jean Desroches, Mathurin Langevin, and Jacques Delaporte already had domestics in their service. Qualified as *habitants* and consequently above those who were not, these lower-class folk thus enjoyed a prestige which one gleans in the reports of the master of servants: these lower-class people commanded others.

It would be interesting to press further in the search for group consciousness among these folk of the lowest class of people; unfortunately, the documentation is very poor and the society in an embryonic state. In any case, it is not, we believe, by group consciousness that the Montrealers elected as churchwardens in

November of 1657 the brewer Prudhomme and the carpenter Barbier: churchwardenship was not yet but a simple community service without social prestige. And when the lower-class people constantly sought godfathers and godmothers for their children in the superior classes, the lesser folk could not feel left out for these dominant people also were systematically the object in the nobles' sponsoring of children and likewise in that of the merchants'.

THE ASCENSION OF THE NEW MEN

A phenomenon which was not exclusive to America, upward social mobility of "the new men," could proceed with greater frequency and facility in a society which, like that of Montreal, was not yet more than in an embryonic state: the social structures were not yet formed; at the beginning, everyone found himself, so to speak, on an equal footing before the great adventure. The lowest individual, if he had sufficient dynamism, could occupy sectors of an economic activity which was not yet organized. He could likewise hoist himself rapidly even to the nobility: the latter, very scant in number of representatives, had to remain open if it did not want to disappear, and the recruitment of this dominant group could not be made but from below.

An extraordinary case well illustrates this situation appropriate to a nascent society – the example is drawn from the history of Trois-Rivières. Pierre Boucher, the son of a joiner, arrived in Canada in 1634, aged twelve years. In 1637 he went to Huronia as a servant, the lowest estate of European society; in 1641 his Huron experience had made him an interpreter, which by the very nature of the fur trade led him into a role as clerk; from 1644 he was simultaneously interpreter and clerk at Trois-Rivières. Passing from the rank of principal clerk, he was soon named in 1649 captain of the fort at Trois-Rivières, and in 1653 we see him a judge of the tribunal of the Hundred Associates and he became seigneur of Grosbois; the year following he was officially named governor of Trois-Rivières. He was always a commoner, but because of the elevated position he occupied, they gave him the title Squire; finally, in 1661 he received letters patent of nobility. In twenty-five years Pierre Boucher had passed from the lowest to the most elevated; in a single generation he hoisted himself to the summit of society. Did this exceptional case – the most spectacular of the climbs of individuals in the seventeenth century – have its match in Montreal or something approaching it? What was it like in the first generation of Montrealers?

In regard to the astonishing climb of Pierre Boucher we cannot but cite that somewhat less surprising climb of Charles Le Moyne. The son of an innkeeper and the nephew of the influential surgeon Du Chesne, he arrived in Canada in 1641 at the age of fifteen. He was engaged to the service of the Jesuits in Huronia in the capacity of "a child," in 1643 he was styled similarly as a domestic servant. Thus he, too, commenced right at the bottom of the ladder. In 1645 he served Trois-Rivières as an interpreter and soldier; then the following year he went to establish himself at Montreal as an interpreter.[12] Where Pierre Boucher had had the time to become judge and governor and receive squiredom, Charles Le Moyne was always officially no more than an interpreter. But he was busy laying solid foundations. He busied himself little by little with commerce and took charge of the store of the Company of Inhabitants at Montreal in 1651. Three years later he had conceded to him an *arpent* within the town (where he already had a house) and ninety *arpents* in the country; thus he was given two or three times more than an ordinary individual, and he consequently became very influential in his milieu. In 1657 he was recognized as a merchant;[13] September 24 of the same year he received a seigneury in gaining title to the fief of Longueuil. This ascension, less rapid than that of Pierre Boucher, came to completion a little beyond the limits of our period. Promoted to king's prosecutor, military leader, diplomat, and seigneur who ceaselessly enlarged his domain, the former servant of the Jesuits received his letters patent of nobility in 1668. And we know the following: his eldest son augmented the prestige of the new family by becoming Governor General *pro tem* and by having himself created Baron, not to forget the other sons (among them Iberville and Bienville) who were to be illustrious in the army and in high levels of administration.

If Charles Le Moyne raised himself in twenty years from the rank of servant to that of influential merchant and seigneur, other Montrealers accomplished a much more modest ascension. It was a matter in certain cases of simple promotions in an army career: Zacharie Dupuy, major of the garrison, became commandant of Montreal in the absence of Chomedey; Lambert Closse, sergeant-major, succeeded to the post of commandant in the same circumstances. Claude Robutel de Saint-André, a lesser noble of Picardy, fell back to merchandising and applied himself to maintaining his rank and his social level. He betook himself to France in 1658 to marry a girl of the nobility; he had at least one servant; he had two pieces of land ceded to him. In 1660 he bought a house for 1,000 *livres* of which he paid half in merchandise. In 1661 he became *percepteur des droits de censive* (the collector of land rents).[14] The merchant Jacques Le Ber acquired much prestige: in 1658 he married the sister of the merchant and seigneur Charles Le Moyne and associated himself in business with the latter, thus preparing the establishment of a family consortium. In 1660 he was a member of the *Conseil de Ville-Marie*. Sought after as a godparent, he took that place fifteen times from 1658 to 1663.

It is among the lower-class people, men of trades or manual labourers, that we can gather most of the examples of a start at climbing socially. Mathurine Godé, the daughter of a joiner, contracted marriage with a notary of the lesser nobility, Jean de Saint-Père; the commoner and widow of a commoner, Barbe Poisson, married the lesser noble Celle du Clos; Jean Leduc, pit sawyer, established himself on some land and had at least one servant. Gilbert Barbier did not depart from his status as a carpenter, but he enjoyed a certain prestige: an act of the civil state in 1657 characterized him "*incolu notus*," and consequently he appeared no less than thirty-seven times as a witness or a godfather; and Dollier de Casson pays him homage for his services "to this island, which is nearly all constructed by his hand or by those whom he has taught."[15] Arriving in 1653 the carpenter Marin Janot was elected three years later syndic of the Company of Inhabitants and lived there until 1660.

There were those of the lower class who clearly raised themselves from their class to that of merchant. André Charly arrived in 1651, only a young soldier. In 1655 he already possessed a building site in town and a grant of thirty *arpents* in the country. In 1656 he acquired the house and surrounding property of Jean Chapleau for the price of 350 *livres* and he immediately paid fifty *livres* in deposit, agreeing to pay the rest in French merchandise and beaver pelts; from 1659 he was presented as a baker, which put him into the merchant class. The Charly Saint-Ange family, which would soon be important in the middle class, laid its first foundations at this time. Jean Gervaise, recruited in 1653 as a land-clearer and baker, in 1655 obtained a grant in the country and a building site in town; he often served as godfather or witness, and from 1657 to 1661 he filled the post of churchwarden. Finally, an important stage, he was qualified as a merchant in 1662. Jacques Testard *dit* Laforest was nothing more at first than an ordinary corporal in the garrison, but see how in 1660 he passes for a merchant; he had a house on the site he owned in town between the merchant Le Ber and the merchant and seigneur Le Moyne. In 1661 he was elected *procureur syndic*. At his burial in 1663 one still wrote Testard *dit* Laforest, but the impetus had been given: the second generation would be Testard de Laforest.

Apart from Charles Le Moyne, who proceeded by decisive leaps, passing from the service of the Jesuits to the state of influential merchant and seigneur, the others did hardly more than to disengage themselves a little from the herd. Le Ber, for example, reinforced his prestige; the soldier Charly and the land-clearer and baker Gervaise acquired the capacity of merchants; Corporal Testard prepared solidly for the social promotion of his sons. New men, of whom the number certainly is limited (but one is just at the first generation), these new men came just in time to join a colony being born.

Finally, in this establishment at Montreal, which the founders had insisted be apostolic, upward social movement was accomplished through commerce and most surely through the fur trade: Charles Le Moyne, Jacques Le Ber, Claude Robutel, André Charly, and Jacques Testard prove this. If the year 1642 marks the birth of Montreal, one can affirm that the year 1655, when the king authorized the establishment at Montreal of a store for the Company of Inhabitants, determined the economic destiny of this colony. This was the point of departure for the dazzling career of Charles Le Moyne, just as it was the beginning of the social rise of various lower-class people through the trade in furs. From 1655 the Île de Montréal rediscovered its first vocation, imposed by the geography, that of financial centre for the fur trade. Consequently, we affirm what we discover in the other places in New France: in a nascent colony of which the economic fulcrum is the fur trade, business becomes the essential springboard to the social promotion of the individual.

NOTES

1. They gave him the title *Ecuyer* (Squire) in 1661 and bestowed on him the *Sieur* ("mister" of address) in the registers of the civil state. At this period those registers in Montreal never gave this title to the lower class.

2. "It is good for married persons to take notice of the advice St. Paul gives them, and of the practice of the early Church; and to conform themselves to the exhortation to live in continence during times of prayer, fasting, and the solemn ceremonies of the Church." Bishop Jean-Baptiste de la Croix de Chevrières de Saint-Vallier, *Rituel du diocèse de Québec* (Paris, 1703), 282.

3. We expect to publish soon the roll of the population of Montreal at the end of June 1663 before the arrival of the ships. This roll has been reconstructed with the help of the civil state registers, notarial acts, as well as from two particularly convenient sources: engagement contracts entered into at Montreal in the autumn of 1662 and during the winter of 1662-1663 (contracts which bound ninety-four adults), and a roll of the militia from February 1663, which enumerates 143 men. As twenty of those betrothed and sixty-eight of the militiamen had been married, we will be able at the same time to add to our list the wives and children. As to persons who do not appear in any document after four or five years, we have discarded them. Of these 605 persons, only ten or so are doubtful cases. The census of 1666, well-known for being incomplete, gave Montreal but 625 persons, after the arrival nevertheless of significant recruits.

4. Jachereau de la Ferté de Sainte-Ignace, Jeanne-Françoise et Marie-Andrée Duplessis, de Sainte-Hélène, *Les annales de l'Hôtel-Dieu de Québec, 1636-1716*, ed. Albert Jamet (Québec, 1939), 108.

5. The following are the nobles as of June 1663:
   Ailleboust des Muceaux, Charles-Joseph
      his wife Catherine Legardeur de Repentigny
       their children Barbe, Louis, Pierre, Paul, and Nicolas
   Artus de Sailly, Louis
      his wife Anne-Françoise Bourduceau
       their children Angélique-Anne and Suzanne
   Boullongne, Barbe de, widow of Louis d'Ailleboust and aunt of
      d'Ailleboust des Muceaux
   Celle du Clos, Gabriel
      his children Marguerite, Gabriel-Lambert, and Barbe
   Chomedey de Maisonneuve, Paul
   Dupuy, Zacharie
   Gauchet, Catherine
   Moreau de Brésoles, Judith, superior of the Hospitalières
   Moyen des Granges, Elisabeth, widow of Lambert Closse
      her daughter Jeanne-Cécile Closse
   Moyen des Granges, Marie
   Mullois de La Borde, Madeleine
   Picoté de Belestre, Perrine
   Robutel de Saint-André, Claude
      his wife Suzanne de Gabriel

their children Jeanne-Paule and Anne-Françoise
Saint-Père, Agathe de

6. He died 22 June 1663. We speak of him here, but we do not retain him in the total for the population (a total which holds to 30 June 1663). Neither do we retain the merchant Louis de Pont, who seems to have made only a brief visit to Montreal 12 May 1663.

7. Archives Judiciares de Montréal, Minute Basset, 22 August 1660.

8. A surgeon and a joiner.

9. If the trade of a man is not known from the census of 1666 or of 1667, we do not take it into account: there was too much instability in occupations in this period to conclude that one's trade in 1666 was the same as in 1663.

10. É.-M. Faillon, *Histoire de la colonie française en Canada*, 3 vols. (Montréal, 1865-66), III, 10ff.

11. Ordinance reproduced in *ibid.*, III, 11.

12. R.G. Thwaites, ed., *The Jesuit Relations and Allied Documents*, 73 vols. (Cleveland, 1896-1901), XXVII, 99; Archives Judiciares de Montréal, registres d'état civil.

13. This was the capacity assigned to him for the first time on 24 November 1657 in the civil state registers of Montreal.

14. PAC, Documents St. Sulpice, pièces, judiciares, 1636-55; Archives Judiciares de Montréal, Minute Basset, 17 March 1660; E.-Z. Massicotte, *Répetoire des arrêts, édits, mandements, ordonnances conservés dans les Archives du Palais de Justice de Montréal, 1640-1760* (Montréal, 1919), 2.

15. François Dollier de Casson, *Histoire du Montréal, 1640-1672* (Montréal, 1868), 41.

Seigneurial Property and Social Groups in the St. Lawrence River Valley, 1663-1760

by Fernand Ouellet

The seigneurial regime, like all the institutional networks of the Old Regime – including the tithe – was a system of allocation of land revenue which favoured certain privileged groups: the clergy and the nobility. This is why the analysis of the movements of seigneurial ownership depends on certain of these social structures: it clarifies in particular the role of nobles and clergy, their relationship with the peasantry, and touches importantly on the dynamic which bound the nobility to the middle class. Hence Fr. Léon writes on the subject of seventeenth- and eighteenth-century France:

> In this society which rests largely on the possession of land, investment in land constitutes the best means of elevating oneself. It is also a good investment. . . . Access to property ownership is, for the rich, at one and the same time a promotion and a consolidation. . . . The middle class thus extricates itself, in fact, from the plebian condition. . . .[1]

Naturally, the blooming of the clergy and nobility (upon which the elites of the Old Regime depended) relied as far as their land revenues were concerned on the mass of the population's sub-

Translation from the French of Fernand Ouellet, "Propriété seigneuriale et groupes sociaux dans la vallée du Saint-Laurent (1663-1840)," *Revue de l'Université d'Ottawa*, XLVII, 1-2 (1977), 183-95, 212-13. Reprinted by permission of the publisher.

mitting to the *rentes* [seigneurial dues] and to the conditions that prevailed in the agricultural sector. But the possession of a fief, which concerned the noble or merchant, also had a symbolic value of a sort that is not coincidental, for he who bought a seigneury made both a social and an economic investment. All this poses the problem of the constitution of the nobility in the colonial milieu, of its relationship with the large property holdings and its incessant recruitment in the bosom of the middle class.

There is no doubt that in its colony in the St. Lawrence River Valley, France had anticipated the setting up of a society of the Old Regime and that she had utilized the seigneurial system to this end. The strategy that she followed with perseverance in the gratuitous distribution of fiefs aimed not only to provide for the first of the "orders," the clergy, but particularly to favour the entrenchment of a strong nobility capable of fully assuming its military, political, and social roles. Principal beneficiary of the granting of fiefs, of royal favours, of honours, of military no less than civil responsibilities, of patronage in the trading of furs, this nobility – for whom the military antecedents are of such significance on the whole – existed from the beginning of the colony and drew its vigour for the most part from the almost permanent state of war which constituted the very fabric of the history of New France. It was war that first attracted the nobility to this country and it was war, as they were waiting till the majority of the population should be sufficient to support them, which secured them for the duration according to their most ancient vocation. In New France the nobility was situated with the clergy at the summit of the social hierarchy. This is why the nobility exerted so much attraction on the commoners, whether they were merchants or civil servants. The pursuit of noble rank was but one of the means used by the middle class to infiltrate the aristocracy, which in general had little propensity for the middle class. The acquisition of a seigneury, whether or not it would be a prelude of ennoblement, constituted part of this strategy which resulted in social conversion. Thus Chaussinand-Nogaret wrote: "The ennobled *bourgeois* instinctively bows to the aristocratic rules of play. . . ."[2]

The military nobility which emerged in the French period, based on seigneurial property and for whom the field of action extended beyond the territory of New France, saw their ambitions seriously limited by the English Conquest of 1760.

Numerous nobles, certain of losing the advantages of patronage and of not being integrated into the regular British army, quit the colony and parted with their fiefs. The major part of their domain was bought by anglophone aristocrats and military men, who along with the old nobility contributed to the perpetuation of aristocratic values in colonial society. Reduced in effectiveness, cut off from the commerce of the fur trade, excluded from the ranks of the British army, the francophone nobility became a landed nobility preserving nevertheless the hope of recovering their old status not so much in the army as in trade and administration.

The nobility were forced to follow their landed calling at the moment from which it became henceforth possible to live on their rents: in 1765 the percentage of seigneuries where the number of tenant families exceeded seventy-five (representing about a hundred *censitaires*, or settlers, paying the feudal dues) was about 42 per cent; in 1790 this percentage rose to 75 per cent.[3] This is to say that the clergy and a good number of the lay seigneurs could draw substantial incomes from their fiefs. Furthermore, to the particular benefit of the tracts of land near towns, the holdings had begun to take on good values before 1760. Accelerated commercialization of the agricultural sector after 1760 promised similar added growth of revenues for owners of fiefs and inspired merchants to acquire seigneuries not only with social promotion in view but for profit. It is uniquely after 1781 that these purchases at the expense of the nobles fundamentally modified the middle-class presence at the level of the great landholders.

In New France the concessions of seigneuries were not made haphazardly and on demand. They were the fruit of a consistent policy which reflected a social design. When Intendant Hocquart declared that it "is never fitting that a simple *habitant* possess fiefs,"[4] he expressed perfectly the views of the king and administrators on the type of society that they wanted to see flourish in the colony. Their model was that of the mother country which calls for a hierarchical society, "ordered," dominated by the nobility and clergy. The concept of three orders, clergy, nobility, and the third estate, was thoroughly alive in the time of Talon and of Frontenac and it remained the same under the British regime.[5] This policy of social structure took shape from the beginning of the colony and was applied during the whole French period.

The transfer of concessions of seigneuries for the period prior to 1663 has been studied in the greatest detail by Professor Marcel Trudel in his book *Les débuts du régime seigneurial*. The enormous distribution of fiefs during the years 1636-1640 and 1651-1656 was allied to the granting of massive land areas which took place in the townships from 1798 to 1807. In both periods the motivations were political and social but did not aim to satisfy the demands for land of a famished peasantry. Close to 14 million *arpents* of land thus passed into the hands of the ecclesiastical and lay upper classes before 1663.

The Seigneurs and Their Estates in 1663[6]

	Number	Percentage	Area
Nobles	32	47%	70%
Middle class	30	44%	14%
Clergy	5	7%	16%

From the outset the nobility were advantaged. The following families received the largest blocs of land: D'Ailleboust, Chavigny, Bermen de la Martinière, Cailhaut de la Tesserie, Chartier de Lotbinière, Damours, Denys, Leneuf, Du Mesnil, Legardeur, Peuvret, Ruette d'Auteuil, and De Lauson. As in this social class the distance between men and their wives was much less marked than in the rest of the population, the nobles were not forced to go to find their marriage partners among the simple *habitants*. They could proliferate without fear of forfeiture of prestige.

It is evident that the noble class would not have been able to extend itself if it had supported itself only on feudal dues. The population was too small to keep alive an exclusively landed nobility. The image of the poor seigneur yoked to his plough like a peasant has no place here. This nobility was bound to the real property as they ought to have been, but they had other justifications for being and growing. Their first but not exclusive vocation was military. In this regard the situation favoured them to the utmost. From the beginning of the Iroquois wars to the end of the Seven Years' War, New France knew less than fifty years of peace and that, one must add, of armed peace.

It is this context that explains the militaristic character of colonial society. Professor Eccles goes so far as to say that "The whole fabric of the Canadian society was imbued with the military ethos."[7] All males from sixteen to sixty years of age were part of the militia and could be summoned in emergencies. In addition to the militia, one finds contingents of regular troops which the mother country sent to the colony according to needs and circumstances. The colonial nobility, within the limits established by immigration, recruited for themselves principally among the officers of these regular troops. W.J. Eccles estimates at 800 the number of officers and soldiers of the Carignan-Salières regiment that settled in the St. Lawrence River Valley.[8] This phenomenon seems to repeat itself to a certain extent in each generation, at least as far as concerns the nobility.

Not less significant for the development of the nobility is the fact that the regular army became welcoming with regard to the sons of Canadian nobles. They could make careers in the *troupes de la marine* [forces of colonial regulars] and hope for promotions. At the end of the century, thirty-five of the eighty-seven officers of the *troupes de la marine* stationed in Canada had been born in the country.[9] On this subject Eccles writes: "the members of the Canadian dominant class were avid for commissions for their sons as soon as they were big enough to handle a musket. . . ."[10] In 1760, there were about 200 Canadians, officers and hopefuls, in the French troops. The interesting number of Canadians who wore the Croix de Saint-Louis or had been made Chevaliers de Saint-Louis illustrates well the phenomenon of the emergence of a nobility which was colonial, to be sure, but which also possessed an imperial character due to its military calling. The departures* of 1760 are in part related to this situation.

This nobility, offspring of the rural lesser nobility and the French military – those that Chaussinand-Nogaret described as the most traditional – exercised control of the military outposts in the interior the same as in the colony. It is sufficient to glance at the list of governors general and local, of king's lieutenants and majors in the three districts in order to be convinced of it.[11] By way of example, we cite the names of the governors of Montreal:

1. P. Chomeday de Maisonneuve
2. F.-M. Perrot

---

* Many nobles and other leaders of French-Canadian society returned to France after the Conquest. [editors' note]

3. L.-H. Callières
4. P. Rigaud de Vaudreuil
5. C. de Ramezay
6. C. Lemoyne
7. J. Bouillet de la Chassaigne
8. J. Boisberthelot de Beaucours
9. C. Lemoyne, baron de Longueuil
10. F.-P. Rigaud de Vaudreuil

In this group Perrot was the only commoner. But even he was in the military, a merchant, and related to Talon. The nobility dominated equally the commandants of military outposts, which permitted them to draw appreciable benefits from the fur trade.

But in New France as in France the service of the king was not limited to the army. For those of the "nobility of the robe" (those who rose through government service or the judicial system), for all those who felt no disposition for a military career, civil service postings were doubtless those which had the greatest value. The Reutte d'Auteils and the brothers Daine are typical cases from this point of view. But the administrative posts were not the prerogative of a single group. The military men coveted them as well as royal gratuities, pensions, and honours. An analysis of the personnel of the Sovereign or Superior Council, councillors and officers, shows beyond a shadow of a doubt the predominant role of the nobility in this institution, which was the dispensory of influence and power. All of the foregoing clarifies the political function of the aristocracy.

The nobility were anxious about their titles which were otherwise authentic. In this regard, if one is to believe Chaussinand-Nogaret, who affirms that four generations or a century is necessary to establish nobility of ancestry in France, the Canadian nobility withstood the challenge.[12] This was manifested similarly with much diligence when it was a matter of confirming their rights.[13] Attached to their values, bearers of a fixed culture revolving about the most ancient traditions, they did not know how to conceive of anything outside of all that was deeply rooted in the holding of great property. It is true that the absence of a demographic base for a long time prevented them from living decently on the feudal dues, but that is not the essential point. The possession of a fief appeared indispensable to their existence. Those responsible for the concessions of seigneuries were equally convinced of this. The officers of the Carignan regiment who agreed to settle in the colony were richly endowed with fiefs: Saurel, Berthier, Chambly, Bécancourt, Morel, Du Gué, Deschamps, Lanoraie, and Villieu benefited from a policy which consisted in procuring country seats from the nobility. In this fashion the domain of the nobility, as much as it was tied to the concessions, never ceased to extend itself from one generation to the next during a century. The old families always found themselves again among the grantees at the moment when new ones were taking their places among the seigneurs. A few names among these suffice to demonstrate this evolution: Beaujeu, Bleury, Contrecoeur, Gaultier, Joybert, Lanaudière, Lery, Noyan, Noyelles, Péan, Ramezay, St-Ours, Taschereau, Vaudreuil, and Verchères.

Grantees of Fiefs (1670-1760)[14]

	Extensions		*New Concessions*	
Nobles	19	70%	170	66%
Middle class	7	25%	78	30%
Clergy	1	3%	6	2%
Total	27		254	

It would be difficult to support a contention that the administrators of New France distributed land without discernment and engendered a group of seigneurs unrecognizable in a social perspective. After 1663 the intendants and governors maintained a policy which favoured the military nobility first and tended to give them a landed vocation.[15]

The role of the nobility was not only military, landed, and political, it was also in a sense commercial. Is that to say that one must speak of noble businessmen[16] or, to use Chaussinand-Nogaret's terminology, of *gentilhommerie bourgeoise*?[17] In regard to France of the second half of the eighteenth century he actually goes on to say: "Henceforth there are no longer *middle-class* gentlemen (*bourgeois gentilshommes*) but pervasively *gentlemen* from the middle class (*gentilhommerie bourgeoise*)." Things were not as simple in the St. Lawrence River Valley as they were in France. There is no doubt that the great majority of nobles were involved in commercial activities, in particular in the fur trade and fisheries. But that does not permit one to affirm the commercial character of the nobility without many qualifications. We know that military investments – the work of fortifications, the construction of forts and outposts spread out across the entire territory – were not uniquely dictated by strategic considerations, but were also a matter of protecting the commerce in furs, or similarly the fisheries. The role of the nobility in these activities derived in part from their military function. This is clear in the case of De Lery and others of the royal engineers. It is also evident in the case of outpost commandants who used their power to extract bribes. These nobles did nothing more in reality than claim feudal dues on the fur trade or the fisheries. But the nobles did no more than invest indirectly in the commercial sector. They put to profit their political influence to obtain permission to trade[18] or to have ceded to them seigneuries well-situated for fishing and the collection of furs. In this regard the names of certain families naturally come to mind: the Damours and the Gaultiers of La Vérendrye; but this phenomenon was much more widespread and general than one would believe. At this level meanwhile, the associations between nobles and commoners do not truly prove the commercial character of the nobility, apart from a few exceptions. This intrusion of aristocrats into commercial activities was the consequence of their political influence, which procured for them the means of imposing a sort of guardianship on commoner merchants. Again, it was most often a matter of a sort of feudal due levied indirectly on an inferior social group: the commoner tradesmen.

The nobility, well-established on their property, thus had a predominant role in society. In spite of the formulae of scorn addressed by the governors and intendants to certain of the more turbulent and unstable members of the nobility, their power was not less recognized whether it concerned the king or his representatives, or the local population. All that would not be measured adequately by the estate inventories after their deaths with their too-often repeated certifications of, as they claim, "poverty at death."[19] The radiance of the aristocracy proceeded certainly from their power and from the influence they commanded, but also from the fact that they were the instruments by which was made felt the influence of the French nobility. The attractiveness of the values they projected incited the middle class in Canada, as in France, to join their ranks. Because the aristocracy was not a caste and the state encouraged up to a certain point the promotion of middle-class people who were successful or meritorious, it was partly among the middle class that they recruited for their class. This penetration of the aristocracy by middle-class elements did not signify that they had taken on bourgeois characteristics. On the contrary, in this relationship the middle-class person made the essential compromise.

The policy of those responsible for free concessions of seigneuries aimed not only, as we said above, at providing for the nobility, but moreover and in part at preparing the way for this accession of the middle class to the nobility – because the granting of fiefs to commoners was inspired by the same criteria as those which prevailed in elevations to the nobility. In this group those who obtained seigneuries were men of substance, and merit, and were experienced in the service of the king. At this level there was interaction between colonial administrators and the candidates for the title of seigneur.

Between 1670 and 1760 about 30 per cent of new seigneurs were commoners: merchants, civil servants, and professionals.[20] This percentage is the same as that which emerges from a list of the proprietors of fiefs arranged at the beginning of three volumes of the *Dictionary of Canadian Biography* (vols. I, II, III).

The Seigneurs, from the *Dictionary* . . .

	Number	Percentage
Nobles	191	66%
Merchants	64	22%
Civil servants	15	5%
Professionals	8	2%
Clergy	8	2%

These proportions vary in the course of the period and it seems to have been more and more difficult for the commoners to obtain concessions. From 1670 to 1699 the proportion of commoners is 35 per cent: the most visible names are Aubert, Jolliet, Riverin, Pachot, Hazeur, Hubert, Perrot, Lefebvre, Martel, Becquet, Bissot, Genaples, and Lepage. From 1700 to 1730 this percentage of new commoner-seigneurs fell to 29 per cent. Again, men of substance predominate: Fezeret, Lefebvre, Haimard, Hazeur, and Dumontier. From 1730 to 1760 the new middle-class seigneurs again lost ground to 25 per cent. It seems that the proportion of administrators in relation to merchants was on the increase. The names are: Foucault, Estèbe, Lanouiller, Cugnet, Rocbert, Rageot, Hocquart, Perthuis, Cressé, and Levasseur. All of this tends to show that as time passed, while the number of nobles to petition increased, the administrators of New France increasingly resisted the demands of commoners, who were thus forced to buy if they wanted to insinuate themselves into the aristocracy or to adopt its style.

Thus the upper strata of the third estate were admitted as candidates to the free concession of seigneuries despite an increasingly severe filtration barrier. But that did not suffice to assuage the hunger for social promotion. From that time on the purchase of a fief became mandatory for those who desired to elevate their social position. It is not that the acquisition of a noble landholding had the legal power of ennobling; but it almost always may be translated as aspiration and social self-consciousness. It is true that merchants very often acquired fiefs because they hoped to draw a profit from them. Such was the case early for seigneurs situated in the Gulf of St. Lawrence region; it became more and more the case in other well-situated locations where the investor could anticipate an impending growth in the population. But the considerations of the economic order did not necessarily eliminate social motivations. Aubert de la Chesnaye, who received noble lands and bought some, is a perfect example in this regard. He was at first a man of the middle class who during one period of his life secretly held aspirations to the nobility and who finally became ennobled. The middle-class gentleman is essentially an individual in transition. The concept is not useful for defining the lay ruling classes in New France.[21]

The proximity between certain middle-class elements and the nobility developed most through marriage. The natural tendency of nobles was to choose their spouses from within their own group. But the diverse circumstances of the society and the hazards of existence worked to impose on them alliances with middle-class families.[22] In this sphere economic considerations carried perhaps the greatest importance. For the middle class these alliances made up part of the dynamic of social promotion.[23] Most certainly if one analyses the marriages among the merchants and takes account only of first marriages, which in general take place before they become successful, one finds that commercial folk preferred to choose their marriage partners from within their group. But an attentive look at subsequent marriages leads one to view things differently.[24] For example, J.-B. St-Ange Charly, a merchant, took to wife for his first marriage a Lecompte-Dupré, the daughter of a merchant. For his second marriage, he allied himself to a D'Ailleboust. His son Louis found a spouse in a noble family, the Godefroy de Tonnancourts, then his daughter entered the Ramezay family. All this well demonstrates (and Cugnet is another illustration) that the aristocratic ambitions of the members of the middle class were not always achieved in formal ennoblement. How many dreams, how many imaginary or symbolic social moves in order to obtain a single letter patent of nobility? How many usurpations of title?

The purchase of seigneuries, marriages, the exercise of certain responsibilities, L'Ordre de St-Louis are all means by which the middle class infiltrated by one fashion or another into the nobility. But none of these gestures was of the slightest value, at least under the legal system, for the obtaining of letters patent of nobility, the ultimate consecration. These were accorded, like the seigneuries, for the recognition of merit acquired in the service of the king and that engendered by success in business. This notion of *merit*, defined by Chaussinand-Nogaret as a value both individual and middle-class,[25] would not only contaminate the ideology of the French nobility but would at the same time contribute to the modification of its character in a radical fashion. It is the phenomenon of the *embourgeoisement* of the nobility, perceptible everywhere, according to him, after 1750. His interpretation of the concept of merit is not so useful to our purpose, because in New France the great majority of elevations to the nobility by letters patent were made before 1710 and in all cases it was the middle-class identity that was lost thereby. Such analysis necessitates the examination of at least three generations.

The letters patent of nobility registered by the Superior Council concern forty-one families. But the majority of these documents are confirmations of nobility and not the acts of entry into the aristocracy. The first interest us less than the second, which in one manner or another call on precisely this notion of merit. Similarly, if merit was acquired in the service of the king, one must conclude that valorous activities altered in the course of the years. At first there were the "pioneers."[26] R. Giffard was one among them: this surgeon by profession arrived in Canada in 1627, bestirred himself as a soldier, as that was the norm, but he was also a sort of driving force in colonization. In 1634 he laid claim to a first seigneury. In 1647 he was made physician in ordinary to the king, then the beneficiary of two concessions of fiefs and was named to the Council of the colony. He was elevated to the nobility in 1658. G. Couillard belongs to the same category: craftsman, soldier, and farmer, he raised himself to the rank of the notables and received his letters patent of nobility in 1654 "in favour of services rendered to the country of Canada." Although his sons had participated in the fisheries and the fur trade and had bought a seigneury, the dynasty that he founded was perhaps the most rural among all the ennobled families.

Toward 1660 the war and relations with the Indians seem to have stabilized the function of the interpreter, who negotiated with the natives. P. Boucher, first engaged by R. Giffard, moved quickly to become a personality of the first type. A soldier and interpreter, he married a Huron maiden in 1649. His second wife, whom he married in 1652, gave him fifteen children. His merit seems to derive as much from his decisive military role as captain and commandant of the town of Trois-Rivières, as from his talents as a negotiator. He was elevated to the nobility in 1661, received the seigneury of Boucherville, and was named governor of Trois-Rivières. P. Boucher retired to his seigneury where he cut a figure as the rural noble; but his sons, who were allied to families of nobles and merchants, opted for military careers, which did not prevent them in spite of circumstances from participating in exploration and the fur trade.

The Godefroy family, a family of interpreters and fur traders, was different in origin. Jean-Paul was the son of a councillor to the king and treasurer general and he married a Legardeur. Pretentions to the nobility had also made their reappearance with the father of Jean and Thomas. After the return to France of Jean-Paul and the death of his brother Thomas, killed by the Iroquois, Jean Godefroy became the sole representative of the family in Canada. He married a Leneuf du Hérisson, was the grantee of seigneuries, and obtained letters patent of nobility in 1668. His sons, numbering eight, followed military careers, remained tied to the seigneurial property, and participated in the traffic in furs and in public administration. For the Hertel family the ascent was much longer. Jacques Hertel, soldier, experienced in the fur trade, became an interpreter and married the daughter of an interpreter. The carrier of the line, François, married a Thavenet, who brought a seigneury in her dowry. After having refused him letters patent of nobility in 1689, the king finally accorded them to him in 1716. His descendants also joined the army.

In time, it seems, the criteria became more severe. They were equally so, we believe, in regard to the merchants. Witness the case of Jean Juchereau to whom the king refused letters patent of nobility in 1668. Nevertheless he bought a seigneury, became the grantee of another, and situated himself advantageously among the notables of the colony. His two sons Jean and Nicolas allied themselves to the Giffard family and figured among the men of influence. Nicolas was for his part the beneficiary of several grants of fiefs. It was only in 1692, after the death of his brother, that he became ennobled. His daughter, spouse of a certain Mr. La Forest, called herself Countess of St. Lawrence. His sons were in the army, civil administration, and the fur trade. Aubert de la Chesnay, son of a middle-class man and perhaps the most important merchant in the colony, had to wait until 1693 before the king would consent to his letters patent of nobility. Before attaining his apogee as a negotiator Aubert had invested heavily in the purchase of seigneuries and he had received several of them from the state. At any given moment he was the proprietor of about ten fiefs. Aubert de la Chesnaye was married three times: in 1664 to a Couillard, in 1668 to a Juchereau, and in 1680 to a Denis de la Ronde. His descendants were numerous: eighteen children. His daughters married nobles and his sons opted above all for military careers. It is clear that the phenomenon we are analysing here is not that of the *embourgeoisement* of the nobility – whatever may have been transporting these commoners into the aristocratic milieu. Charles Lemoyne is a good example in this regard.

Son of an innkeeper, he arrived in New France in 1642 and made his debut in the service of the Jesuits. Then he became a fur trader, interpreter, and soldier. In 1654 he married a commoner, Catherine Thierry, who gave him fourteen children of whom twelve were sons. Lemoyne succeeded in business to the point of becoming the most considerable merchant in Montreal. He received some small fiefs before being raised to the nobility in 1668, and he was made Seigneur of Longueuil in 1672. His sons, like those of other nobles, found places for themselves in the military nobility which, when all's said and done, possessed an imperial character. His elder son Charles was named Baron of Longueuil in 1700, three years before receiving the *Croix de St-Louis*. His brother-in-law, Jacques Leber, on a similar footing as a Montreal merchant, also acquired fiefs and purchased his letters patent of nobility in 1696. The Leber sons, though they remained in contact with the world of furs, were from the outset men of the military.

There is no doubt that the nobility made up part of the substance of New France and that it is not sufficient to speak of peasants and merchants to do justice to the situation. This nobility constituted a real force which radiated power and attracted to it in one way or another the dynamic elements of the third estate. The ennobling of commoners by letters patent, so important in the seventeenth century, ceased despite that after 1710. How does one explain the change? Is it that the society had ceased to produce meritorious individuals? Is it that the king feared the *embourgeoisement* of the nobility, or on the contrary had been frightened by a system that drew out of the third estate its best elements? Could one, in the search for an explanation, go as far as to suppose that the middle class (in the degree to which they had become conscious of themselves) refused to accept a system which weakened them? We think that this radical change, far from transmitting the apparition of a class consciousness among the middle class, aimed rather to restrain the overcrowding of this vigorous and prolific nobility. Toward 1710 this social class appears to have acquired such maturity that it seems to have been able to recruit for its own ranks – without overtly drawing upon the upper strata of commoners through the means of letters patent of nobility. Let us note here that this halting of ennoblements by letters patent coincided with the diminution of concessions of seigneuries to commoners.

All that did not stop the movement which carried the middle class toward the nobility. The possession of certain posts having the virtues of ennoblement, marriages, and the purchases of seigneuries always served this objective. Cugnet is a good example in this regard, just as is Foucault. But these individuals had the prestige and the influence necessary to obtain grants of seigneuries. For others the purchase of a fief was imperative. This is why the changing of hands of seigneurial property was much more considerable than could be justified by the increase in value of landed property. Toward the end of the French regime the middle class possessed almost as much seigneurial land as the clergy.

The Seigneurs and their Properties on the Eve of 1760

	Number	Percentage	Area
Nobles	59	44.3%	53.6%
Middle class	66	49.6%	21.9%
Clergy	8	6.0%	24.4%
Total	133		

Thus, from 1663 to 1760 the proportion of seigneurial soil which finally remained in the hands of nobles diminished – from 70 per cent to 53 per cent – in spite of the policy of the state which gave them the advantage more and more in the plan of concessions. Even if we eliminate the seigneurial domain, that which is described by Trudel for 1663, the enormous seigneury of the Gaspé, this decline is no less noticeable: 60.9 per cent of the territory in 1663 to 53.6 per cent in 1760. That is to say that the purchases and legacies contributed to extend the territory controlled by the middle class and the clergy.

The scheme of a society of the Old Regime could not be realized without generous allotments of seigneuries to the clergy. In this type of society which presupposed the union of the Church and the state, the function of the first "order" was undeniably religious and missionary, but it was significantly extended to teaching, to the care of the sick, and to assistance to the poor. Since the personal revenue of the priests was based upon the tithe, that of the religious institutions depended for a large part of their revenues on their seigneuries. From the very beginning these institutions were abundantly provided with seigneurial land. Trudel[27] estimates at 1,919,052 *arpents* the portion of seigneurial soil conceded before 1663 to male and female orders: the Jesuits, the Sulpicians, the Seminary of Quebec, the Ursulines, the Hôtel-Dieu of Quebec and of Montreal. An important fact, these seigneuries were among the better situated: along the St. Lawrence River, Trudel says, they occupy 29.5 per cent of the seigneurial frontage. These were the ones which were to attract more colonists and to produce the more rapid and significant revenues. The figures given by Cole Harris in regard to the Seminary of Quebec prove it.[28] Common-sense observation serves us quite as well as research for this analysis: the ecclesiastical landed domain was very rarely parted with through sale and was not subject to the tribulations that affected the patrimonies of the laity: the partitioning of property on the death of a father or liquidation in the case of indebtedness. Ecclesiastical property is by definition a domain that grows. Trudel values at 221,041 *arpents* the quantity of seigneurial land bequeathed to the Church by the laity before 1663, which were in the form of donations or dowries.[29]

Toward 1660 the king was perfectly conscious of the danger an uncontrolled expansion of ecclesiastical proprietorship represented for the social and political equilibrium. Also, he decided henceforth to appear more avaricious in the concessions of fiefs in favour of the clergy. From 1670 to 1760 only six new seigneuries were given to clergy. Clerical possessions continued to expand all the same, but in a more moderate fashion than formerly, by donations and by the dowries of noblewomen who entered religious communities. In 1760 the seven great ecclesiastical landowners possessed forty seigneuries and back-section fiefs which allowed them to control a quarter of the seigneurial territory, including the Île de Montréal. At this date the noble proprietors of fiefs possessed, proportionally, 2.2 seigneuries to the 1.2 of the middle class and the 5.7 of the clergy.

This analysis of the relationships between the movements of seigneurial property and social groups takes all its meaning from within the perspective of the progressive emergence of a society of the Old Regime in which the clergy and the nobility were the privileged groups. They were also the groups that held the power and exercised it. The *bourgeoisie*, if one may use this term in all its connotations, was in a situation of dependence which was perhaps resented, but which did not issue forth in an immediate blossoming of class consciousness. To join the aristocracy in one fashion or another was still an aspiration well-rooted in a number of the members of the middle class at the end of the French era.

It seems difficult to deny the economic and social role of seigneurialism. It is not only the history of the nobility and that of the middle class suffering from lack of elevation which shows us that; it is also that of the clergy who escaped the tribulations known to the laity. During almost two centuries the nobility and the clergy constitute the principle forces propelling the institutions of the Old Regime. The downfall of the nobility and, much later, the partial abolition of the seigneurial system could have marked the beginning of a new era. But the old social regime had roots in the milieu too profound to disappear in an abrupt fashion without leaving traces. Espoused by the clergy from the beginning of New France, this old social regime, instead of becoming weaker in the nineteenth century at the same time as seigneurialism, always clung to a society more and more dominated by the clergy. The Church worked in concert with other elements in the society to perpetuate a collection of institutions which only industrialization would be able to shatter. To speak of the seigneurial regime is to pose the problem of the evolution of society in the only perspective which is truly significant: the historical overview.

NOTES

1. Pierre Léon, *Les derniers temps de l'âge seigneurial aux préludes de l'âge industriel, 1660-1789*, vol. II of Fernand Braudel and Ernest Labrausse, eds., *Histoire économique et sociale de la France* (Paris, 1970), 632-5.
2. Guy Chaussinand-Nogaret, *La noblesse au XVIIIᵉ siècle* (Paris, 1976), 40.
3. Richard Colebrook Harris, *The Seigneurial System in Early Canada* (Madison, Wisc., 1966), 78-87. The author establishes fifty as the minimum number of families necessary for the subsistance of the seigneur.
4. *Ibid.*, 44.
5. Marcel Trudel, *La population du Canada en 1663* (Montréal, 1972), 119. See Fernand Ouellet, *Histoire économique et sociale du Québec, 1760-1850* (Montréal, 1966).
6. Trudel, *La population du Canada*, 121-30.
7. W.J. Eccles, "The Social, Economic, and Political Significance of the Military Establishment in New France," *CHR*, LII, 1 (1971), 1.
8. *Ibid.*, 2.
9. *Ibid.*, 8.
10. *Ibid.*, 9.
11. P.-G. Roy, *Les officiers d'État-Major des gouvernements de Québec, Montréal et Trois-Rivières* (Lévis, 1919).
12. Chaussinand-Nogaret, *La noblesse*, 60ff.
13. P.-G. Roy, ed., *Lettres de noblesses, généalogies, érections de comtés et baronies insinuées par le Conseil souverain de la Nouvelle-France*, 2 vols. (Beauceville, 1920).

14. This statistic was developed from the six volumes of P.-G. Roy, ed., *Inventaire des concessions en fief et seigneurie* (Beauceville, 1927-29).

15. "Because almost everyone in the colony could acquire a seigneurie, the amorphous group of lay seigneurs is extremely difficult to characterize . . .": Harris, *Seigneurial System*, 44. The figures which we give here put this thesis in question.

16. G. Richard, *Noblesse d'affaires au XVIIIe siècle* (Paris, n.d.).

17. Chaussinand-Nogaret, *La noblesse,* 60.

18. Fernand Ouellet, "Dualité économique et changement technologique dans la vallée du Saint-Laurent, 1760-1790," *Histoire sociale/Social History*, IX, 18 (1976), 260ff.

19. Louise Dechêne, *Habitants et marchands de Montréal au XVIIe siècle* (Paris, 1974), 382-6.

20. Roy, *Inventaires des concessions*, 6 vols.

21. Cameron Nish, *Les bourgeois gentilhommes de la Nouvelle-France* (Montréal, 1968).

22. Trudel, *La population du Canada*, 122-8.

23. Nish, *Les bourgeois gentilhommes*, 171ff.

24. Jose Igartua, "The Merchants of Montreal at the Conquest: Socio-Economic Profile," *Histoire sociale/Social History*, VIII, 16 (1975), 275-93.

25. Chaussinand-Nogaret, *La noblesse*, 56ff.

26. We have, in order to reveal individual profiles, used in our article the biographies contained in the first three volumes of the *Dictionary of Canadian Biography* (Toronto/Quebec, 1967-74).

27. Marcel Trudel, *Les débuts du régime seigneurial* (Montréal, 1974), 51-4.

28. Harris, *Seigneurial System*, 84.

29. Trudel, *Les débuts,* 53.

III
The Working Class

Most *Canadiens* were peasants and soldiers. Those who worked in non-agricultural pursuits were few in number and were limited to the towns – Montreal, Trois-Rivières, Quebec, Louisbourg. The fur trade was the largest employer of wage labour, with the voyageurs and traders in the west and those working at processing and shipping furs at Montreal and Quebec. Nevertheless, the working class was increasing in size and importance as the colony grew more sophisticated. In fact, because of its international trade and the military presence, New France was highly urbanized for the time. A larger percentage of the people lived in towns than would dwell in urban places for the first century of British rule.

As Peter Moogk describes in his article, the problems of working people, familiar into the twentieth century, were present in New France. Their struggle to find organizations which would improve their working conditions was similar in broad outlines to that of generations of craftsmen until trade unions became common in the late nineteenth century. Throughout, it would be skilled craftsmen who would lead the campaign for improvement. Moogk's thesis about the failure of organizations in New France and the impact of that on the Québécois is a controversial one. Many historians would reject that connection and even reject the characteristics of French Canadians it suggests. Exactly because it is a bold and sweeping analysis, however, the Moogk essay is stimulating.

FURTHER READING:
The literature is slim. Some useful items are: Peter Moogk, "The Ancestor of Quebec's Craft Unions – the Montreal Shoemakers' Protest of 1729," *Histoire des travailleurs Québécois: Bulletin RCHTQ*, V, 1 (1978), 34-9; Jean Hamelin, *Economie et société en Nouvelle-France* (Québec, 1968); Jean-Pierre Hardy et David-Therry Ruddel, *Les apprentis artisans à Québec 1660-1815* (Montréal, 1977).

Peter Moogk teaches history at the University of British Columbia.

In the Darkness
of a Basement:
Craftsmen's Associations
in Early French Canada

by Peter N. Moogk

Many observers of French Canada have noted an historic tendency among the population to trust to another's leadership rather than popular initiative to obtain social improvements. In 1831 Alexis de Tocqueville remarked on the apparent impotence of the *Canadiens* to organize themselves to resist the social, economic, and political threats to their cultural survival. "Au total," wrote Tocqueville, "cette population nous a paru capable d'être dirigée quoique encore incapable de se diriger elle-même."[1] The delayed emergence of self-constituted, secular associations in French Canada has never been fully explained, possibly because a discussion of ethnic characteristics could be confused with racialism. A cultural trait is, of course, something that is learned; it is not innate. A full explanation of why self-help through collective action is a relatively late and rare phenomenon in French Canada would take one beyond the discipline of history. A sociologist might argue that the traditional, patriarchal family discouraged individual initiative in the children. When transferred to politics, the paternalism cultivated by family and religion led to a tendency to seek a strong, fatherly leader to act on behalf of the cultural group and to defend its interests. On the national level, the survival of French Canada re-

Reprinted from *Canadian Historical Review*, LVII, 4 (1976), 399-408, 410-25, 435-9, by permission of the author and University of Toronto Press.

quired ethnic solidarity and this left little room for non-conformists. It is tempting to emphasize the role of religion and the clergy. Undoubtedly, the faith of the *Canadiens* tended to be fatalistic and the Roman Catholic Church, which provided educational and social services to the populace, was reluctant to let the faithful join associations that lacked clerical guidance.

It would be misleading to say that the Roman Catholic clergy in French Canada hindered all popular associations for economic self-help. In this century credit unions and producers' marketing co-operatives have grown under the aegis of the clergy. It is true that the French-Canadian clergy condemned trade unions when they first appeared in late nineteenth-century Quebec[2] and that the priesthood initiated local Catholic unions in 1907 to safeguard French-speaking workers from the secular unions and, later, from what was called "Bolshevism."[3] The secular groups were also a cultural threat in the sense that they were offshoots of English-speaking unions. When senior prelates expressed disapproval of these associations and of industrialization and its social consequences, they spoke more as French Canadians than as Roman Catholics.[4] The Irish Canadians, who were of the same religion, were a leading force in strikes and in the formation of trade unions in nineteenth-century Quebec. A comparison with contemporary Ontario underlines the contrast between the two major language groups. The English Canadians had a tradition of self-organized, voluntary groups for the achievement of social and cultural aims; the French Canadians did not have a comparable heritage. Beyond a brief flurry of literary institutes in the mid-nineteenth century, French-speaking Quebeckers had few of the private associations so commonplace in English Canada. The absence of this tradition among French-speaking industrial workers can be partially explained by the rural background of many of these men. Writing in the 1930's, Everett Hughes pointed out that "in a stable rural community the French Canadian, like other people so placed, need not and does not actively seek companions and collaborators. They are his by virtue of birth into a family and a community."[5]

French Canada has never been an exclusively agricultural society; it has had an urban and commercial element since the late 1600's. Nor has it been entirely without corporate traditions. In the eighteenth century the seigneurs and merchants in this society acted as cohesive groups and they recommended their interests to the Crown, be it French or British, in numerous petitions. One would expect other groups in a colony that was an extension of seventeenth-century France to have their own secular associations. Contemporary France, after all, had a rich institutional life. In addition to those bodies attached to the Church and the monarchy, there were numerous self-governing institutions that represented municipalities, geographical regions, and occupations. It would have been difficult for craftsmen, in particular, to avoid membership in a corporate body. They were concentrated in the towns where artisan life was dominated by guilds and trade confraternities. For the fixed and itinerant journeymen there were the *compagnonnages* that embraced both town and countryside.[6] It seems to be generally agreed that the crafts in seventeenth-century France, when the colony of New France was permanently established, had a strong institutional tradition.

The failure of French corporate traditions to take firm root in Canada wants a comprehensive explanation. In the rural areas, as E.R. Adair observed, the near absence of compact villages and common lands led, by corollary, to the disappearance of the village assembly in New France. The parish assembly, whose main business was the election of churchwardens, was, Adair wrote, "the only assembly in the country seigneury that had any elements of self-government."[7] The extraordinary rural assemblies held to consider the erection of church buildings and public works such as bridges and roads were limited to those subjects and they required the sanction of the intendant.[8] Since these projects required labour *corvées* and contributions of building materials, the countryfolk often had to be prodded into holding an assembly.

Colonial circumstances, in this case the pattern of settlement, may have been decisive in the countryside. The nature of the colonial towns was not, however, so different from those in France as to bring about singlehandedly the death of the corporate tradition there, too. A study of the urban population could uncover the other forces at work in the colony. The immigrant craftsmen from France were usually townsmen and they would have been more inclined than any other occupational group to carry over their customary associations to the New World. In their failure to maintain their corporate traditions will be clues to the weakness of voluntary associations in early French

Canada. A study of craft associations in New France will furnish part of the historical explanation for a notable characteristic of the French Canadians.

The French artisans who immigrated to Canada in the seventeenth century were indeed attracted to others of the same trade and they wanted to preserve the traditions and distinctions of their particular craft. They had no wider occupational loyalty beyond that of their trade. In the pre-industrial era most craftsmen laboured in small, specialized shops and, as a consequence, they were particularistic. They had no sense of belonging to a "working class." At Quebec in 1646, when the colony was still in its infancy, the organizers of the annual Corpus Christi procession were reminded "qu'il falloit garder l'ordre de l'honneur des mestiers." The ritual precedence of crafts was, however, relaxed to allow the two oldest craftsmen to come first, after a wag had suggested "qu'il falloit donc que les peres menassent les enfans." Each artisan bore a waxen torch and one of the patriarchs, a stonemason, ornamented his with the emblems of his trade: "marteau, compas & reigle."[9]

Other religious celebrations provided an opportunity for expressing the same attachment to the traditions of one's craft. In 1645 at the midnight mass on Christmas Eve the distribution of *pain-benit*, a blending of the Eucharist with the symbolic feeding of the poor, was revived under the sponsorship of the Quebec toolmakers.[10] Each trade had its patron saint and it was common for the artisans of one craft to sponsor a high mass on the feast-day of their saint. These pious observances were sometimes followed by earthly rejoicings over food and drink. The contrast between the two events scandalized the clergy. In the register of the chapel adjoining the St. Maurice ironworks we find the following admonition from Bishop Dubreil de Pontbriand, dated 1 July 1755:

> Ayant été informé qu'on chante en cette paroisse la grande messe, les vespres et qu'on donne la bénédiction du Très Saint Sacrement les jours de Saint-Eloi, de la Translation et de Saint-Thibault [sic], parce que les forgerons ont choisi les deux premiers jours pour honorer leur patron et les charbonniers le troisième; qu'il arrivait que, sous le prétexte de les fêter, . . . plusieurs du village se laissent à des excès scandaleux, . . . nous chargeons le missionaire d'avertir les habitants de la paroisse que si, dans la suite, nous apprenons

qu'on tombe dans les mêmes dérèglements nous défendrons de faire dans ces jours aucune cérémonie extraordinaire.[11]

Religious confraternities or *confréries* were permanent groups for the support of these annual observances and, at times, banquets. They were the only type of craft organization transplanted to New France. Guilds were precluded by the circumstances of the tradesmen and by government policy. The legal rank of master craftsman with the exclusive right to operate a workshop did not exist in Canada, nor did established artisans have a say in who would be allowed to assume that role. After 1627 the rule was that any tradesman who had practised his craft in the colony for six years would be reputed a master artisan in France. This inducement to skilled workers to accept employment in Canada, which was contained in the charter of the Company of New France, broke down the legal distinctions among the craftsmen who remained there. In law, nothing prevented a journeyman from becoming a self-employed artisan or master if he could afford to set up his own shop. In Western European towns a caste of master craftsmen usually controlled admission to their trade and they exercised a disciplinary authority over members of their guild. These powers were the heart of the guild. In New France the "master craftsmen" had no commercial privilege or disciplinary authority to be preserved by an association. Indeed, since guilds were an avenue of taxation in France, Canadian artisans might have considered themselves fortunate to be without such institutions.

The right of inspection over one trade, *la jurande*, would have justified a craft organization and the artisans in Canada very nearly received that right. In the end the Crown reserved the supervision of manual trades to itself. Regulations issued in 1673 and 1676 had promised the institution of "Maistres jurés de chaque mestier [. . .] esleus et nommés par la pluralité des suffrages des artisans de leur profession" to inspect workmanship in the town of Quebec.[12] These inspectors were to be subject to royal confirmation. There is, however, no evidence that these officials, first proposed by Governor Buade de Frontenac, ever came into being. The regulations were probably superseded by an ordinance of March 1677, issued at the king's order, that suppressed all popular spokesmen or *syndics*, elected or otherwise chosen.[13] Jean-Baptiste Colbert, as minister of the navy and colonies, had already advised Frontenac of his desire to "supprimer insensiblement le syndic qui présente des requestes au nom de tous les habitans, estant bon que chacun parle pour soy, et que personne ne parle pour tous."[14] Henceforth, petitions could only be presented by individuals in their name alone. An elected *maître juré*, like a *syndic*, could claim to represent his fellows and their interests and this would interfere with the Crown's management of the economy. The royal officials felt that they were capable of deciding what was in the public interest. Popular elections and assemblies were unpredictable and, therefore, disorderly. Even the occasional *assemblées de police*, in which townsfolk gave advice on the pricing of meat and bread, were abandoned after 1720. The principle of popular consent to the choice of an official, which was implicit in an election, was no longer acceptable in 1677. The monarchy of Louis XIV claimed to be the exclusive source of legitimate, secular authority within the realm and colonies. In the yet unformed colony of New France there were no long-established institutions, beyond the Church, to contest that claim.

When a profession was officially organized for better regulation, it was another matter. Persons in such a group could collectively petition the Crown without fear of punishment. The administration of New France, however, tended to license only those trades affecting the health of the populace. The food trades had to accept a fixed price schedule and supervision and, in return, the bakers and butchers were to be assured of a profit sufficient to allow them a decent living. As a consequence, they were entitled to an official hearing when their livelihood was endangered. This was the major exception to the Crown's refusal to accept representations from lower-class interest groups. Other trades tried to use this privilege and the accepted grounds for petitioning. The administration, for its part, upheld the distinction between officially organized trades and self-constituted groups and it was usually more attentive to the appeals of persons from the upper levels of society.

In May 1729 a representative of the master roofers of Quebec, who were not officially organized, presented a petition to the *Conseil supérieur*. The petition sought a monopoly of roofing for these craftsmen. The intendant's building ordinance of 1727 had outlawed shingle roofing within the towns because of the fire hazard. The roofers of Quebec, however, had made their living from wooden shingles, the principal roofing material in Canada "de tems que Lon puis dire Immemoriale." They had

left board roofing to the joiners and now this other craft controlled the cheapest lawful form of roofing. The roofers
declared that if slate or some other fireproof type of roofing
were not required by law or if they were not given a monopoly,
"Ils Se trouveront de faire Vivre Leur famille que tres modique-
ment." [15] The council, on the advice of the Attorney General, rejected the petition of "les Soy Disants Maitres couvreurs de
Cette Ville . . . attendu qu'il n'y a En Cette Ville ny maitrise ny
Jurande ny droit Exclusif de travailler de quelque art ou
Metier." As a limited concession, shingling was permitted on the
bends and edges of roofs. [16] The concession was insufficient and
the roofers' fears seem to have been justified; only one roofer
was enumerated in the fairly comprehensive census of Quebec in
1744. [17] When a roofer and a toolmaker appeared before the
same body in 1758 as "syndics des bourgeois et citoyens de la
ville des Trois-Rivières" appealing a lower court decision, they
were dismissed without a hearing. Other courts and officials
were forbidden to deal with these *syndics* since "elles n'aient
justifié du droit qu'elles ont de prendre la dite qualité." [18]

The notaries and surgeons, whose occupations were licensed
and who were socially above most craftsmen, were far more successful in protecting and even in extending their official
privileges. In 1668 the notaries of Quebec won their case against
a seigneurial notary who had drawn up deeds inside the town. [19]
In 1710 the surgeons of Quebec petitioned against allowing
ships' surgeons from abroad to practise medicine in the colony
"attendu qu'il est Important pour Le bien publique que personne nexerce La chirurgie que sa Capacité ne soit connue [. . .]
et pour prevenir le mal que lentestement que plusieurs ont pour
La Nouveauté." The Quebec surgeons were concerned with re-
taining their clientele as well as with the maintenance of medical
standards. All surgeons who wished to work in the colony were
supposed to be examined and licensed by a royal appointee, the
lieutenant du premier chirurgien du Roi or the *médecin du Roi* at
Quebec. Since the Crown's authority was involved, the intendant responded to the appeal of the local surgeons and he imposed a stiff fine and penalties on all unlicensed, non-resident
surgeons who treated patients in Canada. [20]

Because their functions were limited to devotions and repasts,
religious confraternities were a safe means of expressing craft
fellowship. They were tolerated by the authorities after precau-
tions were taken to make sure that the groups did not conceal a

coalition for the restraint of trade and employment. So that pious works would remain their principal function, confraternities were subordinated to the Roman Catholic Church which, under the Gallican Settlement, acted as an arm of the state. In sixteenth-century France all *confréries* were ordered suppressed and new groups were then permitted in a reformed state under clerical supervision. By a ruling of the *Parlement* of Paris in 1660 no one could establish "aucunes assemblées, confrairies [sic] et congrégations" without the king's approval by letters patent.[21] The consent of the diocesan bishop was also required and in Canada clerical approval seems to have been sufficient authorization. In 1674 the *Conseil d'Etat* forbade confraternities from collecting money from the public; they were to be entirely supported by the membership and all of their goods were reckoned to be property of the Church. As a final blow to the independence of the brotherhoods, a decree of the *Parlement* of Paris in 1689 denied them the powers of discipline or compulsion over their members.[22] The objective of these laws, which served as a guide for the colonial administration, was to reduce artisan confraternities to tame adjuncts of the Church.

With all these safeguards, Edmé de Freminville was still cynical about the sincerity of religious brotherhoods. "Ces sociétés," he wrote, "ont toutes eu en vue la religion, & son exercice avec plus d'exactitude; mais elles ont enfin degénéré souvent en brigue, factions & désordres, en se couvrant du voile spécieux de la religion. [. . .] Si l'on en ôtoit les repas qui se font par les artisans & autres, l'on en ôteroit toute la dévotion & le mérite."[23]

It was a natural and easy step from religious observances in honour of a craft's patron saint to the formation of a confraternity, which was a permanent association for the sponsorship of such ceremonies. The French craftsmen who immigrated to Canada in the seventeenth century were certainly interested in perpetuating their craft traditions. The wonder is that few trades in New France established confraternities and those that appeared were, by French standards, anaemic affairs. There were only three documented artisan confraternities in the history of the colony. The two that existed in Montreal had an ephemeral or shadowy existence. The venerable Confraternity of St. Anne at Quebec outgrew its craft affiliation. Government attitudes cannot be blamed for this poor showing; brotherhoods were of no concern to the magistracy as long as the groups kept to their religious intentions. The history of the confraternities suggests that the craftsmen in New France were fast losing the ability to create voluntary associations for any purpose.

The Brotherhood of St. Eloi at Montreal was deficient in many things, notably brotherhood. The *confrères* were evidently more interested in merriment than religion and the brawls that accompanied their annual libations were the undoing of the group. This confraternity gave corporate expression to the unusual fellowship among metalworkers of the region. Their affinity in the seventeenth century is apparent in the church records which show smiths acting as godparents for a fellow worker's child or as witnesses to the marriage of another metalworker. The group also reflected the loss of craft identity among native-born *Canadiens*.

The five men who founded the metalworkers' confraternity at Montreal in 1676 were all French immigrants, though three had lived in Canada for a score of years and two of them had arrived in the colony as adolescents. At this time there were over a dozen metalworkers in and around Montreal and yet the membership of the society never seems to have grown beyond the original five. The composition and size of the group seems odd considering that Canadian society was no longer in the pioneering stage; New France was a well-established colony with a population of 8,500 Europeans in 1676. This small immigrant group was the only known craft brotherhood formed in the Montreal area during the seventeenth century. If this was the best that could be done by a trade with a notable sense of craft loyalty, then the disunity and indifference of other artisans can well be imagined.

In comparison with the *Confrérie de Sainte-Anne,* the Brotherhood of St. Eloi was a rudimentary organization. The charter consisted of one paragraph drawn up on 4 December 1676 and in it the metalworkers declared their intention "de solemniser la feste de St. Eloy, de faire dire une grande messe, donner un pain benit et cotiser Chacun une pistolle [eleven *livres*] pour se regaller et mettre entre les mains de celuy la qui fera dire La messe." They then drew lots to establish the order in which each member would act as the year's organizer for the mass and banquet.[24] The dues were more than enough for a feast. No offices were created although the oldest among them, Pierre Gadois *fils*, assumed the role of *doyen*. A few days later the smiths signed a *concordat* with the churchwardens of Notre Dame de Montréal parish confirming the workers' intention to sponsor a high mass on the feast-day of their patron saint.

The animosity of two members, René Fezeret and Guillory, was at the heart of the conflicts that disrupt Confrérie de Saint-Eloi. Fezeret was to have been the ho. the banquet in 1677, but the hostility of his wife to the e\ compelled the brethren to dine at the home of Gadois.[25] During the meal Guillory started an argument by goading Fezeret and by telling him that the gunsmiths of the company were doing Fezeret, a blacksmith and locksmith, a great honour by suffering his presence among them. Even in this little circle of metal-workers there remained a divisive sense of occupational rank. At least, this dispute did not go beyond words between the two principals.[26]

In 1678 Guillory was the last one to receive *pain-bénit* from the church beadle at the high mass. He and the others believed that Fezeret had a hand in this and they afterwards claimed that he had admitted it. Precedence in a public ceremony reflected one's social standing and to be served last by intent was a grave insult. The others mocked Fezeret when he lost in a game of cards after the supper. A fight then erupted involving Fezeret, Guillory, a third *confrère*, and their respective wives.[27] It was a disorderly conclusion for a day that was supposed to reaffirm the comradeship of the metalworkers.

Three of the members, including Guillory, blamed Fezeret for the troubles and two days after the banquet they added a post-script to the group's charter stating "Nous avons banny de nostre société fezeret estant seditieux."[28] In expelling Fezeret, they had assumed that they possessed the right to be self-governing and that they were not subject to clerical authority. In the eyes of the magistracy, this assumption was presumption indeed and, to the misfortune of the brethren, the expulsion came to the attention of the Bailiff's Court at Montreal in the winter of 1680-81.

In that winter two plaintiffs acted against the Confraternity of St. Eloi. The first was René Fezeret, who complained of being libelled as *un séditieux* and who demanded a public retraction with damages as well as nullification of the expulsion.[29] He had not heard of the ban until 1680 because, through the negligence of his old foe Simon Guillory, there had been no celebration in 1679. Fezeret pointed this out with righteous satisfaction. This information brought the churchwardens before the court to have their *concordat* with the group enforced.[30] As acting *doyen*, Pierre Gadois had tried to compel Guillory to do his duty, he had endeavoured to reconcile Fezeret with the others, and he gave the magistrate assurance that the remaining members would continue to sponsor the religious observances.[31] The judge, Migeon de Branssat, was not moved by Gadois. The combination of an aggrieved *confrère* with the churchwardens was fatal to the independence and secular interests of the brotherhood and the arguments of the plaintiffs gave de Branssat justification enough to chasten the group.

The churchwardens coveted the substantial dues of the confraternity which, they felt, would be better spent on the church than on banquets. They therefore blamed the suppers for the conflicts while also claiming that the meals were "Contre Les ordonnances qui Deffendent Les Réguale [régals]." They asked that the dues be applied to the construction and upkeep of the parish church.[32] On the following day Fezeret presented a supplementary petition desiring that the magistrate enforce "Les ordonences Sur Les Deffences faites a LEsgards des assemblées." He charged the other brethren with holding an illicit gathering to expel "un tres honeste homme comme je prestends Estre Et sans nuls Raisons" in contempt of the king's laws and justice.[33]

De Branssat's judgement in February 1681 dealt a crushing blow to the metalworkers' brotherhood. The group was ordered to fulfil the religious obligations of the charter and to expunge the ban on Fezeret. The three authors of the expulsion were fined six *livres* each, payable to the church building fund, and charged court costs. The worst was to come. The *confrères* were also deprived of disciplinary authority over any member and were henceforth forbidden to hold any more "assemblées ou festins." One assumes that all of the dues would go to the church, though this is not stated. The celebrations in honour of St. Eloi were thereafter to be confined to a high mass with *pain-bénit* and the smiths' obligation to sponsor this service was to be enforced by the churchwardens.[34] The little confraternity was no longer an autonomous body with secular functions; it had been reduced to a band of involuntary co-sponsors for a religious ceremony. It is likely that the loss of the banquet and the forced reconciliation with Fezeret destroyed the members' enthusiasm for the brotherhood. There are no further references to it.

Literacy may have been the undoing of the metalworkers, for their written charter and its defamatory appendix were turned against them. The confraternity of the Montreal shoemakers had no charter – possibly because few members could write more than their names – and it had more freedom of action than the other two brotherhoods. This group was not subordinated to the church and it did serve the members' economic interests, which was something that the authorities had always feared.

The first reference to "la communauté des cordonniers," otherwise known as *la Confrérie de Saint-Crépin et Saint-Crépinien*, dates from October 1728. On the surface the group seemed to be a very loosely organized confraternity with only one gathering a year. Three representatives of the society, Jean Ridday *dit* Beauceron, Edmé Moreau, and Jacques Viger, presented a request to the royal court at Montreal to have a fellow shoemaker provide the *pain-bénit* for a mass on St. Simon's day since he had failed to do it on the feast-day of their patrons "En la maniere accoutumée." The defendant replied "quil N'a jamais refusé d'obeir a lancienne Convention de la Confrairie de St. Crespin Et St. Crespignon," but that no one had contributed to the cost of the mass. He was willing, he said, to pay his share and to provide the holy bread for distribution, though he was bound by no written act to do so. The court ordered him to make good his offer and the magistrate advised the spokesmen of the confraternity that the entire membership ought to share the cost of the annual service if they wanted the association to continue.[35] The casual nature of the brotherhood and the fact that two of the three spokesmen were French immigrants are further evidence of the decline in the tradition of workers' associations in New France. Native leadership was wanting and the structure of this group was even more primitive than that of the metalworkers' confraternity. At the same time, it was a flexible organization that received widespread support from the shoemakers of Montreal.

The evidence that the Confraternity of Saints Crispin and Crispian was more than a religious brotherhood came in the following year. In August 1729 the same three who had represented the confraternity presented a petition to the *lieutenant-général* or magistrate of the Montreal court. The appeal was endorsed by twenty-three shoemakers of the town. It was an impressive showing and even more impressive was the fact that over two-thirds of the subscribers were Canadian-born craftsmen. Since the French immigrants, including a few former soldiers, headed the list, one assumes that they were the initiators of the movement.[36]

The petition pointed out that, contrary to the intendant's ordinance of 20 July 1706, a local butcher called Joseph Guyon Després was engaged in tanning and shoemaking. The ordinance had ordered the separation of these trades to foster competition and to provide butchers, tanners, and shoemakers with "le moyen de subsister en les reduisant . . . aux fonctions qui conviennent à leur profession."[37] The combination of these trades in the hands of one person gave that individual an unfair advantage because he could control the price and quantity of raw materials available to competing tanners and shoemakers. He would, of course, give his own workers the best hides at cost. The abuse was not new. In 1674 four Quebec shoemakers had obtained a provisional decree from the *Conseil souverain* to compel a tanner to supply them with leather and to close his shoemaking shop.[38] The profits from such a closed operation must have been high, for tannery owners in New France commonly manufactured shoes as a sideline.

In 1729 the Montreal shoemakers complained that Després' little empire did "un tort Considerable a tous les Suplians, d'autant que led[it] desprez et Sa femme tirent Les peaux de Leur boucherie, et les Cuirs de Leur tannerie, Et que faisant employer eux même lesd[its] Cuirs Ils peuvent donner les Souliers a un prix bien plus médiocre que . . . tous lesd[its] Suplians." The butcher, they said, was selling his cheap shoes in the rural settlements (*côtes*) of the region as well as in the town. This illegal operation left the independent shoemakers without work. The petitioners used the conventional plea of an endangered livelihood to support their request for enforcement of the 1706 ordinance, a copy of which they attached to the petition. They were, it was said, "fort douleureux qu'après avoir passé une partie de Leur Jeunesse a aprendre led[it] metier de Cordonnier et avoir fait tous Chacuns une Etablissement pour pouvoir En gaignant Leur vies, faire Subsister Leurs familles, Ils se trouvent dans L'impossibilité de le faire N'ayant point d'ouvrages."[39]

The *lieutenant-général* was in an awkward position. Much as he disliked having shoemakers instruct him on his duties, the law had to be enforced. If he complied, however, he would be encouraging an economic pressure group of social inferiors. The tanners, whose number was occasionally fixed by law, might be considered a licensed trade but the allied craft of shoemaking did not really qualify. After hearing both sides, he consulted with the crown attorney and then referred the parties to the current intendant for a decision on the case.[40] Here the records fail us. Perhaps the intendant gave a verbal judgement that was never registered. We know that the author of the ordinance, Intendant Raudot, had compromised his law within a year of its enactment[41] and that his successors were indifferent to its enforcement since it did not affect the health of the public. Had the shoemakers gone to the expense of carrying their appeal to Quebec, they could not be certain that they would be received. Even if the representatives of the shoemakers' association obtained a hearing, it was unlikely that they would have received a favourable decision. The fate of the Quebec roofers' petition in May 1729 was a precedent for rejection.

An earlier petition of the Montreal shoemakers had been rejected. In 1712 they had asked the *Conseil supérieur* for permission to have shoe leather delivered to their shops on Sundays and holy days after mass. The tanneries were located outside the town and the shoemakers may have been anxious to avoid any delay in their work for want of materials. Delivery on the holidays would have permitted labour to begin in the morning of the following workday. The shoemakers said that this was done elsewhere and that if permission were not granted, they and their families would face imminent ruin. The proposal was firmly refused by the Superior Council.[42]

The two petitions set the Montreal shoemakers apart from other unlicensed trades; they were able to organize themselves more than once to petition on behalf of their trade. Since the three spokesmen of the Confraternity of Saints Crispin and Crispian also led the petitioners of 1729, the brotherhood was a factor in drawing the shoemakers together. Their fellowship was reinforced by kinship and intermarriage. The same group may have been behind the 1712 petition, but we will never know. The informality of the association meant that its history was largely unrecorded. The impressive turnout in support of the 1729 petition could indicate that the master shoemakers were united; it might also suggest that they were desperate. They drew attention to the growth of their craft since 1706 and the apprenticeship indentures made in the Montreal region confirm the fact that until 1730 theirs had been the fastest-growing and most popular manual trade of all. After this period apprentices to shoemakers were outnumbered by those engaged in joinery and metalworking, and apprentice shoemakers serving for two or more years no longer paid their masters for training.[43] Shoemaking had lost its appeal and this might have been related to a change in the fortune of the shoemakers that would indeed make them "fort douleureux" in 1729. Whether the butcher Després was entirely responsible for their situation is open to question.

The rebuffs given to workers' associations by the courts and officials in New France would undoubtedly discourage the formation of other craft groups. The Crown saw an advantage in keeping guilds and privileged craft groups out of the colony; the disunity of artisans facilitated the diffusion of skills and encouraged competition among them. Both consequences were desirable in a poor but rapidly growing society. As late as 1741 the governor and intendant could still write of a distant future "lorsqu'il sera temps d'etablir des maitrises, des communautés et des jurandes."[44] Until then, self-constituted artisan groups and demands for economic protection from unlicensed trades were to be turned aside.

The death of a corporate tradition among the craftsmen of New France had something to do with the hostility of the Bourbon administration to popular associations among social inferiors. It would be facile, however, to place the entire blame on those in authority. The impetus to form workers' associations was diminishing in the colony. The dominance of the French immigrants in the confraternities and their leadership of the Montreal shoemakers, even when they were a minority in the society, reflected the divergence between the attitudes of the newcomers and the values of the *Canadiens*. The native-born colonials lacked cohesion and they seemed indifferent to trade associations. They were less likely to act in concert with others of the same trade and from this we can assume that their attachment to their occupational group was weak.

The divergence of immigrant and colonial craftsmen was part of a classic New World phenomenon; it was the result of greater social and occupational mobility. The French artisan had grown up in a society in which a majority of craftsmen would always be employees. Advancement from journeyman to master was difficult and advancement to a higher social level was doubly so. The closed organization of urban crafts hindered a changing of occupations. In these circumstances one's lot was tied to the fortunes of the trade and each man gained from the advancement of his occupational group. It was hard, if not impossible, to avoid the effects of a setback to one's craft. In France not only was the artisan more closely associated with his craft, he also had a strong personal incentive to engage in collective action.

The French immigrants to Canada came with the ideals of self-employment and family independence. In the colony it was possible for the ideals to become reality. No man was obliged to accept lifelong subservience when fertile land was free and abundant and when craft mastership was open. In New France servitude became the lot of destitute children, unskilled bachelors, poor immigrants, the aged, and slaves. *Canadiens* with a skill, physical strength, the aid of a wife, and money for their own establishment rejected hired service. Journeymanship became one stepping-stone among others to self-employment as a master tradesman. If one craft were not satisfactory, one could embrace another skill or, as was often done, exercise more than one trade. Loyalty to the family's traditional occupation diminished in Canada and this is evident in the difference between the parental occupation of indentured apprentices and their chosen trade. Even when the father's death forced a child to learn how to earn a living from another, few children elected training in the late parent's occupation. The opportunity for personal advancement and the freedom to change trades in New France undermined craft unity and joint action by artisans.

The evidence that the colonial craftsmen had developed values that would hinder co-operation among themselves is provided by the partnerships and artisans' indentures registered by notaries during the French regime. There are some 1,200 apprenticeship indentures surviving from New France; this is more than triple the number of employment contracts made with craftsmen in the colony to work at their trade. Only a small fraction of these service contracts were with a master who was also an artisan; most of the indentured craftsmen were employees of merchants and entrepreneurs. Very few were true journeymen – craftsmen serving a master artisan – and in early Canada there was no large or stable class of journeymen. On the whole, former apprentices bypassed that condition so common in Europe. In the French colony journeymanship was not a compulsory prelude to self-employment and there were other means of acquiring the capital for one's own establishment. In contrast with service to another artisan, those alternatives paid well and they took less time. A contract with a commercial enterprise or one trip as a voyageur in the fur trade provided sufficient funds for the transformation into a master in most trades. Other craftsmen could not offer comparable wages and, for want of journeymen, they relied on apprentices for skilled help. Apprentices who served for more than two years, when they could grasp the essentials of a trade, customarily received a clothing allowance and, frequently, a small salary. They benefited from the *Canadiens'* disdain for journeymanship.

The aversion for hired service was founded on certain assumptions; it was not, as French officials and the local elite believed, a manifestation of excessive pride. The popular assumptions become evident when one looks at the composition of a group of ninety-three indentured craftsmen from Quebec and Montreal. The sample comes primarily from the first half of the eighteenth century when colonial attitudes were firmly defined. The native Canadians in the group were most likely to be in their twenties and men who were not yet married. The immigrants were, by contrast, usually older and more likely to continue as employees after marriage. The pattern indicates a conviction held by the *Canadiens* that a *père de famille* ought to be his own master, that servitude was an unnatural condition for a married man above the age of thirty. They also had the good fortune to be in a society in which one could choose between servitude and self-employment. Naturally, they preferred the role that offered the greatest independence.

There was, in the minds of the colonials, an association between family independence and self-employment and their pursuit of both goals conflicted with voluntary associations on the smallest scale. To judge from the partnership contracts made in New France, material benefits could not induce the independent master tradesmen to compromise their autonomy. There were obvious advantages to a commercial partnership between two craftsmen. It was more economical to share a shop and tools than to maintain separate establishments. Since a master artisan was both the producer and the seller of his manufactures, it would be more efficient to share these functions with another. Finally, the associates could draw on greater capital and credit than a single individual and they could thereby expand their trade. Despite these attractions, French-Canadian artisans shunned business alliances. As for assistance in operating a workshop, they preferred to use subordinates such as apprentices or the wife and children.

As it was in the case of artisans' indentures, the number of notarized partnerships involving craftsmen is small. No more than 150 appear to have been made in New France. Moreover, craft partnerships, like other forms of association, were falling into disuse. As the population of the colony grew, fewer and fewer contracts were registered. The file of a minor notary at Montreal, Claude Maugue (fl. 1677-96), contains seven *actes de société* with craftsmen and references to six others. In the same region in the second quarter of the eighteenth century one has to ransack the files of eight notaries to find an equivalent number of deeds.[45] At Quebec the same trend was apparent in three successive notarial files of equal size: twelve craft partnerships were passed by Louis Chambalon (fl. 1692-1716) and six were registered by Jean-Etienne Dubreuil (fl. 1708-1734), a former shoemaker with many artisans in his clientele; the records of Claude Barolet (fl. 1728-60) contain only mercantile alliances.[46] In the same period the incomplete censuses of the town in 1716 and 1744 recorded an increase in the number of craftsmen enumerated from 134 to 376.[47] The decline of craft partnerships was absolute and, in relationship to the population, it was spectacular.

This drop coincided with two trends in the population of the colony. The first, which was neutral, was the proportionate increase in married couples and the reduction of bachelors to a minority of the adult males. Because of the small number of nubile, white females in the first years of the colony, the adult population in the seventeenth century had contained a high proportion of bachelors. Unmarried artisans would be more likely to avail themselves of a partnership. Since the natural auxiliaries of a craftsman were his wife and family, it is to be expected that partnerships between strangers would decrease as more of the males acquired the assistance of a family. The second trend was the growth in the proportion of native Canadians in the population. By the eighteenth century they, and not the immigrants, were the majority and in the decline of artisan partnerships we may see the consequence of their preoccupation with family autonomy.

Alliances involving craftsmen survived into the eighteenth century, but the few that were made indicate that the *Canadiens* only accepted collaboration with a stranger when it was forced upon them. Partnerships were concentrated in trades that demanded great physical exertion and substantial operating capital; in short, they required the resources of more than one person. Of eighteen agreements made at Quebec in the years 1692-1740 the distribution by occupation was as follows: five in metalwork, four in butchering, three in baking, two in masonry construction, two in tanning, and one each in pottery and milling.[48] The range of eight partnerships made in the Montreal area in the period 1727-59 was more limited: four in metalwork, three in tanning, and one in shoemaking.[49] Accords between two butchers and between a single butcher and a butcher's widow, who possessed facilities for the trade, were expressly "pour leur faciliter led[it] Commerce et trouver plus facilement Le Credit dont ils pouront avoir besoin."[50] Tanning was a very costly enterprise and it accounted for a fifth to a quarter of all notarized craft partnerships. Baking and the forging of iron not only required a heavy investment in raw materials and facilities; they also demanded simultaneous labour at different tasks. A smith, for example, disposed of a hearth and a wide array of tools; he kept a good store of charcoal and bar iron and, to work metal, one person had to pump the bellows while the other wielded the hammer.

Close inspection of the parties to craft partnerships and the terms of the agreement reveals the effect of the same values that were perceived in artisans' indentures. Most of the service indentures did not involve journeymanship and most of the craft partnerships were not true co-partnerships – that is, alliances of equals. One rarely finds a business association in which both parties were craftsmen of equal standing and capable of matching the other's contribution; such partnerships were usually confined to metalworking and masonry construction. In over three-quarters of the cases a single craftsman would be teamed up with a merchant-investor, a lesser speculator, an elderly artisan, or the widow of a tradesman. There were always a few entrepreneurs willing to invest in a secondary industry. All of these people lacked the physical ability to operate a manufacturing enterprise by themselves; they needed a skilled and healthy assistant. . . . Most were unequal partnerships. There was, typically, a senior party in his forties or older who was to provide the facilities and equipment for the tannery, forge, bakery, or brewery. There would be a junior partner, usually an unmarried man in his twenties, who was invariably a craftsman. As a group, the junior partners closely resembled the native Canadian craftsmen who accepted indentured service.

The similarity between indentured *Canadien* artisans and the junior partners in craft alliances is the clue to what had happened to manufacturing partnerships in New France – they had become a substitute for a service indenture. Partnerships overcame the prejudices of the colonial tradesman by elevating him from the ranks of the servile before he could do it for himself. The arrangement was beneficial to the senior partner, too. The worker-partner was likely to work harder than a hired man for he profited in proportion to his productivity; a worker-employee on a fixed, annual salary had no such incentive. The evidence that the junior partner was taking the place of an indentured craftsman is contained in the terms of the agreement. The artisan, like an employee, was usually fed and housed at the company's expense; he was to labour assiduously for the benefit of the company. Some contracts followed the example of service indentures and inserted penalty clauses for absenteeism and premature departure. Sick leave might also be limited to eight days in the year. The intention was to keep the worker-partner on the job. The duties of the investor-partner or senior party were more loosely defined, if they were defined at all. He would occasionally help in buying materials and assist in retailing the product; most were passive and left the business in the hands of the artisan, who was to give a regular accounting. In brief, the senior partner's role was very close to that of an employer.

The fact that would-be employers had to entice skilled workers with the status of a partner shows how much the *Canadiens* prized their independence. A partnership was also used to retain the services of a former apprentice or journeyman. One of the first *actes de société* between craftsmen in New France was made in 1653 between a toolmaker and his journeyman, who was to aid the senior partner at the forge and on his farm "a partager moitié par moytié."[51] The transition from subordinate to associate was more complex in the case of Léonard Paillard, an immigrant from Poitiers. In 1672 he apprenticed himself to a carpenter living outside Quebec for three years with an annual salary of sixty *livres*. Two years later his master sold the indenture of his partially trained apprentice to another carpenter, who recognized the value of his new ward by tripling his salary for the third and last year of service. A month before the expiration of the indenture the second carpenter engaged his helper as a partner for another three years in return for further training, a third of all profits, and an additional forty *livres* a year, which may have been a living allowance.[52] The same sequence was to be seen in the career of Gabriel Lenoir Rolland in early eighteenth-century Montreal. He was successively apprentice, journeyman, and then partner to a tanner. This promotion and even the hand of his former master's daughter in marriage did not ensure his fidelity; Lenoir attempted to move to another tannery in violation of his partnership.[53]

Lenoir may have regretted the length of his commitment which was for five years. This was the average duration of a tanning partnership. Since a tannery and its attendant works cost 3,000 or more *livres*, a partnership in that trade had to last from three to seven years to justify the investment. Colonial artisans were loath to tie themselves down, even as partners, for such a long time. Partnership, like hired service, was a stepping-stone to self-employment; it was not accepted as a lifetime career. Craftsmen in New France rarely accepted an association for more than three years and they almost never renewed their commitment. If further proof be needed of the colonials' disinclination for economic co-operation, it may be found in the brevity of craft partnerships. Five months to three years was as much as they would accept for small-scale ventures using existing or limited facilities. The favourite term was one year which was, significantly, the median term for artisans' indentures of service.

To gratify artisan-partners and to retain their services, they were given a share of the profits that was disproportionate to their contribution to the undertaking. The dominant form of craft partnership in New France was a hybrid of two traditional forms of association. These were defined by the royal ordinance of March 1673 known as the *Code Marchand*. The first was termed *société générale* or, as an index to its frequency, *société ordinaire*. It was an agreement "entre deux ou plusieurs personnes, & dans laquelle les associés conferent également leur argent & leurs soins."[54] The partners were customarily equal contributors and both were actively involved in the joint venture. Above all, they shared equally in the profits and losses of their trade.[55] In the light of their contributions and work, this was a reasonable division of the rewards. The second type, *société en commandite*, was "entre plusieurs associés, dont l'un ne fournit que son argent & les autres donnent leur argent & leur travail, ou leur travail seulement."[56] The share of each partner would be proportional to his investment.

. . . The contracts . . . are largely *sociétés en commandite*. There was a dominant partner who bore almost all the expenses of the business, including the living expenses of the artisan-partner. At most, the craftsman would share the cost of raw materials and other operating expenses, such as the pay of an additional worker engaged by the enterprise. Most investor-partners could demand repayment of their initial outlay before a division of the profits; they did not, as a rule, do this. They were content to retain title to the fixed facilities built at their cost. Since the investor-partner bore most of the expenses and took all the risks, it would be fair if he or she took more than half of the profits. This did not happen in Canada.

With few exceptions, the profits from a craft partnership were shared equally in Canada. The exceptions came when preliminary financial adjustments or the payment of a bonus made the division unequal. Yet, out of deference to the prevailing fashion, the accord gave the customary assurance that the fruits were to be "partagé entre eux également par moitié." Parity in the division of the benefits seems to have been the rule for small business partnerships in the colony. Half of the profits were given by fur trade concessionaires to their factors and by merchant-owners of stores to their shopkeepers.[57] Owners of small vessels sailing out of Quebec had to offer half of the profits to their *navigateurs*.[58] That, evidently, was the price that had to be paid for the services of skilled persons who balked at being salaried employees. The ability of the craftsmen to command the partnership rights of a *société ordinaire* in what were essentially *sociétés en commandite* is a testimony to their bargaining power in dealing with prospective employers. This anomaly, the brevity of the indentures and partnerships, their small number, and the terms of the agreements are witness to the reluctance of the *Canadiens* to abandon even momentarily their goals of self-employment and family independence.

This obsession with self-sufficiency distinguished the Canadians from their French cousins and hindered the development of secondary industries as well as limited the size of workshops. The typical workshop in New France was a small affair employing the master craftsman, his family, and, perhaps, one or two apprentices. It was exceptional to find more than one artisan-employee under one roof. A few would be found in a tannery and, in the construction trades, there was a seasonal concentration of several artisans under one employer. The general dispersal of craftsmen in the colony confirmed their disunity; this was the result of the workers' social ambitions. It would be a reversal of cause and effect to say that the scarcity of large, secondary industries employing wage-earners produced this disunity. Such an argument also assumes that only employees will be inclined to engage in collective action. As we have seen, the master craftsmen had common material interests to be defended and a major threat to those interests could force them to act together.

In the eighteenth century there were two places in New France where hired craftsmen were gathered in large numbers. In the 1730's the St. Maurice ironworks were established near Trois-Rivières; this was the home of the disorderly workers reprimanded by Bishop Pontbriand. In 1738, the same year that the ironworks began production, the intendant of the colony received authorization to undertake the construction of warships and transports in Canada. The royal shipyards were located at Quebec and they employed some 200 craftsmen. Both enterprises depended heavily on imported labour to make up their work force. Few Canadians remained at the shipyards for, as the intendant remarked of one of them, "il prefére sa Liberté a estre assujeti a une Cloche." [59]

The royal shipyards at Quebec were the site of Canada's first recorded strike by skilled workers. In the light of what we know about the individualistic mentality of the colonial artisans, it is not surprising to find that the strikers were all French immigrants. One could plead that since the *Canadiens* disdained the role of employee, they were rarely in the position of having to strike against an employer. There were, however, Canadians in this shipyard and, while they did not share the grievance of the French workers, they showed no sympathy for the strikers. Our only source on the event is an official dispatch of October 1741 in which it was reported that "Les charpentiers envoyez de Rochefort [in France] ont bien fait leur devoir, M. Hocquart [the intendant] s'est cependant trouvé dans la nécessité de reprimer dans les Commencements et une seule fois par la prison et les fers leur mutinerie qui estoit allé au point de résister au Commandement et de ne vouloir point travailler sous des hangards du Roy, quoyqu'ils soient engagés au mois, lorsque les Canadiens estoient congediez à cause du mauvais temps." It seems that the French shipwrights felt that if the weather were bad enough to justify the laying off of the Canadians, who were paid by the day, then they, too, ought to be exempt from labour. We have the assurance of the authorities that, because of the intendant's firm action, the rebellious workers "ont reconnu leur faute et sont très dociles." [60]

This episode underlines two factors in the decline of co-operation and collective action among the craftsmen of early French Canada. There was the attitude of the administration that equated "bon ordre" with the subordination of the lower ranks of society. The magistrates' concern with social discipline and with keeping down the cost of goods and labour made them intolerant of self-constituted workers' groups with secular interests. The second factor, the mentality of the colonial artisans, meant that they would never really threaten the status quo. The first loyalty of the *Canadien* was to himself and to his family. Loyalty to one's trade was reduced to the level of a traditional vocation of a few families and fidelity was conditional on the assurance that the trade would provide a good living and respectability to the practitioner. In New France respectability was associated with self-employment. Service to the king was honourable; service to others for material gain was generally regarded as degrading. This concern for being one's own master was combined with social conservatism so that on the rare occasions when workers coalesced to protect their economic interests, their collective representations took the orthodox form of a petition to those in power, to whom the workers attributed the power for rectification. There is no evidence of profound or enduring social discontent among the craftsmen and they did not challenge the legitimacy of the colonial government which was, by current French standards, a lenient ruler. The administration could be ruthless in dealing with protesters, as we have seen, but it was unlikely that the Canadian artisans would ever organize themselves to force a change in royal policy. Thus, it appears that the disappearance of a corporate tradition among the craftsmen had as much to do with the workers themselves as it did with the colony's administration.

The loss of a tradition of self-organization for economic and social purposes among the craftsmen and the legacy of values developed in the French regime had unfortunate consequences for French-Canadian workers in the industrial era. Economic combinations of employees were alien to these workers and they lacked secular associations such as the "friendly societies" of the English-speaking workers that might represent their material interests. Artisan confraternities, because of their legal subordination to the Roman Catholic Church, were not suited for this role. Yet this was the only historic model for workers' associations within the culture of the *Canadiens*. If the industrial labourers had no knowledge of these groups, it is certain that educated French Canadians were aware of them at the end of the nineteenth century, thanks to the publication of the 1678 charter of the *Confrérie de Sainte-Anne* and articles in such journals as the *Bulletin des Recherches historiques*.[61] It is remarkable that the early Catholic trade unions resembled the Confraternity of St. Anne and it may be that the clerics who founded these groups consciously took that brotherhood as their guide. Further research needs to be done on the matter to establish more than a circumstantial connection between the unions and the confraternity.

If it seems to be a bold jump across 150 years to link the Catholic unions of the Province of Quebec with the craft brotherhoods of New France or the attitudes manifested in the industrial era with the experience of the French regime, let it be remembered that this was French Canada's formative period. Assuming that one can draw an analogy between a society and an individual and that one accepts Sigmund Freud's dictum, borrowed from Wordsworth, that the child is father to the man, then to ignore the events of that early period is consciously to limit our understanding of French Canada. The historical background is not the whole answer, but it is a significant portion of it. There is no doubt that the unionization of labour was slower in the Province of Quebec than it was in the other industrialized regions of Canada, which were ethnically different. Any explanation of that fact must take into account the historic and cultural background of the *Canadiens* as well as the economic and social circumstances of the industrial period. Clerical attitudes have been emphasized in explanations of why it took French Canada so long to accept the world of industry as though the clergy could dictate social values. The *Canadiens*, however, are notorious for going their own way and it seems that the priests reflected, rather than determined, a social climate that was cool to self-constituted, secular unions.

Not only did the French-Canadian workers before the First World War lack an historic model for banding together to act on behalf of their common interest, they also lacked a working-class mentality to sustain trade unions. In a society nurtured on the dream of self-employment and material independence, wage labourers would not readily accept their condition as permanent. To admit that would be, in terms of their culture, a confession of failure. This attitude is usually ascribed to the rural background of many of the factory workers and to the social teachings of the Roman Catholic clergy who advised French Canadians of humble origins to prefer agricultural life to work in industry. The farm was held to be the ideal environment for the fulfilment of the spiritual vocation of the *Canadiens* and for the maintenance of their culture. This creed could be seen as an aspect of a general and long-established disdain for the role of the employee.

The agrarian myth was supplemented by an artisanal myth. In the pre-industrial period craftsmanship had provided French Canadians with a measure of self-respect and a modest prosperity. As late as 1936 Abbé Lionel Groulx could still appeal to the golden memory of the self-employed artisan in a speech given before the young businessmen and lawyers of the Province of Quebec. He called upon the schools to revive "la passion d'être son propre patron, son propre maître." After exhorting farmers to perfect their skills, Abbé Groulx addressed himself to other manual workers:

> petits industriels, petits ouvriers de chez nous, retrouvez le goût du travail patient, de l'article fabriqué avec perfection et amour; à la production quantitative, massive, opposez la production qualitative, à la française; . . . persuadés que le plus modeste patron canadien-français travaillant pour soi et pour les siens, que le petit artiste en fer forgé ciselant son oeuvre dans le trou d'une cave fait plus, pour l'émancipation de sa nationalité, que le plus grand de nos salariés au service d'une firme étrangère.[62]

His description of the humble artisan working in the darkness of a basement was an indirect acknowledgement that the age of the independent and contented craftsman had passed. With the death of that dream, the workers of French Canada had to rediscover the pattern that the Bourbon administration had suppressed and their ancestors had abandoned: the co-operation of workers for the advancement of their trade.[63]

NOTES

1. J.P. Mayer, éd., *Oeuvres, Papiers et Correspondances d'Alexis de Tocqueville*, 12 vols. (Paris, 1951-64), V, 215.
2. Jean Hamelin et Yves Roby, *Histoire économique du Québec: 1851-1896* (Montréal, 1971), 57.
3. J.P. Archambault, *Les Syndicats catholiques, un digue contre le Bolchévisme* (Montréal, 1919).

4. The principal exponents of the view that the French Canadians had a spiritual vocation that would be betrayed by involvement in industry were Mgr. Louis F.R. Lafleche and Mgr. Louis-Adolphe Pâquet. Mgr. Pâquet's "Sermon on the Vocation of the French Race in America" (1902) has been reprinted in translation in G.R. Cook, ed., *French-Canadian Nationalism: An Anthology* (Toronto, 1969), 152-60.

5. Everett Hughes, *French Canada in Transition* (Chicago, 1963), 122.

6. Luc Benoist, *Le Compagnonnage et les Métiers* (Paris, 1966); Emile Coornaert, *Les Corporations en France avant 1789* (Paris, 1941); Pierre Goubert, *The Ancien Regime: French Society, 1600-1750* (New York, 1974), 217-19. In *L'Organisation corporative de la France d'Ancien Régime* (Paris, 1938), François Olivier-Martin describes "l'étonnante variété des corps dont notre ancienne société etait largement faite." His case seems to be overstated and may have been influenced by contemporary interest in the corporate state. The theory that France in the old regime was a society of orders based on occupation goes back to Charles Loyseau in the early seventeenth century and its current exponent is Roland Mousnier.

7. Edward R. Adair, "The French-Canadian Seigneury," *CHR*, XXXV, 3 (1954), 206.

8. *IOI, passim*.

9. C.H. Laverdière et H.R. Casgrain, éds., *Le Journal des Jésuites* (Montréal, 1892), 48-9.

10. *Ibid.*, 20.

11. Benjamine Sulte, *Les forges Saint-Maurice* (Montréal, 1920), 123-4.

12. *OCGI*, I, 135; *JDCS*, II, 67.

13. Ordinance of Governor Buade de Frontenac, 23 March 1677, *RAPQ*, 1927-28, opposite xvi.

14. Colbert to Frontenac, 13 June 1673, *RAPQ* (1926-27), 25.

15. Archives du Quebec (AQ), NF 11, Registres du Conseil supérieur, XXXV, 129-129v; NF 13, Dossiers du Conseil supérieur, II, 54-6.

16. See AQ, NF 11, XXXV, 129v; Thomas Dupuy, who had issued the ordinance of 7 June 1727 on house construction, made the same concession in a particular case on 13 June. See AQ, NF 13, II, 56. The Récollet friars were given an exemption from the ordinance for their church's roof in August 1728. See *IOI*, II, 35.

17. "Le recensement de Quebec, en 1744," *RAPQ* (1939-40), 1-154.

18. Pierre-Georges Roy, *Inventaire des jugements et délibérations du Conseil supérieur de la Nouvelle-France de 1717 a 1760*, 7 vols. (Beauceville, 1932-35), VI, 127.

19. PAC, MG 8, B 1 (Québec Prévôté), II-1, 96-7, 303-5.

20. AQ, NF 2, Ordonnances des Intendants, IV, 68; a marginal note states that several copies of this ruling were made for distribution.

21. De Freminville, *Dictionnaire*, 184; Archives de la Charente-Maritime, Série B, registre 1326 (1660-70), 13 December 1660.
22. Coornaert, *Les Corporations en France avant 1789*, 234-6; Claude-Joseph de Ferrière, *Dictionnaire de Droit et de Pratique*, 2 vols. (Toulouse, 1779), I, 116; De Freminville, *Dictionnaire*, 185-6.
23. De Freminville, *Dictionnaire*, 184.
24. AQ (Montréal), Pièces judiciares, 15 December 1680 (copy of the charter of the Confraternity of St. Eloi).
25. *Ibid.*, 8 January 1681. There are two pertinent documents under this date. The first is a written explanation by Pierre Gadois and Simon Guillory for the expulsion of Fezeret from the confraternity. The second is Fezeret's "Reponces" giving his version of the events that they described. As one might expect, the accounts differ. For example, the two *confrères* state that when they arrived at Fezeret's home for the supper in 1677 "nous le trouvames apres disputé aveq sa femme Laquelle luy deschira sa Cravate par morceau en n[ot]re Presence et Voyant Un tel bruit, nous fusmes contraint d'aller chercher a diné ailleurs." Fezeret's story was that his wife "Luy osta En Effet Sa Cravatte Salle pour Luy En mestre une blanche" and that it was agreed by all, after the mass, that they should sup at the house of Pierre Gadois since "Le poisle [*sic*] dudit gadoise Estoit plus commode que Le Logis de fezeret." The two brethren seem to have distorted events by emphasis and the omission of certain details, while Fezeret seems to have altered the facts. The first detailed account of this confraternity was given by Edouard-Zotique Massicotte in "La Saint-Eloi et la corporation des armuriers à Montreal, au 17ème siecle," *BRH*, XXIII (1917), 343-6. His essay "homogenized" the conflicting testimony and tended to treat the disputes as an amusing internal affair in which the Church and the magistracy had no vital interest.
26. AQ (Montréal), Pièces judiciaires, 8 January 1681 (explanation of expulsion by Gadois and Guillory).
27. In this instance the *confrères* were as much to blame as was Fezeret. In their account they emphasized the *pain-bénit* episode, which involved provocation by Fezeret, and glossed over the card game, saying only that after losing at cards Fezeret "prit querelle aveq [Jean] Bousquet." This is inadequate. Fezeret's version is more plausible. The brethren, he said, were playing cards after supper to win sugarplums (dragées) for their wives, who were present. Fezeret lost all of his candies and offered some money to buy them back. Jean Bousquet, he said, took his money and kept it while the others mocked Fezeret, who then made ready to leave. Bousquet gave him a parting shove at the doorway and the fight erupted. Fezeret portrayed himself as the passive victim of malicious abuse; it is more likely that he lost control of himself after being slighted. The *confrères* stated that after being

separated from Bousquet, Fezeret fell on Guillory shouting "c'est a toy à qui J'en Veult, il y'a dix ans, que je t'en doit." Evidence that there was a long-standing feud between the two comes from their behaviour in the confraternity and from a court case of 12 December 1679 over borrowed goods and services owed to one another. See *ibid.*, Bailliages 1665-82, 293v.

28. *Ibid.*, Pièces judiciaires, 15 December 1680 (transcription of the charter). At the court hearing of 23 December 1680 the text was given as "Nous avons banny de nostre associeté Fezeret estant seditieux." See *ibid.*, Bailliages 1665-82, 373; Pièces judiciaires, 23 December 1680.

29. *Ibid.*, Pièces judiciaires, 14, 18 December 1680 (petitions of René Fezeret to the *bailli* of Montreal). It is a minor curiosity that in both documents Fezeret described himself as an armourer and not as a blacksmith.

30. *Ibid.*, Bailliages 1665-82, 373; Pièces judiciaires, 25 December 1680 (petition of Antoine Forestier and Abraham Bouat, church-wardens of the parish of Montreal).

31. In December 1679 Gadois asked the court to compel Guillory to fulfil his obligations as that year's sponsor. See *ibid.*, Bailliages 1665-82, 292 (5 December 1679, "Le jour et feste de Ste Eloy"). His efforts at reconciliation are borne out by Fezeret's admission that "Gadoise . . . Linvita avec plusieurs prieres Et Bien de L'empressement d'aler disner chez Luy avec Les autres." Fezeret, however, interpreted this as evidence "que ces confreres avoient Resolu de Le Maltraitter." See *ibid.*, Pièces judiciaires, 8 January 1681 (Fezeret's "Reponces"). The assurance by Gadois that the remaining brethren would continue to sponsor the religious services is contained *ibid.*, 21 January 1681 (statement by Pierre Gadois). Olivier Quesnel, an armourer, also affirmed before the court that he would do his duty as sponsor when his turn came up; he was not a party to the disputes. See *ibid.*, Bailliages 1665-82, 382v (4 February 1681).

32. *Ibid.*, Pièces judiciaires, 7 January 1681 (Petition of "Les Marguilliers Procureurs De Leglize parroissiale de montreal"). They described the annual service of the confraternity as "une grande Messe avec L'offrende d'un pain benit orné de six sierges . . . avec diacre et soubzdiacres avec deux Chantres au Ceour (*sic*) et autres Prettres y Assistans."

33. *Ibid.*, 8 January 1681 (supplementary petition of René Fezeret). He specifically accused the brethren of committing "un mespris Considerable Et [contre] des ordres du Roy Et de La justice" by raising themselves up as "Maistres apsolus de Leur differand come géans sans souverains ny sans Loy." His challenge to the legality of the group's proceedings seems to have been inspired by the church-wardens' complaint.

34. *Ibid.*, Bailliages 1665-82, 383. The final decree was anticipated, in part, by the preliminary sentence rendered on 23 January by the *substitut du procureur fiscal* in which the original charter was upheld and the expulsion nullified. See *ibid.*, Pièces judiciaires, 23 January 1681 (sentence passed by Jean Gervaise).

35. *Ibid.*, Juridiction royale, Registre des Audiences, XI, 1726-29, 317-317v (26 October 1728). A fairly accurate transcription of the court minutes was published by E.Z. Massicotte as "La communauté des cordonniers à Montréal," *BRH*, XXIV (1918), 126-7.

36. *Ibid.*, Pièces judiciaires, 19 August 1729 (petition of the master shoemakers of Montreal to the *lieutenant-général*). The petitioners were listed in the following order and their place of birth, taken from Cyprien Tanguay's *Dictionnaire genealogique*, is indicated thus: (C) = Canada; (C*) = probably Canada; (F) = France; (F*) = probably France; no designation = unknown and no attribution possible. The petitioners were Edmé Moreau (F), Jean Ridday *dit* Beauceron (F), Louis Menard (F), Jacques Viger (C), Joseph Dumay (C), Pierre Dubois (F), Pierre Brossard, Joseph Guerin (C), Jean-Baptiste de Sève (C), Joseph de Sève (C*), Charles Laprise, René Laprise, veuve Maurice Lafantaisie (C*), François Lamarche, Jean La Rivière, Pierre Darcy (F*), Pierre Cardinal (C), Cardinal le jeune (C*), Baptiste Yvon (C), Jean-Baptiste Bourg *dit* Lachapelle, Jasinte Reaume (C*). Also signatories, but not listed in the petition, were J.G. Maurice (C*) and René La Rivière (C*).

37. *Edits, ordonnances royaux, déclarations et arrêts*, 3 vols. (Québec, 1854-56), II, 265-6. H.A. Innis, ed., *Select Documents in Canadian Economic History, 1497-1783* (Toronto, 1929), 301, transcribed the original text as "le moien de subsister en les reduisant (. . .) aux fonctions qui conviennent à leurs professions."

38. *JDCS*, I, 884.

39. See the petition cited in note 36.

40. AQ (Montréal), Juridiction royale, Registre des Audiences, XI (1726-29), 456 (19 August 1729).

41. *Ibid.*, NF 2, Ordonnances des Intendants, I, 140v. This ordinance of 3 November 1707 gave the Montreal tanner, Charles Delaunay, permission to employ four journeymen shoemakers and one apprentice shoemaker on the grounds that the independent shoemakers could not satisfy the public's need for footwear. The self-employed shoemakers, for their part, complained that Delaunay only supplied them with inferior leather.

42. *JDCS*, VI, 376-7.

43. This trend was noted in Peter N. Moogk, "Apprenticeship Indentures: A Key to Artisan Life in New France," Canadian Historical Association, *Historical Papers* (1971), 76.

44. Innis, ed., *Select Documents*, 410.

45. AQ (Montréal), Greffes des notaires du régime français, G. Barrette (0), R. Chorel de Saint-Romain (1), F. Comparet (O), J. David (0), N.A. Guillet de Chaumont (O), C.J. Porlier (0), J.C. Raimbault (1), F. Simonnet (6).

46. The files of Barolet do contain a partnership between a carpenter and a court clerk of indeterminate duration. The carpenter was to build a horse-powered grist mill in Quebec using a site and materials supplied by the clerk; they agreed to share the cost of the miller's salary. This has not been classified as a craft partnership since, beyond his initial labour, the artisan-partner functioned as a passive investor. See *ibid.*, J.C. Barolet, 18 May 1734.

47. Louis Beaudet, éd., *Recensement de la Ville de Québec pour 1716* (Québec, 1887); "Le recensement de Québec, en 1744," *RAPQ* (1939-40), 1-154.

48. AQ (Montréal), Greffes des notaires du régime français, L. Chambalon, 20 May 1694, 7 March 1695, 1 September 1698, 3 November 1699, 9 June 1700, 17 April 1701, 10 August 1701, 8 February 1702, 14 April 1704, 26 April 1707, 31 December 1708, 5 January 1709; J.E. Dubreuil, 27 August 1715, 24 February 1720, 15 December 1721, 11 November 1725, 14 March 1726, 18 April 1728.

49. *Ibid.*, R. Chorel de Saint-Romain, 12 April 1731; J.C. Raimbault, 17 August 1727; F. Simonnet, 7 November 1738, 4 February 1743, 7 November 1745, 17 June 1749, 10 January 1753, 6 September 1756.

50. *Ibid.*, L. Chambalon, 31 December 1708, 5 January 1709.

51. *Ibid.*, G. Audouart, 10 October 1653.

52. *Ibid.*, P. Duquet, 14 September 1675; G. Rageot, 26 October 1672, 14 October 1674.

53. Joseph-Noël Fauteux, *Essai sur l'industrie au Canada sous le régime français*, 2 vols. (Québec, 1927), II, 422-4.

54. Jousse, *Nouveau Commentaire sur les Ordonnances des Mois d'Août 1669, & Mars 1673* (Paris, 1775), 234-7.

55. Claude de Ferrière, *Corps et Compilation de tous les Commentateurs anciens et modernes sur la Coutume de Paris*, 4 vols. (Paris, 1714), III, 262.

56. Jousse, *Nouveau Commentaire*, 234-7.

57. AQ, Greffes des notaires du régime français, C. Barolet, 3 October 1736, 17 May 1747, 5 October 1752, 12 September 1753, *passim*.

58. *Ibid.*, C. Barolet, 5 April 1734, 12 October 1740, 3 May 1755 (in this particular case the junior partner's share amounted to a third of the profits).

59. Intendant François Bigot in 1740, quoted in Jacques Mathieu, *La Construction navale royale à Québec* (Québec, 1971), 57.

60. PAC, MG 1, C 11 A, LXXXV, 356.

61. The first reference to the Confraternity of St. Eloi was contained in the *Bulletin des Recherches historiques*, IV (1898), 376.
62. Lionel A. Groulx, *L'économique et le national* (Montréal, 1936), 17-18.
63. The preparation of this article was greatly assisted by the comments of my colleagues, Roderick J. Barman and John M. Norris, and those of my friend and teacher, William J. Eccles.

IV
Violence and Protest

Certain forms of violence were characteristic of pre-industrial societies. Common were food riots, over the shortage or price of staples. Social control by the community caused violence, as in the charivaris, riotous gatherings which punished "unnatural" weddings, such as those between old men and young girls. The military, often a poorly paid and despised rabble, was another source of frequent violence. These and other forms were present in New France, although not enough historical work has been done to document their frequency.

Even less documentation exists on what must have been a violent situation, the fur trade. The lack of social control under which many fur traders lived and the competitive nature of the trade surely bred frequent violent confrontations. Even settled New France, however, was all too familiar with the violence of warfare and Indian incursions. It created an atmosphere of violence which existed in tension with the stern legal mechanisms of French government.

FURTHER READING:
An example of military violence is discussed in Allan Greer, "Mutiny at Louisbourg, December 1744," *Histoire sociale*, X (1977), 305-36. More general disorders are treated by John G. Reid, "Styles of Colonization and Social Disorders in Early Acadia and Maine: A Comparative Approach," La société historique acadienne, *Cahiers*, VII (1976), 105-17. For labour

unrest, see Peter Moogk, "The Ancestors of Quebec's Craft Unions: The Montreal Shoemakers' Protest of 1729," *Histoire des travailleurs Québécois: Bulletin RCHTQ*, V, 1 (1978), 34-9. An important work on Indian-white violence is G.T. Hunt, *The Wars of the Iroquois* (Madison, 1940). A special sort of violence, the Jesuit courting of martyrdom, plays a large role in the best seventeenth-century memoir, Joyce Marshall, ed., *Word from New France: The Selected Letters of Marie de l'Incarnation* (Toronto, 1967).

Terence Crowley, whose major work is on Louisbourg, teaches at the University of Guelph.

"Thunder Gusts": Popular Disturbances in Early French Canada

by Terence Crowley

Popular disturbances in the form of crowds, mobs, and armed uprisings were an intrinsic part of society and government in the Western world during the seventeenth and eighteenth centuries. Although the word "revolt" was often used by those in authority to describe these momentary but frequently violent upheavals, such a term is generally inappropriate at least before the 1760's when revolutionary ideas became more widespread. Popular disturbances were essentially defensive and reactionary: people reacted against what was perceived as a departure from traditional ways, especially in the form of new taxes or seigneurial obligations, or to prompt authorities to relieve situations such as food shortages. Seldom did they involve petitions or any general ideas other than those surrounding the specific grievance at issue. In France, the period from 1620 to 1650 was particularly rife with peasant uprisings. The imposition of new taxes provided the fuel that ignited the wrath of the peasants in the uprisings of the *croquants* of Saintonge, Angoumois, Poitou, and Périgord as well as the *nu-pieds* in Normandy in the 1630's. These violent outbursts occurred during the chaotic reign of Louis XIII and were abetted by local officials influenced by ideas of resistance to tyranny. Yet even during the reign of Louis XIV, there were large-scale uprisings such as that of the

From Canadian Historical Association, *Historical Papers* (1979), 11-31. Reprinted by permission of the author and the Canadian Historical Association.

torrébens of Brittany in 1675, which was principally directed against the domanial rights of seigneurs.[1] The uprisings of the millenarian *camisards* of Languedoc, combining what has been described as "the explosive mixture of prophetic neurosis and antitax ferment," were the last of the great French peasant uprisings of the *ancien régime*.[2]

By the eighteenth century peasant uprisings were more common in Eastern than Western Europe, but mobs and crowds remained as forms of popular protest in the towns and countryside, even though they were more restrained than in the preceding century. One of the prime reasons for this change was that merchants and governments had begun to construct national markets in grains to ensure the movement of the substance of life.[3] Yet food shortages remained as the most common circumstance fomenting collective protest. France alone witnessed some twenty major food riots from the late seventeenth to the early nineteenth centuries.[4] Collective protest became more common in urban areas where the circumstances prompting such activity were more diverse. Urban disturbances were associated less frequently with food and more often with political and religious issues, customs and excise, public rejoicings, counterfeiting, depressions in industry and trade, and military and naval recruitment.[5]

George Rudé, the foremost student of popular protest in this period, has attempted to differentiate those popular disturbances he calls the "pre-industrial" crowd from what became more characteristic in the nineteenth and twentieth centuries. Eighteenth-century popular disturbances, Rudé writes,

> tend to take the form of direct action and the destruction of property rather than of petitions or peaceful marches or demonstrations; and this was as true of peasant rebellion as it was of industrial machine-breaking, the imposition of the 'just' price in food riots or the 'pulling-down' of houses or the burning of their victims in effigy in city outbreaks. Yet such targets were generally carefully selected and destruction was rarely wanton or indiscriminate. Such movements tended to be spontaneous, to grow from small beginnings and to have a minimum of organization; they tended, too, to be led by leaders from the 'outside' or, if from 'inside,' by men whose authority was limited to the occasion. They were generally defensive, conservative and 'backward-looking,' more con-

cerned to restore what had been lost from a 'golden' age than
to blaze a trail for something new; and, accordingly, such
political ideas as they expressed were more often conservative
than radical and they tend (with some notable but rare exceptions) to be borrowed from conservative rather than radical
groups.[6]

Rudé also notes that political issues tended to play a relatively
insignificant role in early eighteenth-century protest and that
England, with its measure of political democracy, witnessed
disturbances that were more militant, sophisticated, and col-
oured by political concerns than were their counterparts in
France.[7] The same observation may also be applied to the
English colonies in North America where the frequency of
crowds and mobs increased as the conflict with the mother country intensified in the 1760's and 1770's.[8]

In Canada the systematic study of popular protest and collective violence is in its infancy. Labour historians have naturally
been interested in strikes in the modern period, but studies of
popular disturbances have been largely confined to the nineteenth century – apart from Kenneth McNaught's interpretive
essay on collective and governmental violence in Canadian
history.[9] In examining the two preceding centuries, information
is less diverse in origin and rich in detail. Like historians of
seventeenth-century France, the colonial historian must rely on
official sources, what Pierre Goubert has called the archives of
repression.[10] The official correspondence of the governors and
intendants remains the principal primary source because there
were no newspapers in New France, relatively few diarists and
memorialists, and the participants in these events were rarely
brought to trial. As there is little descriptive documentation for
popular movements in Canada before 1760, such as the infor-
mative letters written to Chancellor Séguier between 1633 and
1649 which have permitted French historians to examine French
peasant protest during the *ancien régime* at its height, only rarely
can the faces in the crowd in New France be identified or an
estimate given of their numbers.

The nature of settlement in New France and the small number of
colonists precluded popular protest on the scale or frequency of
that witnessed in France, while the absolutist inspiration of
French colonial government inhibited the formation of political
disturbances that were seen in England and her colonies. France

and England had total populations of over thirty million people by the early eighteenth century; Paris had grown to 500,000 residents by 1700 and London to 575,000 by 1750.[11] In contrast, the population of the Quebec colony, generally referred to as Canada, numbered only 55,000 in 1754, with some 8,000 people residing in the town of Quebec and 4,000 in Montreal. The population of the French colonies on Prince Edward Island (Île Saint-Jean) and Cape Breton (Île Royale) amounted to 8,596 in 1752, with nearly one-half residing in the capital of Louisbourg.[12]

Conditions that often fomented popular discontent in the mother country were not present in her colonies. Settlement in New France was greatly dispersed and there were only six villages outside of the towns. The most common cause for French peasant revolt, high taxes, was absent from the colonies. Taxes on the export of beaver pelts and moose hides were removed in 1717, leaving the 10 per cent customs duty on wine, spirits, and tobacco imported into Quebec as the only continuing form of taxation.[13] Seigneurial obligations in Canada were controlled by contract and subject to regulation by the intendant. Seigneurial dues appear to have been relatively light during the French regime and *corvées* were rare.[14] The tithe for the Church was not heavy either, for although it had originally been set at one-thirteenth of the fruits of human labour and production of the soil, it was subsequently reduced to one twenty-sixth.[15] "Si, en France," Louise Dechêne concluded in her study of seventeenth-century Montreal, "la paysannerie d'Ancien Régime est définie par rapport à la classe qui l'exploite et la domine, au Canada, la population rurale est autre chose: des petits propriétaires parcellaires, à qui le régime demande un certain nombre de tributs – redevances, corvées, milices – mais qui, sur le plan matériel, bénéficient d'une sorte de trêve."[16] Nor in the towns were there large numbers of journeymen apprentices who were a frequent source of disturbances in England. Only at the St. Maurice forges, the Quebec shipyards, and Louisbourg were there any concentrations of skilled craftsmen. In Quebec that gave rise in 1741 to the first recorded strike in Canadian history, but among craftsmen recently arrived from France rather than among the Canadian workers.[17]

Despite these differences the distinction between the colonies and the mother country can be exaggerated. New France was far from being a pastoral paradise inhabited only by prosperous farmers and freedom-loving *coureurs de bois*. Demands placed on the people, especially by means of the three tributes of seigneurial dues, *corvées*, and militia service mentioned by Dechêne, did produce discontent. Runaways among apprentices and indentured servants and desertions from the ranks of the colonial regulars also testified to grievances but, apart from the Louisbourg mutiny of 1744, such discontent did not assume collective expression in the form of mobs and crowds.[18] It was the conditions created by war that were most likely to lead the people to protest in New France, just as in the mother country the increased tax burden during periods of military conflict was the most conspicuous harbinger of opposition from French peasants. In the century and a half of settlement in Canada during the French regime, there was only one period of extended peace between 1713 and 1744, and even that was marked by localized conflicts such as the Anglo-Abenaki and Fox Wars. Militia service was compulsory for all men sixteen to sixty, a heavy burden on the population and one which certainly caused resentment, but surprisingly little is known about the operation of the militia organization on the local level.[19] The billeting of regular soldiers in the towns of Quebec and Montreal also caused disputes. More significantly, however, war interrupted shipping to the colonies and aggravated the unstable economic situation created by pre-industrial agriculture and rudimentary communications systems.

On at least a dozen occasions, people in New France took to the streets, paraded to the walls of towns, or otherwise assembled for direct action in defiance of the law. Food shortages were the root of at least four demonstrations and commodity prices were at the centre of an equal number. Religious issues and resistance to forced labour for the government accounted for other forms of collective action. In several instances, officials and the middle classes used such disturbances or collective violence for their own purposes, but more often the motivation and leadership came from within the crowd than from without.

Demonstrations were the only collective means by which the *habitants* and lower classes could influence those in authority, although they were sometimes used for political purposes. Governmental structures in New France were highly autocratic, just as they continued to be during the opening decades of the British regime. Power was concentrated in the hands of the governor and intendant who reported to the Ministry of Marine in France. Merchants, seigneurs, and favoured individuals were able to exercise a continuing though informal influence on the administration by virtue of their economic power, social prestige, or proximity to decision-making; but the lower classes were totally excluded except when the intendant authorized a local assembly to discuss a specific matter, such as the construction of a church or the price of beaver.[20] Otherwise, assemblies were unlawful in a time and place where there were no political rights, only privileges inherited through custom or bestowed by the king. Following Colbert's dictum that "chacun parle pour soy, et que personne ne parle pour tous," collective petitions were also prohibited although they appeared occasionally.[21] In New France the Church alone provided the only continuing means for collective popular expression and representation when parishioners gathered annually to elect churchwardens for their parish.

The first large protest erupted in 1704 during the War of the Spanish Succession and assumed the form of an attempt by rural *habitants* to force a reduction in the price of an essential commodity, salt. In France such conduct was known as the *taxation populaire*, which usually implied price setting by the crowd through force, generally seizure of the commodity or of premises. Salt was in short supply in New France in the fall of 1704 due to the failure of the ship, *La Seine*, to arrive at the port of Quebec. As salt was vital to the preservation of meat at the time of the annual fall slaughter of animals which could not be maintained over the long winter, Intendant François Beauharnois decreed a set price for salt in the Quebec district. Seeing the opportunity to turn a quick profit, some Montreal merchants quickly purchased all available local supplies of salt at prices ranging from three to ten *livres* a bushel. Angered by this injustice, *habitants* from the vicinity around Montreal gathered on November 18 and marched on the town. The commander of the garrison ordered the gates closed but asked the superior of the Sulpician Seminary and seigneur of Montreal, the Abbé Belmont, to speak to the people. Asked what they wanted, the demonstrators replied that they were not intent on insurrection but only desired that the price of salt be reduced to four *livres* and that the reprehensible merchants be punished. When told that such gatherings were illegal, they disbanded. However, the governor of Montreal, Claude de Ramezay, subsequently met with merchants, established a set price for salt, and inventoried supplies in the town with a view toward rationing.[22]

Philippe de Rigaud de Vaudreuil had been Governor General of New France for barely a year when this incident occurred. Informed of the upheaval four days later, he determined to go to

Montreal and deal with the situation himself. Ramezay had overstepped the bounds of his authority in setting prices, since this prerogative belonged to the intendant. Vaudreuil therefore rescinded his order but satisfied the people by having the merchants return their excessive profits.[23] Beseeched by Belmont and local notables not to deal harshly with the protestors, the governor himself sympathized with their plight. They had only demanded justice out of misery, he noted to his superior, the Minister of Marine, Jérôme de Pontchartrain, and, once they had made their voice heard, they had returned to their homes without violence. Not desiring any retribution, Vaudreuil simply promulgated an ordinance forbidding any such gathering under penalty of being considered seditious.[24] He did not take stronger action, he informed France, because he believed "qui'il convenoit mieux d'Entrer dans la misère du peuple que de le réduire au desespoir."[25] Moreover, disquieting rumours of an impending assault on Canada, following a successful English raid on Port Royal the previous July, had unsettled the people and so had counterfeit money then circulating in the Quebec district. But Lamothe de Cadillac, the governor's arch-rival in the colony, interpreted Vaudreuil's clemency as weakness in a letter to the minister. Pontchartrain adopted this criticism and accused Vaudreuil of lacking firmness in handling the demonstration.

Having shown clemency, Vaudreuil had little alternative but to act more resolutely when a second disturbance in the Montreal district erupted in the fall of the following year. Despite attempts by the local administration to alleviate the problems caused by the salt shortage, they could do little: Canada needed 7,000 to 8,000 bushels of salt per year and only 2,000 had arrived in 1705.[26] Prices paid to producers remained low while the cost of merchandise was high, and the *habitant* was further distressed by the failure of eel fishing in the St. Lawrence. Emanating from Mille Isles and Lachenaie on the north shore across from Île Jésus, the protest spread to Boucherville on the south shore. The exact nature of this second demonstration is not known, but this time Vaudreuil ordered Governor Ramezay to arrest two *habitants*, François Séguin *dit* Ladéroute of Mille Isles and Jean-Baptiste Lapointe of Île Jésus. A trial was instituted by the intendant in the *Conseil supérieur* and information gathered in the Montreal district by the intendant's sub-delegate. A total of nine witnesses were called, but there was insufficient evidence to make an example of Ladéroute and Lapointe. On 6 January

1706 they were released with a reprimand and a fine of ten *écus*.[27]

In 1714 the Quebec district provided the scene for a similar protest, the only one in that district during the French regime. The prospect of a meagre harvest and a rise in commodity prices had fomented discontent in the parishes of Lorette and St. Augustin. People decided to express their grievances and demand remedy, but the means were not initially agreed upon. The local curé named Desnoyers had counselled against a march and in favour of a request directed to the intendant, but his advice went unheeded and people gathered to demonstrate before the walls of Quebec. Some of the mob were armed and threatened to enter the town if their remonstrances were not heard. Their object was to force merchants to lower the cost of their merchandise, but Governor Vaudreuil and Intendant Bégon were unsympathetic and moved quickly to end the protest. The officials were willing to acknowledge that the cost of goods had increased but felt that the value of crops had risen more than apace. Wheat that had been selling for three *livres* a bushel the previous year had risen to eight in 1714.

The governor assembled the colonial regulars and the militia of the town to march against the crowd, leading it to disperse and flee for the cover of nearby wooded areas.[28] Court proceedings were begun in the *Conseil supérieur* by the Attorney General on 2 September 1714 and a councillor, François Mathieu Martin de Lino, was delegated to investigate. Louis Dugal, a thirty-five-year-old resident of St. Augustin, was taken into custody and questioned by de Lino but was released because authorities apparently believed his assertion that he had been falsely accused by his enemies.[29] Other testimony led the Attorney General to conclude that Laurent Dubault of St. Augustin and Charles Routtier of Lorette had gone from house to house in the area inciting people to join the demonstration. Routtier was imprisoned and not released until 12 August 1715 when he was sworn to remain in the town for further questioning.[30] The court decided that more information was needed, but the matter was not again discussed in the *Conseil supérieur*.

While uprisings in response to the imposition of new taxes were a common and frequently violent source of popular protest in France, one would not expect this pattern of behaviour to have been repeated in the colonies where the tax burden was so much lighter. Yet the imposition of the *corvée* in 1717 did lead to a similar response in the seigneury of Longueuil, where the men who participated were heavily armed. This protest had its origins in the review of colonial defence undertaken by the *Conseil de Marine* following the death of Louis XIV in 1715. As a result, the Court had decided not only to build a massive fortress at Louisbourg, but also to construct a seventeen-foot wall around Montreal. Louisbourg was totally financed by the Crown, but the construction at Montreal was to be partially funded by an annual tax of 2,000 *livres* on the Seminary of St. Sulpice and 4,000 on the other religious communities and residents of the town.[31] *Habitants* in the area were forced to provide their labour through the *corvée*.

All segments of the Montreal district were disgruntled with this new head tax, but rural people were doubly concerned. *Corvées* for royal projects were much more uncommon in New France than the mother country, even though work for a seigneur was frequently included in the contract by which land was ceded to the *censitaire*. This particular *corvée* had come at a distressing time. Rains had failed in 1715 and 1716, harvests had been reduced, and fires had scoured the countryside. When the following year was also unusually dry, public prayers for rain were offered and it was estimated that three-quarters of the colony's farmers would have difficulty reaping an amount equivalent to what they had sown that spring.[32] Moreover, rural residents failed to see why they should be forced to work on a wall which would afford them little protection if the Iroquois again ravaged the area at a time when they were needed on the farm to tend what appeared to be yet another meagre harvest.

In August 1717, farmers in the seigneury of Longueuil took up arms and refused to submit to forced labour. Vaudreuil, who had been in Montreal since March to oversee the construction, crossed the St. Lawrence and met the dissidents in the manor house of Longueuil. During these discussions some men who answered the governor impudently were jostled by Vaudreuil's guards. As a result no satisfactory resolution to the conflict was found. The governor returned to Montreal, but received word that the armed demonstration continued. This time he determined to make an example of the demonstrators, but the curé of Boucherville, the commandant of militia for the South Shore, and several others pleaded with him not to deal harshly with them. When Vaudreuil ordered the arrest of ten men identified as ringleaders, they gave themselves up voluntarily and were thrown in prison in Montreal. Feeling that his point had been made, the governor released them before winter for, as he wrote, "les cachots de Montréal sont si affreux qu'ils courreroient risque d'y périr." [33]

Over the next three decades such collective protest in New France subsided, despite either disastrous or very poor harvests in 1736, 1737, and from 1741 to 1743, as well as the War of the Austrian Succession. Conditions created by the Seven Years' War once again led people to unite to demand action from the government. Harvests were poor beginning in 1756 and shipping was interrupted by the British navy. The augmentation of the colonial garrison and the presence of several thousand French army regulars created additional strains and led to food shortages. The outbreak of smallpox during the winter of 1757-58 probably had a further unsettling effect on a war-weary population. In December 1757, when the Marquis de Vaudreuil-Cavagnal, son of the previous Governor Vaudreuil and himself Governor General of New France, was at Montreal, shortages necessitated the termination of the one-quarter pound of bread distributed to the people. And as this was the time of the fall slaughter, the administration decided that only a combination of one-half horsemeat and one-half beef would be provided to the public at the reduced price of six *sols* per pound.

Women appeared at the door of the governor's residence in response and demanded to speak with him. Vaudreuil-Cavagnal acceded to their request and found that they had come to demand bread. The governor replied that he had none to give them, nor even to the troops. The king was not obliged to furnish bread to the people, Vaudreuil-Cavagnal continued, but to assist them in this time of scarcity the governor had arranged to have cattle and horses slaughtered and offered for sale at a reduced price. Unsatisfied, the women retorted that "elles avoient de la répugnance à manger du cheval; qu'il étoit l'ami de l'homme; que la religion défendoit de les tuer et qu'elles aimeroient mieux mourir que d'en manger." [34] Vaudreuil-Cavagnal dismissed their claims as a figment of their imagination; horsemeat had always been eaten. To ensure quality, he said, he had ordered that the slaughter be conducted in the same manner as for beef. It was the only assistance he could give the people in such trying times. To allay their fears, the governor ordered the Marine commissary, Martel, and the *lieutenant-général* of the Montreal royal court, Jean-Joseph Guiton de

Monrepos, to conduct the women on an inspection of the butchery to observe for themselves the fine state of the meat. The women agreed, but continued to protest that "elles n'en prendroient pas, ni personne, pas même les troupes."

Having handled the demonstration with some acumen, the governor let the women depart for their tour with the threat that, if they rioted again, he would throw them all in jail and hang half of them. The Chevalier de Lévis, who recounted this incident, noted that, while the commissary and *lieutenant-général* were supposed to have arrested the ringleaders of the demonstration, they did not in fact do so. The attention of Lévis, at least, was directed more toward the conduct of the soldiers of the Béarn regiment and that of the Marine troops in Montreal who, influenced by the popular agitation, twice refused to accept their reduced rations in November and December and who also complained about having to eat horsemeat. By force of argument, threat of punishment, and the example of eating horsemeat in the company of Béarn grenadiers, Lévis calmed the mutinous spirit among his soldiers.[35]

Protests during these years did not end there. In April of 1758 the women of the town of Quebec took to the streets. Bougainville remarked in his journal that "La misère augmente. Le peuple de Québec à été réduit à 2 onces de pain. Il y a eu un attroupement de femmes à la porte de Mr Daine, lieutenant général de police."[36] For the next month the food situation remained extremely critical, but further protests were averted by the arrival at Quebec on May 21 of nine ships from a convoy of twelve. The next winter food scarcity was again a problem and the response was the same. There were rumours that bread rations, already costly, would be lowered to only one-quarter pound a day. This time the Marquis de Montcalm noted "Grande misère à Québec."[37] In this last popular disturbance of the French regime, some 400 women paraded to seek out the intendant's palace and protest the rumoured reduction in bread. François Bigot, the intendant, assured them a half-pound a day and had wheat brought from Lachine in order to fulfil his promise and avert the further wrath of *les femmes québécoises*.

The same indignation that led people to assemble against the government also produced resistance to Church authority, but generally in a less dramatic or individual manner. In religious matters the extreme piety apparent in the early years of French colonization was displaced by greater social convention. As in all pre-industrial Western countries, the parish church in New France provided the only institutional focus for rural life outside the family and as such it reflected a people characterized as "remarkably independent, aggressive, self-assertive, freedom-loving and outspoken."[38] But the power of the Church, despite the occasional threat of religious or civil sanction, rested largely on moral suasion and the hierarchy accepted the role of mediator in local disputes. The election of churchwardens to the *fabrique* (church council) and the calling of parish assemblies under the authority of the intendant when contributions were needed to build or repair church buildings tended to reduce the need to resort to extra-institutional means. Still, the tithe or payments of any kind to the Church were frequently the object of popular contention. Many individuals refused to pay, while others attempted to defraud by calculating the tithe on only part of the harvest or making payment in inferior grain. In one dispute at Île-aux-Coudres in the 1740's, people joined together to prevent the curé from taking the sacrament to the sick and, at St. Antoine de Tilly in the same period, a gathering of *habitants* levelled the rectory fence in a protest centring on the use of the rectory for meetings. Some forty men in the parish of St. Thomas at Pointe à la Caille, rent by internal divisions, collectively objected to the priest naming those who had failed to attend Easter Mass, a time obligatory for religious observance but also one before which all tithes were to have been paid.[39]

Next to contributions, rural *habitants* were most vociferous regarding the church they would attend when a new parish was erected or an existing one divided. As this was a matter that directly affected communal life, people made their opinions known to the Church hierarchy. On one occasion, at least, the bishop's refusal to accede to local opinion led to both concerted action and threat of violence. In 1714 Abbé Belmont, the grand vicar of Bishop Saint-Vallier, provided for the divorce of Côte St. Leonard from the parish at Pointe-aux-Trembles and attached it to the newly erected parish at Rivières-des-Prairies. The people of St. Leonard protested to the bishop, but when Saint-Vallier decided in favour of his subordinate some parishioners decided to take matters into their own hands. A group set out to meet Joseph Pepin, a young man of twenty-six, as he was carrying the communion bread to Rivière-des-Prairies. They tried to persuade him to take it to the old parish church rather than the new, but when he refused they snatched the bread from him and made off for the home of the man identified as their ringleader, one Jean La Chapelle. The priest and churchwardens of Rivières-des-Prairies instituted court action and a bailiff was sent to serve writs.[40] Word of his presence in the parish spread rapidly and, when the bailiff neared the La Chapelle house, he discerned in the distance eight women and a man who, he said, threatened "avec des roches et des perches en Les mains pour massasigner." He attempted to avoid them, but they came after him across a swamp shouting "areste voleur nous te voulons tuer et jette dans le marais."[41] The bailiff had little alternative but to beat a hasty retreat to Montreal.

Different in kind from these protests that sprang directly from the lower classes were those that originated in political disputes. Such outbreaks were less spontaneous, involved fewer people, and were more likely to cause bodily harm. The first two such demonstrations occurred in the latter part of Frontenac's tumultuous first term as Governor General when the Quebec administration was irrevocably split into a fraction supporting Frontenac and another backing Intendant Jacques Duchesneau. While personality differences strongly influenced these quarrels, there were also disputes over policies concerning the regulation of the fur trade which masked pecuniary interests. Little is known about the first incident in 1677 except that, due to what was termed a seditious movement in Montreal in which a *syndic* had participated, Frontenac promulgated an ordinance prohibiting "aucune assemblée, conventicule, ni signatures communes."[42] By the following year two gangs of youths had formed in the town, seemingly with the encouragement of Montreal's governor, François-Marie Perrot, in order to counter new regulations limiting the activities of the *coureurs de bois*. When Jean-Baptiste Migeon, judge of the Montreal royal court, and some of his bailiffs tried to arrest one of the *coureurs de bois* for contravention of the regulations, they were met by the two gangs armed with clubs and by Perrot who brandished both a club and a sword. One of the bailiffs was wounded and Perrot quite unwarrantedly threw Migeon into jail. When the *Conseil souverain* attempted to intervene, Frontenac, who was at this time an associate of Perrot in fur-trading activities and his protector, forbade the court to take any action. The Council referred the matter to France where a royal edict was issued prohibiting local governors like Perrot from fining or imprisoning individuals without orders from the Governor General or *Conseil souverain*.[43]

A protest at Louisbourg in 1720 was similarly motivated by political considerations and involved royal officials. At issue was the price of wine and brandy which had been recently fixed at two *livres* a *pot* for brandy, a *livre* for red wine, and fifteen *sols* for white wine. In that year, a new man, Jacques-Ange Lenormant Demesi, had arrived to become the chief commissariat official of the colony (*commissaire-ordonnateur*). A jealous and irascible defender of the nobility of the robe, Demesi immediately clashed with Governor Saint-Ovide de Brouillan. A series of personal and jurisdictional squabbles nearly immobilized the administration. One of these concerned the setting of wine and brandy prices. Demesi was seemingly not consulted before the governor promulgated the ordinance and decided to embarrass the governor publicly. When some fishing outfitters expressed their displeasure with the set prices, the *ordonnateur* grasped the opportunity to lead the disgruntled residents to the governor's residence. Saint-Ovide was away, but when they regrouped the next morning the governor disbanded them. Demesi said that only seven or eight individuals were involved, but the governor discerned "l'air de révolte."[44] Displeased with this breach of public decorum and open challenge to the governor's authority, French officials reprimanded the *ordonnateur* and threatened both officials with punitive action if they did not settle their differences.[45] Still, the demonstration was not without effect since spirit prices were lowered.

Collective protest in New France was, therefore, more common than historians have previously recognized. Popular disturbances were not simply spasmodic reactions of mindless people succumbing to momentary whims or losing themselves in the collective identity of the crowd. As in Europe, people in New France assembled to seek remedy to immediate but well-defined grievances, to "representer la misère de la Coste," as one witness to the disturbance of 1714 admitted.[46] Demonstrations emanating from the countryside appear to have originated among the local residents themselves rather than being the result of leadership from outside the area. They were not declarations of political principle but requests for official intervention or indignant reactions against what were perceived as unfair practices or unjust impositions by government. The discussions preceding the 1714 march, the steadfastness of the men of Longueuil pro-

testing the royal *corvée* in 1717, the impudence of women con-
fronting Governor Vaudreuil-Cavagnal in 1757, and even the
reactions of the officials themselves suggest that such forms of
collective behaviour were accompanied by some notion of legiti-
matization, which revealed that the protestors were supported
by the consensus of the larger community or were defending a
traditional right.[47] But in contrast to Europe, no disturbances
associated with popular festivities or feast-days have been
uncovered in New France. The charivari, or mock serenade of
newly married couples, was imported into the colonies from the
mother country and created the raucous behaviour normally
associated with that public ritual. Although the charivaris did
not burst into anti-government or anti-Church activity, Bishop
Laval found that they lead to "désordres et libertés scan-
daleuses" where "des actions très impies" were committed, and
he officially banned them in 1683.[48]

The study of collective protest quickly turns to an examination of the society which first produced and then reacted to it.
The essentially non-political character of most of these disturbances and the absence of large-scale popular protest fomented
by the middle classes reflects not only political structures during
the French regime, but also the mentality of the middle classes
and their numerical weakness in the social structure.[49] There
were no Bacon's or Leisler's rebellions, nor any Regulators, in
New France as there were in the English colonies. At the same
time the strong military presence in the French colonies accounted for at least part of the restraint shown by demonstrators. New France was an armed camp where authorities
could threaten effective counter-violence through the use of garrisoned regulars. There were no police forces as such but, unlike
officials in England and her dependencies, French colonial administrators did not have to rely on only the "hue and cry," the
posse commitatus, or the militia for law enforcement in such
situations. Towns were garrisoned with colonial regulars ready
for the call and French officials showed that they were prepared
to use force if disturbances persisted or became unruly. Officials
even argued that the garrisons should be increased because
soldiers were necessary "pour maintenir l'ordre de la Colonie et
reprimer L'insolence des habitans."[50]

Popular protest in New France was sparked more by a sense
of injustice, a fear of privation, and a desire to invoke government protection than it was prompted by any single economic

factor. There is no mechanical correlation between the incidence of popular disturbances and the price of the dietary staple, wheat. Demonstrations in 1704 and 1705 occurred when wheat prices were falling, while those in 1714, 1717, and 1757-58 transpired within the context of advancing prices being paid to producers.[51] More important than the price of wheat was the nature of markets during the *ancien régime* and its effects on popular psychology. Markets in the colonies demonstrated the same characteristics as those described by Pierre Goubert for France: limited in extent, poorly provisioned, inelastic, and subject to speculation. As a result, the popular mind was haunted by "la peur panique de la cherté et de la disette, nourrie par des souvenirs collectifs (souvent exagérés) des famines anciennes."[52] New France did not experience famine where people died as they did in Europe, but shortages due to interruptions in shipping or poor harvests and rapid escalations in prices were sufficiently numerous to alarm people when such indicators first appeared. For this reason protests erupted in the fall or spring when the prospect of a difficult winter loomed ahead, or when shortages were beginning to be perceived before the arrival of ships or the appearance of spring crops.

Fears that a difficult situation might suddenly deteriorate further, or indignation that others had denied them access to essential commodities, were nurtured by the fundamental instability of pre-industrial markets. Fears and indignation as elements of popular psychology help to explain why popular protest erupted more over food or prices than actual instances of destitution or starvation. Similarly, Charles Tilly has concluded that in modern Europe conflicts over the food supply occurred not so much where people were hungry, but where people believed that others were depriving them of food to which they had a moral and political right.[53] That such conflicts in New France never reached the level of great societal redressing rituals that they attained in Europe is indicative of better economic conditions in the New World and a lesser degree of social antagonism. It also testifies to the success of government regulation of the economy of New France. Older historians of New France such as Francis Parkman, George Wrong, and L.H. Gipson, who were imbued with the principles of nineteenth-century *laissez-faire* liberalism, saw such government activity as a fettering of trade, excessive benevolence, and a paternalism which hampered the untrammelled free spirit.[54] W.J. Eccles, in contrast, has more recently argued that government intervention in New France was inspired by the aristocratic ethos of the age and dictated by the nature of the colony's economy.[55]

Government intervention in the marketplace during the seventeenth and eighteenth centuries derived not just from concepts of society and Canadian economic deficiencies, but also from the practical necessity of overcoming deficiencies in pre-industrial economies in order to avoid popular protest in the form of crowds, mobs, and riots. Consequently, Britain and her American colonies practised the same regulation of supply and prices as did the French colonies and their mother country, but a serious study of differing amounts of regulation in the French and British Empires remains to be undertaken. E.P. Thompson has found that one of the threads running through eighteenth-century English crowd activity was the attempt to invoke government intervention for the greater good, what Thompson refers to as the "moral economy of mercantilism."[56] The need for such regulation was apparent because markets were unstable largely due to their dependence on agriculture and poor transportation facilities. Agriculture "as an industry was always in difficulty" in the early modern world, Fernand Braudel has written.[57] The central problem of agriculture in New France, as in Western Europe, was an overconcentration of one crop, wheat.[58] Life depended on the production of wheat, but wheat crops were sensitive to climatic changes and insect manifestations. Poor or disastrous harvests were recorded in New France in at least the following years: 1689, 1691, 1714-17, 1723, 1732, 1736-37, 1741-43, 1750-51, and 1756-58.[59]

Officials during the French regime regularly set the price of wheat, flour, bread, and meat, as well as that of a variety of services, just as town and provincial authorities did in the English colonies. In years of scarcity when harvests were poor, the Quebec administration requisitioned supplies from merchants and required farmers to sell, at prices it had established, an amount of grain or flour required for the colony as a whole. In 1714, the year of the march on Quebec, the intendant had issued an ordinance in August allowing Quebec bakers to requisition wheat from farmers for eight *livres* a bushel wherever individuals had more than a three-month supply. The next month another ordinance required that all *habitants* in the Quebec district bring a fifth of their wheat crop to the king's stores in Quebec within six months. This was followed by a third decree in October which ordered residents of Neuville, Les Ecureuils (the two parishes closest to St. Augustin and Lorette where the demonstration had originated), and Pointe-aux-Trembles to bring a tenth of their wheat to Quebec to feed the townspeople.[60] In particularly difficult times, officials withheld part of the grain from the market so that it could be distributed as seed the following spring and exports were prohibited.

Special attention was paid to the towns, for it was in and around the towns that popular disturbances could and did erupt most easily. The terrible crop failures in 1736 and 1737 reduced many habitants to wandering beggars who migrated to the towns in search of assistance. In 1738 the Intendant Gilles Hocquart wrote:

> Je ne puis vous exprimer, monseigneur, la misère causée par la disette qui se fait sentir dans toutes les campagnes. Le plus grand nombre des habitants, particulièrement de la coste sud, manquent de pain depuis longtemps et une grande partie ont erré pendant tout l'hiver dans les costes du nord, qui ont été moins maltraitées, pour y recueillir des aumônes et quelques peu de bled pour semer. D'autres ont vécu et vivent encore d'un peu d'avoine et de bled d'Inde et de poisson. Les villes on été remplies tout l'hiver de ces coureurs misérables qui venaient y chercher quelques secours de pain ou d'argent. Les habitants des villes, particulièrement les journaliers et artisans, sont dans une situation aussi fâcheuse manquant tous de travail.[61]

Hocquart was forced to provide aid from the king's stores just as officials in Louisbourg did when shortages were experienced in 1729, 1733, and 1737. Following the caterpillar infestation that devastated the crop in 1742, Bishop Pontbriand lent Church support to such government activity through a *mandement* which enjoined the rural faithful to bring their harvests to town.[62]

The last intendant of Quebec, François Bigot, was acutely aware of the possibility of popular disruptions in the towns. Alarmed at how fast the town of Quebec had grown, he promulgated an ordinance in 1749 which prohibited anyone from establishing in Quebec without his express permission. If the pace of the town's economic growth slowed, he reasoned, those who had left the countryside to work there would soon find themselves "réduits à la mendicité, ce qui pourroit exposer une partie d'entre eux à de facheuses suites, et de venir à charge au public."[63] In 1751 Bigot took quick action to avoid any trouble in Montreal and Quebec when poor harvests resulted in shortages of bread. Some areas in the Montreal district that year were able to reap enough wheat for only four months of subsistence. By the beginning of November, Montreal was without bread. Bigot noted that "L'Emeute se mettant dans le peuple qui manquoient de pain, on Eut recours à moi."[64] He and Governor LaJonquière set the price of wheat at five *livres* a bushel, since it had been selling for up to seven. But as the price of bread was already too high and bakers dared not raise it more, there was no initiative for securing the flour and making bread. The governor and intendant therefore commandeered wheat in the Montreal district and paid farmers the set price, just as they did in the Quebec district during the winter. Some grain was kept for seed while the rest was converted into flour, distributed to bakers, and warehoused for use by the troops. Only the arrival of supply ships from France in the spring averted starvation.

That New France did not witness popular protest on the scale or frequency observed elsewhere may therefore be partially attributed to the activities of her officials. Through intervention in the marketplace they bypassed the buyers and their agents, who filtered through the countryside to purchase farm products, and either moderated or prevented speculation and price collusion among decidedly small merchant communities in Montreal and Quebec. Official regulation of the food supply in New France was made easier and was ultimately more successful than that in many areas of France for two reasons. As settlement during the French regime was strung out along the avenues of the St. Lawrence and the Atlantic, the colonies did not experience the transportation difficulties encountered in parts of France where there were few waterways and only poor roads. Secondly, despite the weaknesses inherent in agriculture at the time, Canadian agriculture was at least as efficient as that in France as a whole, although it was dependent on clearing new lands.[65] Even with poor harvests, early Canadian agriculture was able to feed a rapidly expanding population and export surpluses of wheat and other foodstuffs to Louisbourg and the West Indies from the 1720's to 1751. Only in 1743 and 1744 was it necessary for Quebec officials to import wheat from France and the English colonies to feed the Canadian population.[66]

These procedures to avoid popular disturbances and the leniency with which the protestors were handled suggest that colonial authorities, like their English counterparts, unofficially recognized the legitimacy of demonstrations as long as they acted within certain bounds.[67] Governors and intendants were overtly hostile to such manifestations in their correspondence with their superiors in France, but their actions belied their words. "Sedition," "mutiny," "revolt," and "riot" were terms they used to describe popular disturbances, but punishments were never harsh. This is explained not only by the non-destructiveness of the crowds, but also by the opinion among colonial officials that the people had no other way to express their plight. Officials in France, especially early in the eighteenth century, feared outbreaks as violent as those seen in the mother country and argued for stiffer sentences. Their subordinates in New France chose, rather, to remedy the complaint and exact only enough punishment to reinforce the appearance of authority.

In 1768 the *New York Journal* referred to the popular tumults that occasionally erupted as "Thunder Gusts" which "do more Good than Harm."[68] By providing a channel for collective expression with a minimum of violence, popular demonstrations can be said to have had a beneficial effect in New France. The British victories of 1758-60 and the transfer of Canada to Britain in 1763 temporarily ended this form of popular expression. Under alien rulers direct collective action would have been considered as insurrection and brought severe reprisals by the British troops now stationed in the colony. Demonstrations protesting food shortages and commodity prices appear to have died completely, less due to the presence of a foreign army than as a result of the return of peace, sound economic policies implemented by British officials, a reduction in inflation, better harvests, and increasing prosperity for rural *habitants*. Quebec did not, therefore, experience the greater frequency and intensity of popular movements observed in Europe after 1760 by George Rudé or the upswing in the number of revolutionary crowds, riots, and popular uprisings that Jacques Godechot had characterized as the Atlantic Revolution between 1770 and 1799.[69]

Popular protest was not altogether absent in the opening decades of British rule in Canada, but initially it assumed an individual form and was essentially passive. During the period of the military regime from 1760 to 1764, *habitants* removed wheels from their carts to avoid unpaid work on the roads and refused to sell wheat to the British on the mere promise of payment.[70] The collective behaviour of Quebec's *habitants* in this period, especially during the American invasion of 1775-76 and during the French Revolution, has been studied extensively by others.[71] The intention here is not to retread old ground, but simply to draw links to popular disturbances seen during the French regime and the collective psychology that accompanied them.

The same sense of fear and injustice that impelled people to collective action during the French regime was now channelled into resistance to British authority whenever the question of enlistment in the militia was raised. Fear of deportation – the fate of the Acadians in 1755 – provided a continuing link in the passive resistance that greeted Governor James Murray's attempt at militia enlistment in 1764, Carleton's efforts in 1775 when the presence of American soldiers on Canadian soil allowed more concerted action, and the Militia Act of 1794 passed by the newly formed Assembly of Lower Canada. Some of these incidents occurred in the places where there had been popular disturbances during the French regime. Lachenaie, involved in the protest of 1705, was one of four parishes just north of Montreal that offered resistance in 1775 to the Sieur de la Corne when he attempted, through violence, to coerce men into enlisting. In the Quebec area, militia officers in St. Augustin, the site of protest in 1714, refused the king's commission in 1775. Ancienne Lorette and Jeune Lorette (the former also implicated in 1714) refused to recognize militia officers named by Governor Guy Carleton in 1775 and were two of the four parishes that mounted armed patrols against the enforcement of the 1794 militia law. The repetition of collective protest in such localities suggests the development of a tradition passed on orally through the generations. Local folklore may help to confirm such a contention.

Debate among historians continues about the effect of the French revolutionary ideas spread through the press and by emissaries in Quebec during the 1790's. Despite the limited dissemination of some revolutionary propaganda among the masses, popular protest which erupted in Quebec in the 1790's shared the same general characteristics of that earlier in the century: spontaneous generation, limited targets, restraint in the use of violence, and defensiveness in the cause it espoused. War between France and England, rumours circulating in the countryside about the Militia Act, the appearance of a French fleet in the St. Lawrence, poor harvests, high prices, and French revolutionary propaganda emanating from the United States created a climate of instability. Not only was there armed opposition to militia enlistment in 1794, but in April of that year a crowd in Montreal seized the pillory where Joseph Léveillé, a canoeman convicted of fraud, was being exposed and threw it in the river. They then proceeded to the home of a magistrate, Frobisher, to demand pardon for Léveillé. When Frobisher consented, the crowd dispersed.[72]

Popular demonstrations were much more widespread in reaction to the roads law passed by the Assembly in 1796, because it reintroduced the *corvée* for the upkeep of royal roads and bridges or required a payment in lieu of labour. Even with French intrigues and revolutionary propaganda, the crowd continued to take direct limited action in opposition to the roads law, as it had during the French regime, rather than expressing generalized ideas. In the summer of 1796 residents of Quebec removed the wheels from their carts in opposition to the law and, when five leaders of the demonstration were arrested the following day, a crowd of some 500 women hurled insults at the arresting officers.[73] A constable in Montreal, sent in October to collect a fine imposed against Luc Berthelot for contravention of the roads law, was attacked by several assailants. Berthelot and the attackers were ordered arrested but could not be apprehended. A mob formed in the Place d'Armes outside the court house two days later when judges convened to determine their course of action in the case. Berthelot himself appeared and was recognized and arrested by the sheriff, but then he was snatched from the sheriff by the crowd. An even larger assembly to protest the law was held in the Champs de Mars the following week, but it dispersed when so ordered by magistrates. In the Quebec district there were similar crowd activities. At St. Roch on October 9, an assembly called to elect roads inspectors turned into riotous confusion and had to be dispersed. In January 1797, a mob at Pointe-Lévis led nine roads inspectors to the centre of the parish and forced them to renounce their positions. Court officials later sent to arrest the leaders of this demonstration were driven back across the river to Quebec.[74]

Popular protest revealed in these demonstrations as well as those during the French regime has been described variously as "first stage," "communal," and "reactive," as it involved localized groups outraged by some decision and determined to make their case known through popular demonstration.[75] After more than three decades of adjustment to British rule, the crowd had re-emerged in Quebec during the 1790's impelled by the same sense of injustice seen in New France and prepared to take the same form of limited collective action. What had changed was not the crowd but attitudes of officials, the Church, and Quebec's elite toward popular protest. Aware that crowds and mobs elsewhere had led to insurrection against the government and traumatized by the revolutionary terror in France, there was no intercession by the clergy and local notables to deal leniently with the protestors as there had been in 1704 and 1717. British officials in particular feared revolutionary uprisings against the government at nearly every turn. Consequently, the authorities moved swiftly against the protestors and exacted greater retribution. Nineteen people were brought to trial in March of 1797 in Montreal and thirteen were sentenced to fines and imprisonment varying from three months to a year. Twenty-four were arrested in the Quebec district, with all but one being convicted and sentenced to terms of up to six months in prison.[76]

Crowds and mobs in eighteenth-century Quebec may have been the thunder gusts of popular sentiment, but they did not bring any revolutionary storm. Revolutionary ideas of liberty, sovereignty, and the Rights of Man had only a limited impact on Quebec and they seldom reached the lower classes. Revolutionary ideas must be taken to the people, Lenin argued, and before 1800 Quebec lacked an indigenous group willing to transmit such an ideology. Only in the nineteenth century would popular protest reach the next stage of "associational" or "proactive" violence intent on claiming rights, privileges, or resources not previously enjoyed by at least one segment of the population. Out of the legislative confrontations beginning in the opening decade of the nineteenth century would emerge the leadership capable of channelling popular protest into a force more threatening to the political structure.

NOTES

1. The literature on this subject has grown considerably. See B. Porchnev, *Les soulèvements populaires en France de 1623 à 1648* (Paris, 1963); Roland Mousnier, *Peasant Uprisings in Seven-*

teenth-Century France, Russia, and China, Brian Pierce, trans. (New York, 1970); Leon Bernard, "French Society and Popular Uprisings Under Louis XIV," in Raymond S. Kierstead, ed., *State and Society in Seventeenth-Century France* (New York, 1975). For a review of the more recent literature, see Louis Lavallée, "Les soulèvements populaires en France dans la première moitié du dix-septième siècle," *Histoire sociale/Social History*, XX (1977), 427-33.

2. Emmanuel Le Roy Ladurie, *The Peasants of Languedoc*, translated with an introduction by John Day (Chicago, 1974), 286.

3. Charles Tilly, Louise Tilly, and Richard Tilly, *The Rebellious Century 1830-1930* (Cambridge, Mass., 1975), 17.

4. Louise A. Tilly, "The Food Riot as a Form of Political Conflict in France," *Journal of Interdisciplinary History*, II (1974), 24.

5. George Rudé, *The Crowd in History: A Study of Popular Disturbances in France and England 1730-1848* (New York, 1964); Max Beloff, *Public Order and Popular Disturbances 1660-1714* (London, 1963; reprint of 1938 edition).

6. George Rudé, "Popular Protest in 18th Century Europe," in Paul Fritz and David Williams, eds., *The Triumph of Culture: 18th Century Perspectives* (Toronto, 1972), 278.

7. George Rudé, *Paris and London in the 18th Century, Studies in Popular Protest* (London, 1970), 8, 18.

8. Jesse Lemisch, "The American Revolution Seen from the Bottom Up," in Barton J. Bernstein, ed., *Towards a New Past: Dissenting Essays in American History* (New York, 1969), 3-45; Jesse Lemisch, "The Radicalism of the Inarticulate: Merchant Seamen in the Politics of Revolutionary America," in A.F. Young, ed., *Dissent: Explorations in the History of American Radicalism* (De Kalb, Ill., 1978), originally published as "Jack Tar in the Streets: Merchant Seamen and the Politics of Revolutionary America," *William and Mary Quarterly*, 3rd ser., XXVII (1970), 3-35; Pauline Maier, *From Resistance to Revolution: Colonial Radicals and the Development of American Opposition to Britain, 1765-1776* (New York, 1972), especially ch. I; Gordon S. Wood, *The Creation of the American Republic, 1776-1787* (Chapel Hill, N.C., 1969), especially 319-28. On colonial Latin America, see Chester Lyle Guthrie, "Riots in Seventeenth-Century Mexico City: A Study of Social and Economic Conditions," *Essays in Honor of Herbert Eugene Bolton* (Berkeley, 1945), 243-58.

9. See Martin Galvin, "The Jubilee Riots in Toronto," *Canadian Catholic Historical Association Annual Report* (1959), 93-107; Gregory S. Kealey, "The Orange Order in Toronto: Religious Riot and the Working Class," in Gregory S. Kealey and Peter Warrian, eds., *Essays in Canadian Working Class History* (Toronto, 1976), 13-34; Michael Cross, "The Shiner's War: Social Violence in the

Ottawa Valley in the 1830's," *CHR*, LIV (1973), 1-26; Kenneth McNaught, "Violence in Canadian History," in John S. Moir, ed., *Character and Circumstance: Essays in Honour of Donald Grant Creighton* (Toronto, 1970), 67-83.

10. Lavallée, "Les soulèvements populaires en France," 428.

11. Rudé, *Paris and London*, 35-6.

12. Canada, *Censuses of Canada 1665-1871* (Ottawa, 1876); J.S. McLennan, *Louisbourg: From Its Foundation to Its Fall* (London, 1918), 372.

13. W.J. Eccles, *The Canadian Frontier 1534-1760* (Toronto, 1969), 81. Taxes were even lower at Louisbourg. See T.A. Crowley, "Government and Interests: French Colonial Administration at Louisbourg, 1713-1758" (Ph.D. thesis, Duke University, 1975), 256-7.

14. Richard Colebrook Harris, *The Seigneurial System in Early Canada* (Quebec, 1968), 63-70; Allan Greer, "Seigneurial Tenure in Quebec: The Examples of Sorel and St. Ours, 1670-1850," paper presented to the Canadian Historical Association annual meeting, Saskatoon, June, 1979.

15. Cornelius Jaenen, *The Role of the Church in New France* (Toronto, 1976), 84-90.

16. Louise Dechêne, *Habitants et marchands de Montréal au XVIIᵉ siècle* (Paris, 1974), 486.

17. Peter N. Moogk, "In the Darkness of a Basement: Craftsmen's Associations in Early French Canada," *CHR*, LVII (1976), 399-439.

18. Jean-Pierre Hardy and David-Thiery Ruddel, *Les apprentis artisans à Québec 1660-1815* (Montréal, 1977), 74-80; André Lachance, "La désertion et les soldats déserteurs au Canada dans la première moitié du XVIIIᵉ siècle," *Mélanges d'histoire du Canada français offerts au professeur Marcel Trudel,* Cahiers du Centre de Recherche en Civilisation Canadienne-Française (Ottawa, 1978), 151-61; T.A. Crowley, "The Forgotten Soldiers of New France: The Louisbourg Example," French Colonial Historical Society, *Proceedings of the Third Annual Meeting,* Alf Andrew Heggoy, ed. (Athens, Ga., 1978), 52-69. Allan Greer, "Mutiny at Louisbourg, December 1744," *Histoire sociale/Social History*, XX (1977), 305-36, suggests that the desertion rate among colonial regulars on Cape Breton was lower than in France, but he uses a specious comparison in which the French figures cover a time period during two wars, when desertion was highest, while those for the colonies cover only a period of peace.

19. Dechêne, *Habitants et marchands*, 356-61, has advanced our knowledge of the militia on the local level but has found no generalized discontent in Montreal before 1715.

20. Representation in various forms is discussed most fully in Gustave Lanctôt, *L'administration de la Nouvelle-France* (Montréal, 1971, reprint of 1929 edition), ch. VII, "La participation du peuple dans le gouvernement." On the influence of factions and interest groups, see Guy Frégault, "Politique et politiciens," *Le XVIIIe siècle canadien: études* (Montréal, 1968), 159-243; and Crowley, "Government and Interests," 283-316, 367-81.

21. Colbert to Frontenac, 13 June 1673, *RAPQ* (1926-27), 25. See also Francis Hammang, *The Marquis de Vaudreuil, New France at the beginning of the Eighteenth Century* (Bruges, 1938), ch. I.

22. Yves Zoltvany, *Philippe de Rigaud de Vaudreuil, Governor of New France, 1703-1725* (Toronto, 1974), 57.

23. Vaudreuil to Pontchartrain, 4 November 1706, *RAPQ* (1938-39), 163.

24. *OCGI*, 326.

25. Vaudreuil to Pontchartrain, 28 April, 30 October, 1, 4 November 1706, *RAPQ* (1938-39), 109.

26. *Ibid.*, Vaudreuil, Beauharnois, and Raudot to Pontchartrain, 19 October 1705, 82.

27. *Ibid.*, Vaudreuil and Raudot to Pontchartrain, 30 April 1706, 112-13. *IOI*, I, 5, 8.

28. Vaudreuil and Bégon to Pontchartrain, 20 September 1714, *RAPQ* (1947-48), 277.

29. Archives Nationales du Québec à Québec, NF 13-1, Matières de Police, 30 September 1714, 98ff.

30. *Jugements et déliberations du Conseil Supérieur de Québec* (Québec, 1891), VI, 834-5, 837-9, 997-1000.

31. Mémoire du roi à Vaudreuil et Bégon, 15 June 1716, *RAPQ* (1947-48), 302-3. See also *Inventaire des papiers de Léry conservés aux Archives de la Province de Québec* (Québec, 1939), I, 43, 45; Zoltvany, *Philippe de Rigaud de Vaudreuil*, 66; Camile Bertrand, *Histoire de Montréal*, vol. I: *1535-1760* (Montréal, 1935), 191-2; Robert Rumilly, *Histoire de Montréal* (Montréal, 1970), I, 321-3; Gustave Lanctôt, *A History of Canada*, vol. III: *From the Treaty of Utrecht to the Treaty of Paris, 1713-1763*, Margaret Cameron, trans. (Toronto, 1965), 10.

32. Guy Frégault, *La civilisation de la Nouvelle-France 1713-1744* (Montréal, 1969), 70.

33. AN, Colonies, C11A, 38: 121, Vaudreuil au Conseil, 17 October 1717.

34. Henri-Raymond Casgrain, ed., *Collection des manuscrits du maréchal de Lévis,* 12 vols. (Montréal and Québec, 1889-1895), vol. I: *Journal des compagnes de Lévis en Canada de 1756 à 1760,* 118-19.

35. *Ibid.*, 112-24. Similar disturbances among the soldiers have not

been noted in the town of Quebec, nor are they mentioned in Gilles Proulx, "Soldat à Québec, 1748-1759," *Revue d'histoire de l'Amérique française*, XXXII (1979), 535-64.

36. "Le Journal de M. de Bougainville," *RAPQ* (1923-24), 318, 320, 321.

37. *Collection des manuscrits du maréchal de Lévis,* vol. VII: *Journal du marquis de Montcalm,* 492.

38. Jaenen, *The Role of the Church,* 155.

39. Archives de l'Archevêché de Québec, Registre C, fol. 164-5, 166-7, "A Saint-Thomas: Divisions," 8, 23 November 1741; Registre C, fol. 200, "A Saint Antoine de Tilly: Desordres au Presbytère," 23 October 1749, in Claudette Lacelle, "Monseigneur Henry-Marie Dubreil de Pontbriand: ses mandements et circulaires" (typed copy in the possession of the author, 1971), 114-20, 193-4; A. Mailloux, *Histoire de L'Ile-aux-Coudres depuis son établissement* (Montréal, 1897), 5. I would like to thank Claudette Lacelle of Parks Canada (Ottawa) for allowing me to consult the above manuscript as it contains all the unpublished *mandements* and circular letters issued by Bishop Pontbriand. They are not included in the M.A. thesis of the same title that she presented to the University of Ottawa in 1971.

40. Archives Nationales du Québec à Montréal, Archives Judiciaires, Feuilles detachées, Déposition de Courtois, 5 October 1715, Delafosse, 11 October 1715, Information, 14 October 1715.

41. *Ibid.,* Déposition de Delafosse, huissier, 14 October 1715.

42. Ordinance of Governor Frontenac, 23 March 1677, *RAPQ* (1927-28), opposite xvi: E.-Z. Massicotte, "Répertoire des arrêts, édits, mandements, ordonnances et règlements conservés dans les archives du Palais du Justice de Montréal, 1640-1760," *Proceedings and Transactions of the Royal Society of Canada,* 3rd ser., XI (1917), ordinance received 3 April 1677; Dechêne, *Habitants et marchands*, 369.

43. AN, Col., C11A, 5: 38v, Duchesneau to Colbert, 10 November 1679; C11A, 6: 112-112v, Extrait des lettres du Canada (n.d.); W.J. Eccles, "François-Marie Perrot," and Jean-Jacques Lefebvre, "Jean-Baptiste Migeon de Branssat," *Dictionary of Canadian Biography,* I (1966), 540-2, 508. Dechêne, *Habitants et marchands*, 177, omits the political context of this demonstration and conveys the impression that it was larger.

44. AN, Col., C11B, 5: 166, Saint-Ovide au Conseil, 22 June 1720; Col., F3, 50: 90-1, Reglements de police faits à l'Ile Royale depuis le début de 1720 jusqu'au présent (n.d.).

45. *Ibid.,* 5: 78, Conseil, 20 August 1720.

46. Archives Nationales du Québec à Québec, NF 13-1, Matières de Police, 30 September 1714, 98ff.

47. E.P. Thompson, "The Moral Economy of the English Crowd in the Eighteenth Century," *Past and Present*, L (1971), 70-136.
48. See Henri Têtu et C.O. Gagnon, éds., *Mandements, lettres pastorales et circulaires des évêques de Québec* (Québec, 1887), I, 114-15; and Jaenen, *The Role of the Church*, 140. For France, see Yves-Marie Bercé, *Fête et révolte, Des mentalités populaires du XVI siècle au XVIII siècle* (Paris, 1976).
49. The character and composition of the bourgeoisie in New France continues to be hotly contested. For an introduction to the debate, see Dale Miquelon, ed., *Society and Conquest: The Debate on the Bourgeoisie and Social Change in French Canada, 1700-1850* (Toronto, 1977).
50. Vaudreuil and Bégon to Pontchartrain, 20 September 1714, *RAPQ* (1947-48), 277.
51. Wheat prices are discussed and charted in Dechêne, *Habitants et marchands*, 324-36, 521; and in Jean Hamelin, *Economie et société en Nouvelle-France* (Québec, 1960), 58-62.
52. Pierre Goubert, *L'Ancien Régime,* Tome I: *Le Société* (Paris, 1969), 42.
53. Charles Tilly, "Food Supply and Public Order in Modern Europe," in Charles Tilly, ed., *The Formation of National States in Western Europe* (Princeton, N.J., 1975), 389.
54. For a review of these interpretations, see Yves F. Zoltvany, *The Government of New France: Royal, Clerical, or Class Rule?* (Scarborough, Ont., 1971), 36-55.
55. W.J. Eccles, *Canada Under Louis XIV 1663-1701* (Toronto, 1964), 57-8; Eccles, *Canadian Society During the French Regime* (Montreal, 1968), 13, 43-4; Eccles, *The Canadian Frontier 1534-1760* (New York, 1969), 75.
56. Thompson, "The Moral Economy of the English Crowd." For the American colonies, see Carl Bridenbaugh, *Cities in the Wilderness* (New York, 1964), 198, 201-3; Bridenbaugh, *Cities in Revolt* (New York, 1955), 37, 83-5.
57. Fernand Braudel, *Capitalism and Material Life 1400-1800*, Miriam Kochan, trans. (New York, 1973), 81-2.
58. See Ralph Davis, *The Rise of the Atlantic Economies* (London, 1973), 111-20.
59. Alice J.E. Lunn, "Economic Development in New France, 1713-1760" (Ph.D. thesis, McGill University, 1942), 95-105; Hamelin, *Economie et société en Nouvelle-France*, 65.
60. *Inventaire des ordonnances des Intendants,* I, 142-4, ordinances of 18 August, 23 September, 27 October 1714.
61. Emile Salone, *La colonisation de la Nouvelle-France* (Paris, 1905, reprinted Trois-Rivières, 1970), 375.
62. Têtu et Gagnon, *Mandements*, II, 22-4, 28-9.

63. *Arrêts et régulations du Conseil Supérieur de Québec et ordonnances et jugements des Intendants du Canada* (Québec, 1855), 399-400.
64. AN, Col., C11A, 98: 111, Bigot to Rouillé, 8 May 1752.
65. Dechêne, *Habitants et marchands*, 326-8; W.J. Eccles, *France in America* (Toronto, 1972), 121-2.
66. Lunn, "Economic Development," 101.
67. David Grimstead, "Rioting in Its Collective Setting," *American Historical Review,* LXXVII (1972), 362.
68. Cited in Maier, *From Resistance to Revolution,* 23.
69. Rudé, "Popular Protest in 18th Century Europe," 295-7; Jacques Godechot, *France and the Atlantic Revolution of the Eighteenth Century, 1770-1799,* Herbert H. Rowen, trans. (New York, 1965), 3, 5. While agreeing with elements of the "common context" of the Atlantic interpretation of Godechot and his followers, Rudé argues against forcing all protest in this period into a similar mould. He advocates placing each form of popular protest in its national as well as the international context. This is as essential for understanding popular disturbances in Quebec after the British Conquest as it is for such events as the Gordon riots in England, the Pugachev rebellion in Russia, and the French grain riots in 1775.
70. Hilda Neatby, *Quebec: The Revolutionary Age 1760-1791* (Toronto, 1966), 25.
71. S.D. Clark, *Movements of Political Protest in Canada 1640-1840* (Toronto, 1959), 93-102, 176-89; Michel Brunet, *Les Canadiens après la conquête 1759-1775* (Montréal, 1969), 51-80; Gustave Lanctôt, *Canada and the American Revolution 1774-1783,* Margaret Cameron, trans. (Toronto, 1967), 57-8, 68-75, 80-2, 116-19; Claude Galarneau, *La France devant l'opinion canadienne (1760-1815)* (Québec, 1970), 235-48; Jean-Pierre Wallot, *Un Québec qui bougeait, trame socio-politique du Québec au tournant du XIX siècle* (Montréal, 1973), 254-69; Raoul Roy, *Résistance Independantiste 1793-1798* (Montréal, 1973), 107-23; Fernand Ouellet, *Le Bas Canada 1791-1840, Changements structuraux et crise* (Ottawa, 1976), 70-3. In 1812 there were again demonstrations against militia enlistment, but they were localized in the Lachine area. See J.P. Wallot, "Une Emeute à Lachine contre la 'conscription' (1812)," in his *Un Québec qui bougeait,* 107-32.
72. William Kingsford, *The History of Canada,* 10 vols. (Toronto, 1877-98), VII, 396; Galarneau, *La France,* 242.
73. Wallot, *Un Québec qui bougeait,* 268.
74. Thomas Chapais, *Cours d'histoire du Canada* (Montréal, 1919-32), II, 118-21; Galarneau, *La France,* 248-50.
75. Mousnier, *Peasant Uprisings,* 306-7; Charles Tilly, "Collective

Violence in European Perspective," in Hugh D. Graham and Ted Robert Gurr, eds., *Violence in America: Historical and Comparative Perspectives* (New York, 1969), 14-16, 38-40; Tilly, Tilly, and Tilly, *The Rebellious Century*, 49-52.

76. Galarneau, *La France*, 250.

V
Social Control

The Indian was perhaps the most pervasive and important influence on the development of New France. From the beginning of the colony it was a pre-eminent goal to establish friendly relations with the natives and, even more, to shape the Indians to the needs of the French. This drive took various forms over the history of New France. At times the Catholic missionary and the fur trader competed, the one seeking to create an unspoiled Christian Zion in the wilderness, the other to make the Indians into passive suppliers and consumers. To the north, the English Hudson's Bay Company preferred to minimize white impact on the natives, believing that they functioned best economically if left alone. Fur trade competition ended the debate. The missionaries became as much agents of economic control as were the traders themselves, and the Bay Company eventually adopted the tactics of its rivals. The natives were pressed to produce furs, decimated by trade-inspired wars, seduced by trade goods, and debauched by liquor. The competition between Montreal and the Bay continued until 1821 and by then most Indians had their cultures distorted beyond repair by the agents of white control.

Bruce Trigger discusses the early stages of the process in the work of the Jesuit missionaries in Huronia, the area around Midland in central Ontario. Before they and the Huron nation were destroyed by the Iroquois in 1649, the Jesuits were able to alter fundamentally the once stable and successful culture of the Hurons.

The attempt to make the Hurons conform to new social values was an especially clear-cut example of the social control which operates in any society. The Church also tried to impose different values on the white population; having failed to make a theocracy of the Old World, the Church wanted to redress that failure in the New World. The courts, too, dispensed values as well as justice. The people themselves, in their family organization and their community attitudes, imposed control in the wilderness.

FURTHER READING:

On Indians and social control, see G.F.G. Stanley, "The Policy of 'Francisation' as applied to the Indians during the French Regime," *Revue d'histoire de l'Amérique française*, III (1949-50), 333-48; Arthur N. Thompson, "A Study of the Conflict Between Civilization and the Fur Trade," *Journal of the Canadian Church History Society*, XII, 3 (1970), 44-57. Sigmund Diamond gives a more general interpretation of social control in "An Experiment in 'Feudalism,' " *William and Mary Quarterly*, third series, XVIII (1961), 3-34.

In French, see André Vachon, "L'eau-de-vie dans la société indienne," Canadian Historical Association *Report* (1960), 22-32; André Lachance, *La Justice criminelle du Roi au Canada au XVIIIᵉ siècle* (Québec, 1978).

Bruce G. Trigger is an anthropologist at McGill University.

The Deadly Harvest: Jesuit Missionaries among the Huron

by Bruce G. Trigger

By an unlucky coincidence, the return of the Jesuits to the Huron country coincided with the beginning of a series of virulent epidemics that were to reduce the Huron population by approximately 50 per cent within six years. These same diseases infected all the tribes who had dealings with the French and penetrated along the trade routes into areas no European had yet visited.

Prior to the arrival of the Europeans, the American Indians had never been exposed to many infectious diseases common in the Old World and had little natural immunity against them; hence when these diseases were transmitted to the Indians, they died in great numbers. The most dangerous killer was smallpox although various respiratory illnesses accounted for many deaths. Even childhood diseases that had a low mortality rate in Europe, such as measles, chickenpox, and whooping cough, killed many people of all ages when they broke out in Indian communities. As these diseases gradually spread westward across North America, aboriginal populations were cut drastically. Entire peoples lost their identity through depopulation.[1]

Epidemics of this sort may explain the marked decline that took place in the population of the southeastern United States and in the level of cultural development in that area in the six-

Reprinted from Bruce G. Trigger, *The Children of Aataentsic: A History of the Huron People to 1660* (Montreal, 1976), II, 499-500, 516-19, 522-6, 588-9, 595-8, 709-11, 714-22, 724. Reprinted by permission of McGill-Queen's University Press.

teenth century.[2] It has also been suggested, though without evidence, that epidemics played an important role in the dispersal of the St. Lawrence Iroquoians.[3] In the summer of 1611 numerous Algonkin died of a fever[4] and in the winter of 1623-24 many Weskarini perished of disease and hunger in the Ottawa Valley.[5] It is impossible because of inadequate reports to determine whether or not these were epidemics of European diseases. Although there were such epidemics along the east coast of the United States prior to 1620, there is no evidence of a major epidemic in eastern Canada prior to 1634. Nor is there evidence that the Huron had been affected by European diseases prior to that time. The reason for the swift succession of epidemics beginning in 1634 is unknown, but it may be connected with the rapid increase of European settlement along the eastern seaboard of North America.

While the Indians of eastern Canada died by the thousands between 1634 and 1640, the French rarely became ill and, when they did, they almost always recovered. When the Indians failed to arrest these epidemics with their inadequate pharmacopoeia and rituals that were meant to appease malevolent spirits, they became convinced that they were victims of a powerful witchcraft. Since the French had the power to remain well, or to cure themselves, it seemed inexplicable that they did not use this power to assist the Indians unless they wished to see them die. A remorseless logic, innocent of any knowledge of the varying susceptibility of different populations to the same infection, led the Indians to conclude that the French were using witchcraft to destroy them. Many reasons were suggested why the French should do this and the Indians disagreed whether the French should be appeased or slain as sorcerers. The most fatalistic were the Montagnais around Quebec City, whose hunting territories were becoming depleted and who were increasingly poverty-stricken and dependent on the French.[6] They were convinced that the French had determined to exterminate them so they could take possession of their land. . . .

Although Brébeuf* visited Teanaostaiaé and Scanonaenrat in the autumn of 1635,[7] the Jesuits spent their second year in the Huron country, as they had their first, in Ihonatiria. At first

---

* Jean de Brébeuf (1593-1649) was a Jesuit priest among the Huron who was martyred by the Iroquois during their invasion of Huronia in 1649. [editors' note]

they continued to baptize a few children and adults who appeared to be dying. Among those who did die was Sangwati, the headman of Ihonatiria.[8]

In spite of the occasional baptism, the Jesuits feared that their mission work would be jeopardized when they realized that most of the people of Ihonatiria and Wenrio had become convinced that baptism would shorten their lives. To counteract this fear, the Jesuits decided to baptize some young children who either were ill but seemed likely to recover or had shown a special interest in their catechisms. The recovery of a pregnant woman who was extremely ill, after she had agreed to be baptized, marked another turning point in the northern Attignawantan's attitude toward baptism.[9] On 8 December 1635, three young girls were baptized and, before the end of the month, twenty-seven more people had been.[10] Of the eighty-six Huron who were baptized between the summers of 1635 and 1636, ten or fewer died, four being adults. This makes it possible that as many as eighty baptisms were of children.[11]

The Huron began to believe that baptism was a ritual that protected children against sickness and misfortune[12] and children were brought to the Jesuits from distant parts of the country. While the Jesuits knew that the parents interpreted baptism as a physical healing ritual, they saw in their work the saving of many souls, particularly if the children should die young. They also hoped that by reminding the Huron, at a later date, that the souls of baptized children would be separated forever from those of non-Christians, they might persuade the parents of these children to want to become Christians.[13] In order to increase the respect that the Huron had for baptism, the Jesuits made it a rule to baptize healthy children only at solemn ceremonies in their own chapel.[14] Because of this new policy and a healthy winter, the Jesuits soon found themselves cleared of all former suspicions and their rituals again as popular as good shamanistic practices.

As a result of their growing popularity, in the spring of 1636 the Jesuits received numerous invitations to live elsewhere than in Ihonatiria. These came from the Arendarhonon and from important towns such as Teanaostaiaé and Ossossané;[15] however, the most persistent invitation was from Aenons, who won the Jesuits' support for a plan to have the five small villages in the northern part of the Penetanguishene Peninsula, including Wenrio and Ihonatiria, join together to form a single town that could be fortified against the Iroquois.[16] Aenons hoped that if he could persuade the Jesuits to move to Wenrio that village would become the nucleus of the new town and his claim to be its principal headman would be assured. He pointed out that since Sangwati's death, there was no experienced headman in Ihonatiria who could protect the Jesuits and ensure they were treated properly; on the other hand, in the new town, Aenons promised to see that they were provided with all the food they needed and with transportation to and from Quebec.[17]

To convert the Huron, Brébeuf was prepared to follow the example of early Christian missionaries and, where it seemed appropriate, to treat the matter as a political issue. He announced that the Jesuits did not look with disfavour on the plan to found a new village, but they were unwilling to commit themselves to live in that community unless the headmen of the five villages would pledge that they and their "subjects" would become Christians.[18] Brébeuf still misunderstood the nature of Huron society and believed that headmen had the power to treat clansmen as subjects and commit them to a predetermined course of action. The Jesuits were not present at the council that met to discuss the move, but later were informed that the headmen had agreed to their proposal and were coming to transport the Jesuits to the site of the new town.[19] Yet in spite of this conference, the planned merger of the villages did not take place and soon Aenons was asking the Jesuits to move to Wenrio and settle in his longhouse.[20] Most of the people the Jesuits had baptized were living in Ihonatiria and the various disputes that were troubling the northern Attignawantan made any move a delicate matter. The Jesuits therefore decided to remain at Ihonatiria for another year.[21] This pleased the inhabitants of the village so much that they enlarged and repaired the Jesuits' now dilapidated cabin, while accepting only a portion of the presents that the Jesuits offered them. All the men of the village, young and old, joined in this work and completed it within three days.[22]

The transferring of Ossossané to a new location in the spring of 1635 was the occasion for the celebration of a Feast of the Dead among the Attignawantan. During the winter, meetings were held to make arrangements for this feast and at one of them Aenons was commissioned to ask the Jesuits if the bodies of Guillaume Chaudron and Etienne Brûlé might be disinterred and reburied with the Attignawantan. Among the Huron, the burial of their dead in a common grave constituted the most solemn expression of friendship between two groups of people. If the Jesuits would agree, the Attignawantan and the French would be united by the most sacred of alliances.[23]

To their surprise, Brébeuf did not accept this proposal. He explained to Aenons that church regulations forbade that Christians and non-Christians be buried together and that it was not a Christian custom to raise the bodies of the dead.[24] Seeming to meet the Huron halfway, Brébeuf offered to rebury Chaudron and Brûlé near the Ossossané ossuary, but only provided that all the Huron who had died after being baptized could be buried in the same separate grave with them. Brébeuf hoped that in future such a precedent would make it easier to persuade converts to have their bodies interred separately from those of non-Christians and in cemeteries specifically consecrated for that purpose. He also believed that by reburying these bodies within the context of the Feast of the Dead, he could claim official sanction for the public performance of other Roman Catholic rituals and that by erecting a cross over the grave, the Huron would be compelled to honour it publicly. In this way, the Huron might be dissuaded from abusing or desecrating other crosses that the Jesuits might erect.[25] What Brébeuf did not reveal to Aenons was that he had serious moral reservations about moving Brûlé's body, since this would require giving the renegade a Christian burial.[26] Aenons and the other Attignawantan headmen agreed to Brébeuf's proposal. Nevertheless, since the Huron regarded the mingling of bodies as a symbol of unity and friendship, it is highly unlikely that Brébeuf's emphasis on the ritual separation of Christians and non-Christians either pleased or reassured them.

Toward spring a quarrel broke out between the headmen of the five northernmost Attignawantan villages and those of the rest of the tribe. According to Brébeuf, the northern headmen complained that they were being excluded from secret councils and were not receiving a fair share of the reparations payments and other gifts that were made to the tribe as a whole.[27] Because of this quarrel, the five northern villages decided to hold their own Feast of the Dead.[28] It is not certain, however, that the Feast of the Dead was necessarily a tribal ritual and the celebration of separate feasts by the major Attignawantan villages may have been more common than Brébeuf surmised. The proposal that Brébeuf mentions for a single feast embracing all the Attignawantan villages may have been an innovation reflecting a growing sense of tribal unity as a result of the fur trade. Alternatively, it is possible that the argument between Aenons and Anenkhiondic, who were apparently the headmen in charge of the Feast of the Dead in their respective areas, was never about whether there should be two feasts or one, but about the role that each division of the Attignawantan should play in the other's feast. Aenons seems to have nurtured a personal grievance about the southern Attignawantan spoiling an earlier feast he had arranged.

In April, Brébeuf was invited to be present when the principal Attignawantan met to discuss the Feast of the Dead one more time. Brébeuf took advantage of this opportunity to draw attention to Champlain's exhortations of 1635 that all Huron should become Christians if they wished to seal their alliance with the French, and that they should send some Huron children to Quebec the following summer to be instructed by the Jesuits. After preaching a sermon, Brébeuf presented the council with a collar of 1,200 wampum beads that he said was to smooth the way to heaven for the Huron.[29] Although one headman replied that no Huron was enough of a coward to fear torture in the Jesuits' hell,[30] the acceptance of this collar, and the nominal approval of what Brébeuf had said, convinced the Jesuits that these headmen had no strong objections to Brébeuf's teachings or to his proposals. Presumably the Huron respected the right of their French trading partners to ask for Huron children in return for the Jesuits; however, aside from their desire to preserve and strengthen their alliance with the French and to be polite, these headmen manifested no positive enthusiasm for Brébeuf's proposals. . . .

Since at least 1635, one of the Jesuits' main goals had been to gain custody of a number of Huron children whom they could instruct for one or more years. The Jesuits already knew that the Huron respected old people more than young ones and that all important matters of public concern were regulated by mature males.[31] Brébeuf had also learned from equivocal experience that it was easier to discuss theological questions with men than with women and children.[32] In spite of this, the Jesuits clung to the Recollets' belief that the long-term hope for converting the Huron lay in influencing the children, who were as yet uncorrupted by traditional beliefs.[33] In spite of their equivocal experience with Amantacha, they were determined to secure more Huron children to train as a corps of missionary assistants.[34]

To ensure necessary isolation from their families, Le Jeune argued that Montagnais children should be sent to France for two years of training,[35] while Huron should be brought to Quebec.[36] The resulting separation from their families would give the Jesuits a free hand to instruct these children in the French language and customs, since their relatives would be unable to carry them off whenever they wished. Le Jeune feared that the Indians would object to their children being scolded and physically punished, which he regarded as essential to their education. He also argued that the children would experience fewer distractions if they were removed from their own people and that the Huron children would serve as hostages to ensure that the Jesuits and their assistants were well-treated. No doubt, the Jesuits wished to send some Huron children to France for additional training, but after the delays in returning Amantacha to his family, such a request would likely have been turned down by the Huron.

In 1635 Etienne Binet, the French Provincial of the Society of Jesus, authorized Le Jeune to open a school for Indian children at Quebec, since donations were now available to support such an enterprise. The Jesuits judged this project to be of such great importance that it was decided that Fathers Daniel and Davost should return to Quebec to instruct these children, although they were the missionaries who, next to Brébeuf, had been in the Huron country the longest and who best knew the Huron language.[37] The Jesuits began to give special instruction to twelve young boys from Ihonatiria whom they wished to take with them.[38] No girls were chosen, because there were as yet no nuns at Quebec. The Huron were also probably unwilling to allow girls to be taken to Quebec, since this involved exposing them to a dangerous canoe voyage and to life among a strange, and therefore potentially hostile, people. Dangers of this sort were appropriate adventures for young men, but not for young women.

Only one youth seemed anxious to go with the Jesuits. This was Satouta, the grandson of the council chief Tsondechaou-anouan, who was entrusted with all matters pertaining to foreign peoples whom the Huron visited by water, and in whose name the Huron sent formal messages to other tribes and confederacies.[39] Satouta was nearly an adult and was in line to inherit his grandfather's office, which would require him to have many dealings with the French. It is therefore not surprising that in his desire to secure the Jesuits' goodwill, he said he was willing even to go to France, if they should wish it.[40]

When the time came to depart, the women of the households that these twelve boys came from raised so many objections that only three of the twelve boys were permitted to embark with their fathers or uncles.[41] The departure of these boys was a matter of vital concern to their extended families, and in family matters Huron women had a strong voice. The key role ascribed to the grandmothers, or headwomen, of these households clearly indicates that matrilineal and matrilocal principles remained important among the Huron. When the trading at Trois-Rivières was over, Satouta was the only boy whose male relatives were willing to let him stay with the French. To honour Satouta and encourage other Huron to leave their children with them, the French, in defiance of Huron custom, gave him seating precedence ahead of Huron headmen at formal meetings. In spite of this, the relatives of the two other children made excuses for taking them home with them.[42] Du Plessis-Bochart rebuked such behaviour for showing a lack of trust in the French. He promised that if the Huron allowed up to twenty children to come to Quebec, he would send an equal number of armed Frenchmen to defend the Huron villages.[43] Since only three children were present, it is difficult to know whether or not this promise was made in good faith.

Father Daniel warned the Huron headmen that by refusing to leave these children with the French, they were breaking pledges they had made to the Jesuits both individually and in council. To maintain the alliance the Huron must send some of their own people to live with the French, in return for the French who were sent to live with them. This appeal to Huron traditions, accompanied by much individual persuasion, finally resulted in the two other youths being left with the Jesuits. News of this decision encouraged a spirit of emulation among the Huron and a group of traders who came to Trois-Rivières later left three more children with the French. These, too, were taken to Quebec. It is unclear whether these included some of the twelve children that the Jesuits had selected in the Huron country. Not all were, however, since at least one boy had never heard Christian teaching prior to coming to Quebec and some were not Attignawantan.

Still more youths were offered by traders who arrived early in September, but these could not be accepted because all the Huron interpreters, who were necessary for holding a formal council, had returned to Quebec. Before returning home, Endahiaconc came to Quebec to see how his nephew was faring and was persuaded to take home with him one of the Huron boys (not his nephew) who could not get along with the others.[44] Endahiaconc was also accompanied up the Ottawa River by Simon Baron.

Who were the five youths who remained at Quebec and why had their male kinsmen given in to French demands, in spite of the opposition of their female relatives? Satouta, as we have seen already, was the grandson and heir of an important Attignawantan headman who had relatives in both Ihonatiria and Ossossané.[45] Tsiko was a nephew of Endahiaconc, the principal headman of the Attigneenongnahac, and Tewatirhon was the nephew of a council chief named Taratouan who seems to have lived near Teanaostaiaé[46] and of an unnamed war chief.[47] After his return to the Huron country, and possibly after he had married, Tewatirhon lived in Taenhatentaron, which may have been his home village.[48] About the other two boys, Andehoua (Ariethoua) and Aiandace (Aiacidace), we know only that the former came from Scanonaenrat. All of these boys appear to have been matrilineal kinsmen (nephews or grandsons) of important headmen who profited from controlling their clan segments' trade with the French. These men were therefore the Huron who had most reason for wanting to establish close ties with the French. The exchange of children or adults traditionally constituted a bond of friendship between trading partners. Thus Taratouan and other headmen could now boast that they were kinsmen of the French and, in that capacity, lay claim to be counted among the "masters of the St. Lawrence River."[49]

The Huron boys experienced various difficulties adjusting to life among the French. They had to accustom themselves to wearing French clothes and eating French food. Their habit of caressing people as a sign of friendship was also wrongly interpreted. Satouta and Tsiko both became ill and died not long after they had fights with Frenchmen. Although they appear to have succumbed to infectious diseases, the Jesuits attributed their illnesses to overeating, resulting from their unfamiliarity with the solid nature of French food. To prevent a recurrence of this tragedy the surviving boys were fed partly, after the Huron fashion, on corn soup.[50] The deaths of Satouta and Tsiko were witnessed by an Algonkin who knew Satouta's family and the Jesuits feared that he might report they had died from fighting or witchcraft, for which the French would be held accountable.[51] If their relatives believed such charges, it was feared they might retaliate by trying to kill some of the Jesuits in the Huron country.

The surviving boys followed a well-defined daily routine at Quebec: following prayers, attendance at mass, and breakfast, they were taught reading, writing, and catechism. After the noonday meal, there were more prayers, followed by instruction and a free period during which the older boys often made weapons and hunted and fished near the Jesuit house. After supper, there was an examination of conscience, prayers, and early bed.[52] In their free-time activities the younger boys followed the example of the older ones.[53] During the winter, the latter cleared a patch of ground which, since there were no women present, they themselves sowed with corn in the spring. They also built a cabin near the field, in which the harvest could be stored.[54] They urged the Jesuits to baptize them,[55] so they might conclude a closer alliance with the French, and announced that if they could obtain their families' permission, they would persuade some Huron girls to marry them and return to found a Huron colony at Quebec.[56] No doubt, they were attracted in part by the food, clothing, and tools that the French were giving them,[57] but they also may have believed that such a colony would benefit Huron traders.

During their first two years in the Huron country, the Jesuits had made progress in learning to use the Huron language and had begun preaching to the Attignawantan. They had also established themselves as the sole representatives of French officials and fur traders among the Huron and had persuaded the Huron to send some young people to Quebec to be indoctrinated and to serve as hostages for the safety of the missionaries. These successes were based on the Huron accepting the Jesuits in their country as a necessary condition of their trading alliance with the French. Instead of tactfully working to transform this relationship into an even more solid one based on personal trust and confidence, Brébeuf proceeded to exploit the French-Huron alliance and to offend cherished Huron beliefs in the hope of bringing about mass conversions. By so doing, he accomplished little that was positive and did many things that were to harm the

Jesuits in the critical years ahead. Already, his behaviour had created widespread resentment, which was still fairly well controlled on the political level but was giving rise to many rumours that the Jesuits were practising witchcraft. . . .

In the summer of 1639 smallpox spread through the St. Lawrence Valley, killing many Indians who came to trade at Quebec and Trois-Rivières.[58] This epidemic appears to have started in New England and was carried to the St. Lawrence by a group of Kichesipirini returning from a visit to the Abenaki.[59] Soon the Algonkin were dying in such numbers that the living were unable to bury the dead, whose bodies were eaten by hungry dogs.[60] The epidemic reached the Huron country when the Huron traders returned from Quebec. The first Huron who suffered from smallpox landed near Sainte-Marie and was carried to his home in the Ataronchronon village of Ste. Anne.[61] The epidemic lingered throughout the winter,[62] striking an extraordinarily large number of Huron. The Jesuits baptized more than 1,000 people who were in danger of death; of these, 360 children under the age of seven died, as well as 100 more children under the age of seven who had been baptized in previous years. In addition, many older children and adults died.[63] These figures suggest a total mortality of several thousand. By the time the epidemic had run its course, the Huron population was reduced to about 9,000 people, or only about one-half of what it was before 1634. Of the three cycles of epidemics that had attacked the Huron since that date, the smallpox epidemic accounted for by far the greatest loss of life. . . .

Since the Huron and Tionnontaté both agreed that the Jesuits were using sorcery to cause yet another epidemic, it is surprising that the Jesuits managed to survive the winter. Most Huron, including many council chiefs, appear to have wished and called for their death and specific plans were formulated to accomplish this. None of these plans came to anything, however, and when individual Jesuits were attacked, other Huron came to their aid. To a large degree, the Jesuits were protected by the segmentary nature of Huron society, which made not the confederacy but the tribes, villages, clan segments, and even individual lineages responsible for the actions of their members. Each group wanted closer trading relations with the French and was convinced that if it took the initiative of killing or even harming the Jesuits, other groups would profit at its expense. The internal quarrels that had arisen following Brûlé's assassination were too flagrant an example of the disintegrative effects of such behaviour to encourage any group to take responsibility for murdering the Jesuits. Huron headmen spent their time trying to persuade other Huron and non-Huron to kill the Jesuits while refusing to be persuaded themselves. Even the Tionnontaté, who did not trade directly with the French and therefore had less to lose, understood what was going on and refused to become cat's-paws for their Attignawantan neighbours. The Huron discussed refusing to sell the Jesuits any more corn in an effort to force them to stop practising witchcraft, but even this relatively innocuous plan foundered on the self-interest of the groups involved.[64] None of them was willing to forego the supplies of European goods that were received in payment for the corn.

In March 1640 a general council met at St. Louis to discuss what the Huron confederacy as a whole should do about the Jesuits. An entire night was spent debating this issue and the majority of headmen who were present said they were in favour of killing them as soon as possible. One tribe, however, opposed this action, arguing that it would ruin the country.[65] It is not stated which tribe this was, although it may have been the Arendarhonon, playing their traditional role as allies of the French. This led to further argument about which tribe would bear responsibility if the Jesuits were killed, and finally the project was abandoned. It was decided that since it was likely that native sorcerers were also at work, these should be hunted down and slain before further action was taken against the Jesuits.[66] There is no evidence that the Huron attempted to revive the old plan of compelling the Jesuits to return to Quebec the following spring.

The fundamental reason that the Jesuits survived was that the Huron dared not kill them or force them to leave the country. When they were angry, Huron might prevent the Jesuits from preaching, or they might insult or even strike a priest. In spite of this the Huron believed that the French governor gave the Jesuit mission his complete backing. Because of this, they were convinced that the survival of the French-Huron alliance depended on the Jesuits remaining in their midst and being well treated by them. That this knowledge could be converted into sufficient psychological pressure to protect the Jesuits' lives, in spite of the hostility that their behaviour generated, is a measure of the degree to which the Huron were now dependent on the French.

In the beginning, French trade goods had appealed to the Huron as novelties, but over the years these goods had become increasingly vital to the Huron economy. At first the Huron could reduce or suspend trade for a year or more if it was in their own interest to do so; however, by 1636 Aenons said that the Attignawantan (and presumably the rest of the confederacy) could not afford to let more than two years go by without trading with the French. Yet, so long as the Huron did not perceive themselves as dependent on the French, they were able to deal with the latter as equals. The relatively small amount of political or cultural pressure that the French exerted on the Huron prior to 1629 did not challenge this feeling of independence.

In 1634 the Huron headmen found their trading and military alliance with the French transformed into a mechanism for compelling them to allow missionaries to live in their midst whose behaviour was incomprehensible to them and who wished to overturn the traditional Huron way of life. The Huron headmen were convinced that these priests had the backing of the French traders and officials and could only be expelled at the cost of giving up the French alliance. To make things worse, there was no alternative to trading with the French. European goods could no longer be done without and the Iroquois, who were the principal enemies of the Huron, lay between them and the Dutch. The Huron could therefore perceive no opportunity in the foreseeable future of switching their trade from the St. Lawrence to the Hudson Valley. Knowledge that there was no alternative and that they were dependent on the French inculcated a sense of frustration and resignation among a number of Huron headmen. Yet, while a realization of the need for good relations with French traders seems to have been widespread enough to ensure the protection of the Jesuits, its more crippling effects were not generally realized until some time later. The period between 1634 and 1640 was not the time when most Huron first became aware of their loss of independence.

Lalemant records that when the Huron went to trade in 1640, Montmagny punished them for the acts of violence they had committed against the Jesuits during the previous winter.[67] Nothing is recorded concerning the precise nature of this punishment, although it was probably directed against the traders who had been most active in opposing the Jesuits rather than against the Huron as a whole. Punishments meted out to the Montagnais suggest that some traders may have been seized, imprisoned for a few days, and made to pay fines. Alternatively, they may have been denied the right to trade until they promised to behave differently in future. Montmagny warned the Huron of severe penalties that he would inflict on any Huron who in future attempted to harm the Jesuits.

However much the Huron resented such coercion, they were intimidated by Montmagny's threats and did not attempt to defend their honour by making any sort of counter-threats against the French. When the traders returned home, several Huron tribes offered reparations to the Jesuits to atone for the behaviour of those who had sought to injure them. From this time on, however hostile certain individuals may have felt toward the Jesuits, the Huron headmen treated them with circumspection. Lalemant rejoiced at the success of Montmagny's action, which he described as a pious employment of secular power.

This event, though inadequately reported, was clearly a turning point in French-Huron relations. Not long before, the French had feared the loss of the fur trade and were making contingency plans to try to come to terms with the Huron even if the Jesuits were slain. Now that half of the Huron population had died, the French became convinced that the Huron were economically and politically dependent on them, and this encouraged Montmagny to assert his power. As the Jesuits in the Huron country observed the success of this new policy, Montmagny was encouraged to press home his advantage. . . .

By 1640-41 the Jesuits had launched an ambitious scheme to counteract instability in Huron marriages in which one or both partners were Christians. It was noted that one of the main causes of divorce was a man's inability to provide the things that his wife and her family expected of him. Therefore, readers of the *Jesuit Relations* were requested to donate money that could be used to provide assistance to such families.[68] In some cases, perpetual annuities of ten or twelve *écus* were established with the understanding that Huron who were supported by these stipends should be given the Christian names of their benefactors. Although it is unclear how this money was spent, it was probably used to provide the heads of selected families with the trade goods they required. It was hoped that this charity would give the Jesuits sufficient influence to regulate the lives of the recipients and their families much as they wished. While this technique must have been effective only for controlling less productive families, according to Lalemant it resulted in the conversion of a goodly number of Huron.[69] Although this may be a pious exaggeration, we have here an early example of a later world-wide technique for enticing converts: "rice Christians."

The decision to live as the Jesuits required of a Christian must have been a very difficult one for any Huron to make, especially since the rationale for most of the rules that converts were asked to observe was not understood by them. The Jesuits now appreciated the important role that the traditional religion played in everyday Huron life and observed that it was more difficult to keep a Huron Christian than it was to convert him in the first place.[70] The Jesuits also realized that the Huron depended on religious practices to cure the sick, ripen crops, and bring almost every kind of activity to a successful conclusion. In spite of this, to become a Christian the Jesuits still required a man or woman to renounce all of the charms and rituals that had hitherto provided them with a sense of security.[71] On a more general level, the Jesuits observed that the Huron had no concept of hierarchical authority nor did their laws permit the personal punishment of those who had committed crimes. It was concluded that this spirit of liberty was contrary to that of Roman Catholicism, which required men to submit their will and judgement to a law that was "not of this earth and is entirely opposed to the laws and sentiments of corrupt nature."[72]

The Jesuit missionaries recognized the degree to which Christianity was the expression of a coercive, state-organized society. They were, however, unable to transcend this limitation and search for a way to adapt Christianity to the needs of a tribal organization. Instead, while admitting that Huron society functioned well enough, they justified their own beliefs by concluding that Huron society was institutionally, as well as theologically, primitive. In order to provide the Church with the authority required to enforce its decrees and to establish the punitive justice that Christian morality required, the Jesuits now foresaw that the Huron must be made to evolve some rudimentary state institutions. The implementation of such a scheme was impossible, however, until the Christians were in a majority in at least one large community. Until then, the Jesuits could only hope to restrain traditional practices among their followers.

When it came to providing moral support for their converts, the Jesuits were also not very successful. They vigorously attacked any reliance on dreams as guides to action without providing any other guide except an ill-defined and amorphous recourse to prayer,[73] which was also advocated as a general substitute for all charms and shamanistic practices. Because they still did not replace these time-honoured sources of moral support with more specific and more easily recognizable Christian substitutes, the Jesuits continued to undermine their converts' self-confidence. The temptation to have recourse to traditional aids was consequently very strong, and even long-standing converts required careful supervision to prevent backsliding. The situation was made worse by the converts' uncertainty concerning which aspects of their traditional culture were contrary to Jesuit teachings and which were not. Christian families would rehearse their weekly confessions before going to the priest, in the hope of sorting out such problems ahead of time. Most Huron seem to have been totally unable to distinguish between major and minor offences or even between permissible and impermissible behaviour.[74] The result was uncertainty about even the most trivial actions. It seems certain that few if any Huron understood what Christianity as a whole meant to the Jesuits. They were attempting to satisfy the Jesuits by doing in a piecemeal fashion what was required of them.

In order to protect converts from traditional influences, the Jesuits encouraged them to avoid contact with non-Christians as much as possible. As more Huron were converted, Sainte-Marie became the centre where, at the main Christian festivals and once every fortnight during the summer, large numbers of converts gathered for religious observances. At these assemblies converts would encourage one another and, under Jesuit guidance, would hold meetings to plan for the advancement of Christianity and for the eventual elimination of what they were taught to view as the paganism of their fellow tribesmen.[75] A strong sense of Christian identity was also built up by the prayer meetings and church services that were held with some frequency in the larger settlements. In the absence of the priests converts acted as native preachers, instructing potential converts and leading public prayers.[76] These meetings developed a sense of common identity among Christians and distinguished them from non-Christians.[77] In an effort to maintain the ritual purity that was demanded of them by the Jesuits, Huron Christians broke many of their links with the rest of Huron society.

An example of this can be given in terms of its effect on a particular relationship. A non-Christian woman of high status wished to contract a ritual friendship with a Christian woman. This was an accepted thing to do, and as the friendship was greatly to the advantage of the Christian the latter readily agreed to it. The non-Christian sent her a dog, a blanket, and a load of firewood as presents and gave a feast to proclaim their new relationship. Later, however, the Christian woman and her husband learned that the non-Christian woman had sought this friendship after a spirit had ordered her to do so in a dream. As soon as this was known the husband returned the presents and repudiated the friendship on behalf of his wife. The Jesuits rejoiced that there was "no bond of friendship that Faith will not sever rather than see a Christian separated from God."[78] . . .

The majority of Huron were deeply troubled by the growing success of the Jesuits and the breakdown of their traditional way of life. They noted that since the arrival of the Jesuits, one disaster after another had befallen the confederacy, while the Iroquois who had no contact with the Jesuits and had not forsaken the ways of their ancestors were prospering.[79] In spite of this the traditionalists did not seriously consider killing the Jesuits or expelling them from the country. Individual Huron chased the Jesuits out of their houses,[80] and in the winter of 1645-46 a priest in Teanaostaiaé was threatened with an axe during the celebration of the Ononharoia;[81] however, the only priests who seem to have been in any real danger were Brébeuf and Chaumonot and this was because of their visit to the Neutral and their suspected dealings with the Iroquois. In the Huron country, traditionalists as well as Christians took pains to protect the Jesuits from every possible danger. The reason for this was clearly their desire to continue trading with the French. This relationship had saved the Jesuits' lives during the epidemics, hence there was no question of it not being effective when conditions were easier and the Huron's dependence on the French was greater than before. However much the traditionalists may have resented what the Jesuits were doing, there seemed to be no practical way of getting rid of them. This allowed the Jesuits to undermine the traditional Huron way of life with little fear that the Huron would or could do anything to stop them.

If, however, the traditionalists were unable to express their strong disapproval of what the Jesuits were doing, the same was not true of their feelings toward their countrymen who had become Christians. The principal charge that was levelled against converts was that of witchcraft. This resulted from them refusing to perform various traditional functions that the Huron believed were necessary to assure the welfare of their community and of its individual members. Wealthy converts were not only accused of sorcery but also threatened with death for refusing to participate in redistributive rituals.[82] Christians were accused of endangering their communities by failing to join in rituals to avert the threat of crop failures. For example, in 1641 two women in Ossossané refused to obey a public order to burn tobacco in their fields and to stop gathering wild hemp in order to prevent a bad harvest. This resulted in a further proclamation by the town council stating that the Christians were causing a famine and in a general denunciation of these women.[83] It was also said that rosaries and medals could be used to do evil, since they stole away the souls of those who looked at them as well as caused blood to pour forth.[84]

The majority of witchcraft complaints were about the refusal of Christians to join in healing rites, including dream guessing. Frequently, these accusations arose within a convert's own household. A man from Ossossané, who is described as of no particular importance and the only remaining Christian in his household, was driven out by his relatives after the death of his niece who had also been baptized. These relatives urged him to renounce Christianity and when he refused they would not give him anything to eat. Lacking other relatives to whom he could turn, he was forced to beg for food and to do his own cooking, which made him an object of ridicule throughout the community. Men amused themselves picking quarrels with him and if he attended a feast, people would cry out that because he was a Christian he ought not to be there. He was said to bring misfortune wherever he went and people warned him that since he was a sorcerer, he must be prepared to die at any moment.[85]

In Teanaostaiaé a husband and wife who had lived together in the wife's longhouse for fifteen or sixteen years and who had five children were both baptized. As soon as the wife's mother learned about this, she flew into a rage and persuaded her daughter to renounce her baptism. When the husband refused to follow his wife's example, the older woman ordered him out of the house and forced her daughter to divorce him. A young man who refused to renounce Christianity in spite of repeated promises and threats admonished his grandmother that even if he were burned, he would not give in to her. He clearly expected that his stubbornness would result in charges of witchcraft.[86]

Shortly after Charles Tsondatsaa announced to his family that he had been baptized, one of his nephews fell ill, a niece became frenzied as a result of spirit possession, and another nephew was reported drowned. Some of his nearest relatives accused him of being responsible for these misfortunes and a quarrel broke out that nearly led to bloodshed. Tsondatsaa refused to renounce his conversion and, ultimately, all three relatives were found to be out of danger. Sometime later another niece fell ill, and her sickness was diagnosed as being curable by means of the dance of which Tsondatsaa had formerly been the leader; however, Tsondatsaa refused to perform this dance or to permit it to be performed for her. She, too, recovered.[87] After Tsondatsaa refused to fulfil a dream wish for a friend, the friend invited him to join him and some other Huron in a steam bath. There, the traditionalists promised not to tell the Christians if Tsondatsaa would fulfil his friend's wish. At the same time they threatened to suffocate him if he did not. In spite of increasingly violent threats, Tsondatsaa refused to grant this man's request. Finally, he passed unconscious and the Indians who were with him rescued him from the steam bath.[88]

Tsondatsaa was not the only prominent Huron who was persecuted by friends and relatives for becoming a Christian. When the new Atironta refused to allow shamans to attend his ailing son, his wife left him, took the boy with her, and soon remarried.[89] This left Atironta unable to remarry according to the laws of the Roman Catholic Church. We do not know whether this first wife died or returned to him, or whether some special dispensation allowed him to remarry, but when Atironta visited Quebec several years later he was accompanied by a wife and two-year-old son.[90] This quarrel demonstrates the bitterness that was generated by conversions even within the most important lineages of the confederacy.

Christians were also blamed for not taking part in healing rituals that were prescribed by their village councils. Sometimes the organizers of these rituals would tell Christians that the Jesuits had secretly agreed that they might join in them or would argue that by confessing afterwards, converts could obtain forgiveness for their participation. On other occasions, the traditionalists stated that the country was being ruined because the sick were no longer being cared for and would plead with Christians to join in the ceremonies one more time. When such pleas were unsuccessful, the traditionalist headmen frequently became angry and denounced the Christians for conspiring to kill their fellow countrymen. Sometimes hatchets were wielded over the heads of Christians to frighten them into joining in traditional celebrations.[91]

The leaders of the curing societies came to play an active role in persuading converts to renounce the new religion and sometimes were successful in doing so. Threats, promises, and bribes were all used for this purpose. The most strenuous efforts of these societies were directed toward recovering members who had become Christians. One of these was a woman named Andotraaon who lived in Taenhatentaron and was probably a member of the Awataerohi society. A headman who was one of the principal officers of this society informed her that at a secret meeting its leaders had resolved that if she did not rejoin their group, they would murder her the following summer. By scalping her while she was working in her fields, the killing would be made to look as if the Iroquois had done it (as Chihwatenha's had been done).[92] While the curing societies obviously had a special corporate interest in resisting the spread of Christianity, the members of this one were primarily objecting to Andotraaon's unwillingness to help her fellow Huron, which they interpreted as evidence of sorcery.

The shamans also had a vested interest in opposing the spread of Christianity and were among the harshest critics of those who converted.[93] They were able to use their expert knowledge of Huron religion to indicate how Christians were endangering people's lives by refusing to participate in the religious life of their communities. In this way they managed to stir up much hatred of the Christians.[94] Sometimes, however, the Jesuits were able to undermine the resistance of these shamans by converting relatives, thus bringing pressure to bear on them to convert also.[95]

The relationship between Christians and traditionalists was much affected by Jesuit demands that Christians should abstain from all forms of extramarital sexual intercourse. The Jesuits strove to inculcate in their converts what in their opinion was an appropriate sense of shame about sex and although their

teachings ran counter to Huron culture, they appear to have succeeded somewhat in this endeavour. As early as 1642 a fifteen or
sixteen-year-old Christian girl rebuked her traditionalist companions for talking about sexual matters.[96] The Jesuits believed
that some Christian girls tried to appear melancholy in public in
the hope that men would not be tempted to approach them.[97] A
Christian adolescent was approvingly reported to have gone into
the forest and rolled unclad in the snow for a long time in order
to stifle his sexual urges.[98]

The refusal of young Christians to respond in what the Huron
regarded as a normal way to sexual advances astonished other
Huron. It was regarded as yet another example of antisocial
behaviour with sinister connotations of sorcery. This was particularly so when young people met in the woods or in other
remote places where their sexual intercourse would not become
public knowledge and thus be brought to the Jesuits' attention.
Christian men were reported to have fled from one village to
another to make certain that they would not succumb to a
woman's advances,[99] while a girl told her traditionalist admirer
that she would prefer to be slain rather than submit to him.[100]
Most traditionalists regarded such behaviour as folly and told
the Christians that they were making a mistake to deny themselves the pleasures of youth through their fear of an imaginary
hell. Those who were rejected sometimes became angry with the
Jesuits because of it.[101]

Sexual temptation was, however, clearly one of the weak
points of converts, especially young ones. By 1645 the traditionalists were deliberately exploiting such weaknesses in order to
undermine commitments to Christianity. Headmen publicly incited girls to seduce Christian men. The Jesuits viewed this as a
serious threat and took comfort in the steadfastness of those
who resisted such advances. They reported that one woman who
had no success in seducing Christian men concluded that Christianity must indeed confer special powers on the believer and expressed the wish to become a Christian.[102] Gradually, the
prudery of converts seemed to undermine the traditional patterns by which young Huron met and came to know one
another. One young Christian is reported to have asked his uncle
to provide a wife for him, sight unseen.[103]

The traditionalists collectively opposed the spread of Christianity in many ways. Christians were taunted and ridiculed as a
group in an effort to persuade them to give up their religion. In

Teanaostaiaé they were nicknamed Marians, because they were frequently heard invoking the Virgin Mary in their prayers.[104] Children and adults were mocked that they had become Christians because they were cowards and were afraid of the fires of hell.[105] Among the children, such taunts sometimes led to fights and vigorous exchanges of insults between Christians and traditionalists.

Organized resistance to Christianity varied considerably from one community to another. In Ossossané, which was the oldest of the missions, there was little organized opposition. When the Ononharoia was celebrated in the winter of 1641-42, the leading men of the town approached every Christian separately and attempted to bribe or frighten them into joining in the celebration.[106] When the Christians stood firm efforts at intimidation ceased. At the opposite extreme was Teanaostaiaé, where the communal persecution of Christians was violent and prolonged. The first outburst was in spring 1642, when French workmen arrived to construct a chapel in Etienne Totiri's longhouse. People began to say that the progress of Christianity would ruin the village and that converts should be made to renounce it or be expelled from the community. Even Totiri's kinsmen joined in the demand that he and his Christian relatives should leave Teanaostaiaé. One of the council chiefs warned Totiri's nephew that if they did not cease to practise Christianity, they would be torn out of the earth like a poisonous root; this was a stock expression that the Huron used to intimidate suspected sorcerers.[107] Hostility against the Christians continued and rose to a fever pitch when Assiskwa returned from Sainte-Marie and demanded that all Frenchmen should be slain.[108]

This hostility was renewed the following winter when the Christians, who were somewhat more numerous, again refused to join in Huron religious ceremonies. They were accused of practising witchcraft and thereby exposing their countrymen to dangers of war, starvation, and disease. The growing strength of the Iroquois was also attributed to the Christians' public condemnation of the customs of their forefathers. Suggestions were made that a general council should be called that would require all Christians to renounce Christianity or to practise it secretly and without criticizing Huron customs. If Christians would not do this, they should be expelled from the country; meanwhile, all contact should be broken off with them and they should not be allowed to attend any Huron feasts or councils. Public antagonism against the Christians became so fierce in Teanaostaiaé that the Christians were forced to consider ways of conciliating public opinion.[109] When the Ononharoia was celebrated in 1645-46, a serious commotion broke out in the course of which several Christians were beaten and an old man named Laurent Tandoutsont was wounded with a blow from a hatchet. He had raced into the crowd, which was milling about the chapel, shouting "Today I shall go to heaven."[110] The same year the Christians were mocked when they formally erected a large cross in their cemetery. Later the children of Teanaostaiaé pelted the cross with rocks and filth.[111]

The public opposition in other villages appears to have been less persistent and less well-organized than it was in Teanaostaiaé. In 1643-44 a Kichesipirini headman named Agwachimagan wintered at Scanonaenrat and began to denounce the Jesuits and the French. At a secret meeting with the headmen of the village, he compared the teachings of the French with what he had seen at Quebec and Trois-Rivières. On this basis he found their teachings to be lies. Agwachimagan said that the real aim of the French was to destroy the Huron as they had already destroyed the Montagnais and the Algonkin. As proof he described a house at Quebec that was kept full of fleshless skeletons and lame, crippled, and blind people who had resolved to be Christians. This was his understanding of the hospital. He told the Huron that if they converted to Christianity, not one of them would be alive within three years. News of this warning spread terror through the town. Christianity was denounced and many who had requested baptism now decided to postpone it a while longer.[112]

In Taenhatentaron the first persecutions of Christians are recorded for 1645-46, but they may have started earlier. Although they were as violent as elsewhere, they appear to have consisted mainly of individuals being threatened with death rather than of public expressions of opposition to Christianity. Headmen and leaders of curing societies played a prominent role in opposing Christianity.[113] The late dissemination of Christianity to this town, and possibly a lack of headmen among the converts, may explain the form that this opposition took. It may also explain why, in the autumn of 1645, some of the Christians decided to offer a gift to the traditionalist headmen of the village, to induce them not to try to persuade Christians to join in customary Huron rites. When the Jesuits learned about this they removed these converts, because they feared that this example might encourage traditionalists to attempt to extract similar presents elsewhere.[114]

There can be no doubt that the development of Christian factions in various Huron villages gave rise to new tensions that cut across the segmentary structure of lineages, clan segments, and tribes. The traditional religion had helped to unite these disparate groupings and to assure the unity of the Huron confederacy. Moreover, until the coming of the Europeans, new rituals had supplemented rather than conflicted with existing ones. The exclusive nature of Christianity prevented it from fitting into this traditional pattern and its gradual spread created a rift in Huron society between Christians and traditionalists that threatened to cut across all existing social groupings. The unity of Huron society had never before been threatened in this manner and the traditionalists were faced for the first time with an organized threat to the Huron way of life.

Yet, in spite of these efforts to intimidate the Christians, there is no evidence that any Christian was killed or expelled from his village and very few of them were injured. One may conclude that the aim of these attacks was to coerce Christians into conforming with traditional norms of behaviour. What the traditionalists did not appreciate was that under Jesuit guidance the Christians were no longer sufficiently tied to the values of their society for coercion of this sort to be effective. Often the traditionalists found their own norms being used against them. For example, when the cross in the Christian cemetery at Teanaostaiaé was attacked, Totiri summoned a general meeting of all the people in the town and accused the traditionalists of one of the most heinous of all Huron crimes: violating a cemetery. This charge so troubled the traditionalist headmen that they ordered that hereafter the children should leave the cemetery alone.[115]

While the majority of non-Christians remained attached to the old ways and believed that Christianity was responsible for most of the troubles that were afflicting them, the Jesuits noted, with considerable satisfaction, that a growing number of them seemed to feel that there was no longer any hope of resisting the spread of the new religion. The Jesuits believed that such a spirit of despondency and resignation would facilitate the dissemination of Christianity. A certain amount of evidence appeared to justify this opinion. Some headmen, when going through villages to invite people to join in curing ceremonies, publicly declared that Christians need not attend or even encouraged them to remain in their houses.[116] In a similar vein a non-Christian woman, who became the guardian of a little girl after her parents died, refused to have traditional curing ceremonies performed for her. She argued that since the child's parents had been Christians, she must not be separated from them after death. When the child died she buried her body in a separate place away from the non-Christians.[117]

By 1645 the headmen in one of the larger villages complained that the traditional rituals lacked the fervour of former years and attributed this to the growing number of conversions. Yet, instead of attacking the Christians, they went through the community asking that the converts cease to be Christians for twenty-four hours and join in the traditional rites so that they might be performed properly.[118] One result of this growing lack of confidence was the tendency for some Huron to convert in order to emulate those who had already done so. An aged man at Teanaostaiaé sought to become Christian so as not to be excluded when his friends went to the chapel to pray.[119] Another, named Saentarendi, was one of the greatest opponents of Christianity in Taenhatentaron. Nevertheless, when he was near death he inexplicably requested baptism and urged the traditionalists, who had come to drive the priests away, to recommend to everyone that they should become Christians.[120]. . .

CONCLUSION

It is difficult to believe that the Jesuits did not perceive in these stories evidence of growing opposition to their work among what was still a majority of the Huron people. It must be assumed, therefore, that they felt sufficiently sure of their own safety (as guaranteed by the French-Huron alliance) and of the ultimate success of their plans to convert an increasing number of Huron that they no longer saw the need for caution in their dealings with non-Christians.

It is also difficult to believe that the Jesuits were unaware of the divisive effects that their mission was having on Huron society. Christians now observed Huron customs only when they did not conflict with their religion and this meant a growing rift between Christians and traditionalists about many vital issues. The mutual distrust of these two groups made political decisions more complicated and the refusal of Christians to fight along-side traditionalists lessened the military effectiveness of the confederacy at the same time that the growing hostility of the Iroquois made more fighting necessary. While the new factions that were developing among the Huron were not yet openly antagonistic, it must have been clear to the Jesuits that their work was not conducive to the well-being of the confederacy at such a critical period. They may have believed that their goal of converting the Huron was soon to be achieved and that a Christian people would once more be a united people; however, it seems unlikely that they could have believed that this process would outstrip the growing power of the Iroquois. The Jesuits must have known that their efforts to convert the Huron would multiply loyalties and viewpoints precisely when as much unity as possible was required. Their actions therefore make sense only if we assume that the Jesuits placed the conversion of the Huron ahead of all other considerations. The Jesuits may have known that it was impossible, under the circumstances, to be both a good Christian and a good Huron. Nevertheless, in accordance with their own values, they placed the salvation of souls ahead of preventing divisions in Huron society.

NOTES

1. H.F. Dobyns, "Estimating Aboriginal American Population: An Appraisal of Techniques with a New Hemispheric Estimate," *Current Anthropology*, VII (1966), 410-12; E.W. Stearn and A. E. Stearn, *The Effect of Smallpox on the Destiny of the Amerindian* (Boston, 1945).
2. C.O. Sauer, *Sixteenth Century North America* (Berkeley, 1971), 302-5.
3. William N. Fenton, "Problems Arising from the Historic Northeastern Position of the Iroquois," *Smithsonian Miscellaneous Collections,* C (1940), 175.
4. H.P. Biggar, *The Works of Samuel de Champlain*, 6 vols. (Toronto, 1922-36), II, 207.
5. G.M. Wrong, ed., *The Long Journey to the Country of the Hurons* (Toronto, 1939), 263.
6. Reuben G. Thwaites, ed., *The Jesuit Relations and Allied Documents*, 75 vols. (Cleveland, 1896-1901), XVI, 93.
7. *Ibid.*, X, 11.
8. *Ibid.*, X, 11-13.

9. *Ibid.*, X, 67.
10. *Ibid.*, X, 69.
11. *Ibid.*, X, 11.
12. *Ibid.*, X, 13, 73.
13. *Ibid.*, X, 31.
14. *Ibid.*, X, 83.
15. *Ibid.*, X, 235.
16. *Ibid.*, VIII, 105; X, 245.
17. *Ibid.*, X, 241-3.
18. *Ibid.*, X, 245.
19. *Ibid.*, X, 245-7.
20. *Ibid.*, X, 247.
21. *Ibid.*
22. *Ibid.*, X, 247-9.
23. *Ibid.*, X, 305.
24. *Ibid.*
25. *Ibid.*, X, 305-7.
26. *Ibid.*, X, 309-11.
27. *Ibid.*, X, 281.
28. *Ibid.*, X, 307.
29. *Ibid.*, X, 27-9.
30. *Ibid.*, X, 29-30.
31. *Ibid.*, X, 15.
32. *Ibid.*, X, 19.
33. *Ibid.*, X, 21.
34. *Ibid.*, VIII, 181.
35. *Ibid.*, VI, 85-9.
36. *Ibid.*, VI, 153-5.
37. *Ibid.*, XIII, 9.
38. *Ibid.*, IX, 283; XII, 39.
39. *Ibid.*, XII, 53-5.
40. *Ibid.*, XII, 41.
41. *Ibid.*, IX, 283; XII, 41.
42. *Ibid.*, IX, 285.
43. *Ibid.*, IX, 287.
44. *Ibid.*, XII, 45-7; XIII, 125.
45. *Ibid.*, IX, 273; XIII, 119-23.
46. *Ibid.*, XII, 97.
47. *Ibid.*, XII, 95.
48. *Ibid.*, XXI, 173.
49. *Ibid.*, XIII, 125.
50. *Ibid.*, XII, 53.
51. *Ibid.*, XII, 51.
52. *Ibid.*, XII, 63-5.
53. *Ibid.*, XII, 67.
54. *Ibid.*, XII, 77.

55. *Ibid.*, XII, 67-9.
56. *Ibid.*, XII, 79.
57. *Ibid.*
58. *Ibid.*, XV, 237; XVI, 53.
59. *Ibid.*, XVI, 101.
60. *Ibid.*, XVI, 155, 217-19.
61. *Ibid.*, XIX, 89.
62. *Ibid.*, XXI, 131.
63. *Ibid.*, XIX, 77-9, 123.
64. *Ibid.*, XVII, 229.
65. *Ibid.*, XIX, 177.
66. *Ibid.*, XIX, 179.
67. *Ibid.*, XXI, 143.
68. *Ibid.*, XXI, 135-9.
69. *Ibid.*, XXIII, 187-9; XXVII, 69-71.
70. *Ibid.*, XXVIII, 55.
71. *Ibid.*, XXIII, 185-7; XXVIII, 53.
72. *Ibid.*, XXVIII, 49-51.
73. *Ibid.*, XXI, 161-3; XXX, 43-5.
74. *Ibid.*, XXIII, 107-15.
75. *Ibid.*, XXVI, 211.
76. *Ibid.*, XXVII, 67-9.
77. *Ibid.*, XXX, 43.
78. *Ibid.*, XXIII, 125.
79. *Ibid.*, XXV, 35-7.
80. *Ibid.*, XXIII, 39.
81. *Ibid.*, XXX, 101.
82. *Ibid.*, XXX, 19-21.
83. *Ibid.*, XXIII, 55-7.
84. *Ibid.*, XXIII, 135.
85. *Ibid.*, XXIII, 67.
86. *Ibid.*, XXIII, 127.
87. *Ibid.*, XXIII, 85-9.
88. *Ibid.*, XXVI, 243-9.
89. *Ibid.*, XXIII, 165.
90. *Ibid.*, XXVII, 113.
91. *Ibid.*, XXIII, 43-53.
92. *Ibid.*, XXX, 23.
93. *Ibid.*, XXIII, 117-19; XXVII, 33.
94. *Ibid.*, XXIII, 55.
95. *Ibid.*, XXIII, 117-21.
96. *Ibid.*, XXIII, 99.
97. *Ibid.*, XXIII, 71-3.
98. *Ibid.*, XXX, 39.
99. *Ibid.*, XXIII, 63.
100. *Ibid.*, XXVI, 229.

101. *Ibid.*
102. *Ibid.*, XXX, 33-7.
103. *Ibid.*, XXX, 30-9.
104. *Ibid.*, XXII, 135.
105. *Ibid.*, XXIII, 97; XXVI, 229.
106. *Ibid.*, XXIII, 43-55.
107. *Ibid.*, XXIII, 133-5.
108. *Ibid.*, XXIII, 145.
109. *Ibid.*, XXVI, 279-81.
110. *Ibid.*, XXX, 101-3.
111. *Ibid.*, XXIX, 275.
112. *Ibid.*, XXVI, 301-7.
113. *Ibid.*, XXX, 19-25.
114. *Ibid.*, XXIX, 271.
115. *Ibid.*, XXIX, 275-7.
116. *Ibid.*, XXVI, 255-7.
117. *Ibid.*, XXVI, 227.
118. *Ibid.*, XXIX, 273.
119. *Ibid.*, XXX, 99-101.
120. *Ibid.*, XXX, 105-7.

VI
Native Peoples

The native peoples of Canada had been resident for thousands of years before the French arrived and their cultures had been viable and evolving. The fur trade and the colonial wars overloaded many of those cultures, however, and many cracked under pressure. They simply were forced to change and adapt more quickly than was possible. The result was the same as it was for other cultures under similar duress – the rural culture of French Canada in the twentieth century or many immigrant lifestyles. The people could integrate into the dominant culture or fall into stagnation. Not welcome to integrate, the Indians really had no choice.

A sympathetic and rounded analysis of this process has begun to emerge only in recent years. Two of the authors in this book, Bruce Trigger on the Hurons and Calvin Martin in this section, were pioneers in the process. To move beyond the inevitably one-sided studies of government policy and the ethnocentric economic analyses, recent writers have found it necessary to employ more than traditional historical techniques. The insights of anthropology, geography, and, in Calvin Martin's work, ecology have been necessary to develop a sensitive history of native peoples. It is still far from complete. Most of the best work of scholars such as Trigger and Cornelius Jaenen has focused on the early contacts, on the seventeenth century and the East. Both the West and the century before the Conquest await full treatment.

FURTHER READING:
Among the extensive literature are Alfred G. Bailey's ground-breaking, *The Conflict of European and Eastern Algonkian Cultures, 1504-1700*, 2nd edition (Toronto, 1969); Cornelius Jaenen, "Amerindian Views of French Culture in the Seventeenth Century," *CHR*, LV, 3 (1974), 261-91; Karl H. Schlesier, "Epidemics and Indian Middlemen: Rethinking the Wars of the Iroquois, 1609-1653," *Ethnohistory*, XXIII, 2 (1976), 129-45; Bruce Trigger, "The French Presence in Huronia: The Structure of Franco-Huron Relations in the First Half of the Seventeenth Century," *CHR*, XLIV, 2 (1968), 107-41.

Calvin Martin is an historian and anthropologist at Rutgers College.

The European Impact on the Culture of a Northeastern Algonquian Tribe: An Ecological Interpretation

by Calvin Martin

As the drive for furs, known prosaically as the fur trade, expanded and became more intense in seventeenth-century Canada, complaints of beaver extermination became more frequent and alarming. By 1635, for example, the Huron had reduced their stock of beaver to the point where the Jesuit Father Paul Le Jeune could declare that they had none.[1] In 1684 Baron Lahontan recorded a speech made before the French Governor General by an Iroquois spokesman, who explained that his people had made war on the Illinois and Miami because these Algonquians had trespassed on Iroquois territory and overkilled their beaver, "and contrary to the Custom of all the Savages, have carried off whole Stocks, both Male and Female."[2] This exploitation of beaver and other furbearers seems to have been most intense in the vicinity of major trading posts and among the native tribes most affected by the trade (the Montagnais, Huron, League Iroquois, Micmac, and others),[3] while those tribes which remained beyond European influence and the trade, such as the Bersimis of northeastern Quebec, enjoyed an abundance of beaver in their territories.[4]

Even before the establishment of trading posts, the Micmac of the extreme eastern tip of Canada were engaged in lively trade with European fishermen. Thus areas that were important in the fishing industry, such as Prince Edward Island, the Gaspé Pen-

From *William and Mary Quarterly*, third series, 31 (1974), 3-26. Reprinted by permission of the author.

insula, and Cape Breton Island, were cleaned out of moose and other furbearers by the mid-seventeenth century.[5] Reviewing this grim situation, Nicolas Denys observed that game was less abundant in his time than formerly; as for the beaver, "few in a house are saved; they [the Micmac] would take all. The disposition of the Indians is not to spare the little ones any more than the big ones. They killed all of each kind of animal that there was when they could capture it."[6]

In short, the game which by all accounts had been so plentiful was now being systematically overkilled by the Indians themselves. A traditional explanation for this ecological catastrophe is neatly summarized by Peter Farb, who conceives of it in mechanistic terms: "If the Northern Athabaskan and Northern Algonkian Indians husbanded the land and its wildlife in primeval times, it was only because they lacked both the technology to kill very many animals and the market for so many furs. But once white traders entered the picture, supplying the Indians with efficient guns and an apparently limitless market for furs beyond the seas, the Indians went on an orgy of destruction." The Indian, in other words, was "economically seduced" to exploit the wildlife requisite to the fur trade.[7]

Such a cavalier dismissal of northeastern Algonquian culture, especially its spiritual component, renders this explanation superficial and inadequate. One can argue that economic determinism was crucial to the course of Algonquian cultural development (including religious perception) over a long period of time. Yet from this perspective European contact was but a moment in the cultural history of the Indians, and it is difficult to imagine that ideals and a lifestyle that had taken centuries to evolve would have been so easily and quickly discarded merely for the sake of improved technological convenience. As we shall see, the entire Indian/land relationship was suffused with religious considerations which profoundly influenced the economic (subsistence) activities and beliefs of these people. The subsistence cycle was regulated by centuries of spiritual tradition which, if it had been in a healthy state, would have countered the revolutionizing impact of European influence. Tradition would doubtless have succumbed eventually, but why did the end come so soon? Why did the traditional safeguards of the northeastern Algonquian economic system offer such weak resistance to its replacement by the exploitive, European-induced regime?

When the problem is posed in these more comprehensive

terms, the usual economic explanation seems misdirected, for which reason the present article will seek to offer an alternative interpretation. The methodology of cultural ecology will be brought to bear on the protohistoric and early contact phases of Micmac cultural history in order to examine the Indian/land relationship under aboriginal and post-contact conditions and to probe for an explanation to the problem of wildlife overkill.[8]

Cultural ecology seeks to explain the interaction of environment and culture, taking the ecosystem and the local human population as the basic units of analysis.[9] An ecosystem is a discrete community of plants and animals, together with the non-living environment, occupying a certain space and time, having a flow-through of energy and raw materials in its operation, and composed of subsystems.[10] For convenience of analysis, an ecosystem can be separated into its physical and biological components, although one should bear in mind that in nature the two are completely intermeshed in complex interactions. And from the standpoint of cultural ecology, there is a third component: the metaphysical or spiritual.

The ecosystem model of plant and animal ecologists is somewhat strained when applied to a human population, although, as Roy A. Rappaport has demonstrated in his *Pigs for the Ancestors*, the attempt can be very useful.[11] The difficulties encountered include the assignment of definite territorial limits to the area under consideration (resulting in a fairly arbitrary delimitation of an ecosystem), the quantification of the system's energy budget and the carrying capacity of the land, and the identification of subsystem interrelations. Assigning values to variables becomes, in many instances, quite impossible.

The transposition of the ecosystem approach from cultural anthropology to historical inquiry complicates these problems even further, for the relationships between a human population and its environment are seldom amenable to rigorous quantitative analysis using historical documents as sources. Yet this is certainly not always so. In the case of the fur trade, for example, one may in fact be able to measure some of its effects on the environment from merchants' records – showing numbers of pelts obtained from a region over a certain time period – and also from lists of goods given to the Indians at trading posts and by treaties. Even when available, such records are too incomplete to satisfy the rigorous demands of the ecologist, but to say that they are of limited value is not to say that they are useless.

Few historians have used the ecological model in their work.[12] Recognizing the need for the environmental perspective in historiography, Wilbur R. Jacobs recently observed that "those who hope to write about such significant historical events [as the despoiling of the American West] . . . will need a sort of knowledge not ordinarily possessed by historians. To study the impact of the fur trade upon America and her native people, for instance, there must be more than a beginning acquaintance with ethnology, plant and animal ecology, paleoecology, and indeed much of the physical sciences."[13]

In the case of the northeastern Algonquian, and the Micmac in particular, the fur trade was but one factor – albeit an important one – in the process of acculturation. Long before they felt the lure of European technology, these littoral Indians must have been infected with Old World diseases carried by European fishermen, with catastrophic effects. Later, the Christian missionaries exerted a disintegrative influence on the Indians' view of and relation to their environment. All three of these factors – disease, Christianity, and technology – which may be labelled "trigger" factors, must be assessed in terms of their impact on the Indians' ecosystem.[14]

Among the first North American Indians to be encountered by Europeans were the Micmacs who occupied present-day Nova Scotia, northern New Brunswick and the Gaspé Peninsula, Prince Edward Island, and Cape Breton Island. According to Sieur de Dièreville, they also lived along the lower St. John River with the Malecites, who outnumbered them.[15] For our present purposes, the Micmac territory will be considered an ecosystem, and the Micmac occupying it will be regarded as a local population. These designations are not entirely arbitrary, for the Micmac occupied and exploited the area in a systematic way; they had a certain psychological unity or similarity in their ideas about the cosmos; they spoke a language distinct from those of their neighbours; and they generally married within their own population. There were, as might be expected, many external factors impinging on the ecosystem which should also be evaluated, although space permits them only to be mentioned here. Some of these "supralocal" relations involved trade and hostilities with other tribes; the exchange of genetic material and personnel with neighbouring tribes through intermarriage and adoption; the exchange of folklore and customs; and the movements of such migratory game as moose and woodland caribou.

The Micmac ecosystem thus participated in a regional system, and the Micmac population was part of a regional population.[16]

The hunting, gathering, and fishing Micmac who lived within this Acadian forest, especially along its rivers and by the sea, were omnivores (so to speak) in the trophic system of the community. At the first trophic level, the plants eaten were wild potato tubers, wild fruits and berries, acorns and nuts, and the like. Trees and shrubs provided a wealth of materials used in the fashioning of tools, utensils, and other equipment.[17] At the time of contact, none of the Indians living north of the Saco River cultivated food crops. Although legend credits the Micmac with having grown maize and tobacco "for the space of several years,"[18] these cultigens, as well as beans, pumpkins, and wampum (which they greatly prized), were obtained from the New England Algonquians of the Saco River area (Abnakis) and perhaps from other tribes to the south.[19]

Herbivores and carnivores occupy the second and third trophic levels respectively, with top carnivores in the fourth level. The Micmac hunter tapped all three levels in his seasonal hunting and fishing activities, and these sources of food were "to them like fixed rations assigned to every moon."[20] In January, seals were hunted when they bred on islands off the coast; the fat was reduced to oil for food and body grease, and the women made clothing from the fur.[21] The principal hunting season lasted from February till mid-March, since there were enough marine resources, especially fish and mollusks, available during the other three seasons to satisfy most of the Micmacs' dietary needs. For a month and a half, then, the Indians withdrew from the seashore to the banks of rivers and lakes and into the woods to hunt the caribou, moose, black bear, and small furbearers. At no other time of the year were they so dependent on the caprice of the weather: a feast was as likely as a famine. A heavy rain could ruin the beaver and caribou hunt, and a deep, crustless snow would doom the moose hunt.[22]

Since beaver were easier to hunt on the ice than in the water, and since their fur was better during the winter, this was the chief season for taking them.[23] Hunters would work in teams or groups, demolishing the lodge or cutting the dam with stone axes. Dogs were sometimes used to track the beaver which took refuge in air pockets along the edge of the pond, or the beaver might be harpooned at air holes. In the summer hunt, beaver were shot with the bow or trapped in deadfalls using poplar as bait, but the commonest way to take them was to cut the dam in the middle and drain the pond, killing the animals with bows and spears.[24]

Next to fish, moose was the most important item in the Micmac diet, and it was their staple during the winter months when these large mammals were hunted with dogs on the hard-crusted snow. In the summer and spring, moose were tracked, stalked, and shot with the bow; in the fall, during the rutting season, the bull was enticed by a clever imitation of the sound of a female urinating. Another technique was to ensnare the animal with a noose.[25]

Moose was the Micmacs' favorite meat. The entrails, which were considered a great delicacy, and the "most delicious fat" were carried by the triumphant hunter to the campsite, and the women were sent after the carcass. The mistress of the wigwam decided what was to be done with each portion of the body, every part of which was used. Grease was boiled out of the bones and either drunk pure (with "much gusto") or stored as loaves of moose-butter;[26] the leg and thigh bones were crushed and the marrow eaten; the hides were used for robes, leggings, moccasins, and tent coverings;[27] tools, ornaments, and game pieces were made from antlers, teeth, and toe bones, respectively.[28] According to contemporary French observers, the Micmac usually consumed the moose meat immediately, without storing any, although the fact that some of the meat was preserved rather effectively by smoking it on racks, so that it would even last the year, demonstrates that Micmac existence was not as hand-to-mouth as is commonly believed of the northeastern Algonquian.[29] Black bear were also taken during the season from February till mid-March, but such hunting was merely coincidental. If a hunter stumbled upon a hibernating bear, he could count himself lucky.[30]

As the lean months of winter passed into the abundance of spring, the fish began to spawn, swimming up rivers and streams in such numbers that "everything swarms with them."[31] In mid-March came the smelt, and at the end of April the herring. Soon there were sturgeon and salmon, and numerous waterfowl made nests out on the islands – which meant there were eggs to be gathered. Mute evidence from seashore middens and early written testimony reveals that these Indians also relied heavily on various mollusks, which they harvested in great quantity.[32] Fish was a staple for the Micmac, who knew the spawning habits of each type of fish and where it was to be found. Weirs were erected across streams to trap the fish on their way downstream on a falling tide, while larger fish, such as sturgeon and salmon, might be speared or trapped.[33]

The salmon run marked the beginning of summer, when the wild geese shed their plumage. Most wildfowl were hunted at their island rookeries; waterfowl were often hunted by canoe and struck down as they took to flight; others, such as the Canadian geese which grazed in the meadows, were shot with the bow.[34]

In autumn, when the waterfowl migrated southward, the eels spawned up the many small rivers along the coast. From mid-September to October the Micmac left the ocean and followed the eels, "of which they lay in a supply; they are good and fat." Caribou and beaver were hunted during October and November, and with December came the "tom cod" (which were said to have spawned under the ice) and turtles bearing their young.[35] In January the subsistence cycle began again with the seal hunt.

As he surveyed the seasonal cycle of these Indians, Father Pierre Biard was impressed by nature's bounty and Micmac resourcefulness: "These then, but in a still greater number, are the revenues and incomes of our Savages; such, their table and living, all prepared and assigned, everything to its proper place and quarter."[36] Although we have omitted mention of many other types of forest, marine, and aquatic life which were also exploited by the Micmac, those listed above were certainly the most significant in the Micmacs' food quest and ecosystem.[37]

Frank G. Speck, perhaps the foremost student of northeastern Algonquian culture, has emphasized that hunting to the Micmacs was not a "war upon the animals, not a slaughter for food or profit."[38] Denys's observations confirm Speck's point: "Their greatest task was to feed well and to go a hunting. They did not lack animals, which they killed only in proportion as they had need of them."[39] From this, and the above description of their effective hunting techniques, it would appear that the Micmac were not limited by their hunting technology in the taking of game. As Denys pointed out, "the hunting by the Indians in old times was easy for them. . . . When they were tired of eating one sort, they killed some of another. If they did not wish longer to eat meat, they caught some fish. They never made an accumulation of skins of Moose, Beaver, Otter, or others, but only so far as they needed them for personal use. They left the remainder [of the carcass] where the animals had been killed, not taking the trouble to bring them to their camps."[40] Need, not technology, was the ruling factor, and need was determined by the great primal necessities of life and regulated by spiritual considerations. Hunting, as Speck remarks, was "a *holy occupation*";[41] it was conducted and controlled by spiritual rules.

The bond which united these physical and biological components of the Micmac ecosystem, and indeed gave them definition and comprehensibility, was the world view of the Indian. The foregoing discussion has dealt mainly with the empirical, objective, physical ("operational") environmental model of the observer; what it lacks is the "cognized" model of the Micmac.[42]

Anthropologists regard the pre-Columbian North American Indian as a sensitive member of his environment, who merged sympathetically with its living and non-living components.[43] The Indian's world was filled with superhuman and magical powers which controlled man's destiny and nature's course of events.[44] Murray Wax explains:

> To those who inhabit it, the magical world is a "society," not a "mechanism," that is, it is composed of "beings" rather than "objects." Whether human or nonhuman, these beings are associated with and related to one another socially and sociably, that is, in the same ways as human beings to one another. These patterns of association and relationship may be structured in terms of kinship, empathy, sympathy, reciprocity, sexuality, dependency, or any other of the ways that human beings interact with and affect or afflict one another. Plants, animals, rocks, and stars are thus seen not as "objects" governed by laws of nature, but as "fellows" with whom the individual or band may have a more or less advantageous relationship.[45]

For the Micmac, together with all the other eastern subarctic Algonquians, the power of these mysterious forces was apprehended as "manitou" – translated "magic power" – much in the same way that we might use the slang word "vibrations" to register the emotional feelings emanating (so we say) from an object, person, or situation.[46]

The world of the Micmac was thus filled with superhuman forces and beings (such as dwarfs, giants, and magicians), and animals that could talk to man and had spirits akin to his own, and the magic of mystical and medicinal herbs – a world where even inanimate objects possessed spirits.[47] Micmac subsistence activities were inextricably bound up within this spiritual matrix, which, we are suggesting, acted as a kind of control mechanism on Micmac land-use, maintaining the environment within an optimum range of conditions.

In order to understand the role of the Micmac in the fur trading enterprise of the colonial period, it is useful to investigate the role of the Micmac hunter in the spiritual world of pre-contact times. Hunting was governed by spiritual rules and considerations which were manifest to the early French observers in the form of seemingly innumerable taboos. These taboos connoted a sense of cautious reverence for a conscious fellow-member of the same ecosystem who, in the view of the Indian, allowed itself to be taken for food and clothing. The Indian felt that "both he and his victim understood the roles which they played in the hunt; the animal was resigned to its fate."[48]

That such a resignation on the part of the game was not to be interpreted as an unlimited licence to kill should be evident from an examination of some of the more prominent taboos. Beaver, for example, were greatly admired by the Micmac for their industry and "abounding genius"; for them, the beaver had "sense" and formed a "separate nation."[49] Hence there were various regulations associated with the disposal of their remains: trapped beaver were drawn in public and made into soup, extreme care being taken to prevent the soup from spilling into the fire; beaver bones were carefully preserved, never being given to the dogs – lest they lose their sense of smell for the animal – or thrown into the fire – lest misfortune come upon "all the nation" – or thrown into rivers – "because the Indians fear lest the spirit of the bones . . . would promptly carry the news to the other beavers, which would desert the country in order to escape the same misfortune." Likewise, menstruating women were forbidden to eat beaver, "for the Indians are convinced, they say, that the beaver, which has sense, would no longer allow itself to be taken by the Indians if it had been eaten by their unclean daughters." The fetus of the beaver, as well as that of the bear, moose, otter, and porcupine, was reserved for the old men, since it was believed that a youth who ate such food would experience intense foot pains while hunting.[50]

Taboos similarly governed the disposal of the remains of the moose – what few there were. The bones of a moose fawn (and of the marten) were never given to the dogs nor were they burned, "for they [the Micmac] would not be able any longer to capture any of these animals in hunting if the spirits of the martens and of the fawns of the moose were to inform their own kind of the bad treatment they had received among the Indians."[51] Fear of such reprisal also prohibited menstruating women from drinking out of the common kettles or bark dishes.[52] Such regulations imply cautious respect for the animal hunted. The moose not only provided food and clothing, but was firmly tied up with the Micmac spirit-world – as were the other game animals.

Bear ceremonialism was also practised by the Micmac. Esteem for the bear is in fact common among boreal hunting peoples of northern Eurasia and North America, and has the following characteristics: the beast is typically hunted in the early spring, while still in hibernation; it is addressed, when either dead or alive, with honorific names; a conciliatory speech is made to the animal, either before or after killing it, by which the hunter apologizes for his act and perhaps explains why it is necessary; and the carcass is respectfully treated, those parts not used (especially the skull) being ceremonially disposed of and the flesh consumed in accordance with taboos. Such rituals are intended to propitiate the spiritual controller of the bears so that he will continue to furnish game to the hunter.[53] Among the Micmac the bear's heart was not eaten by young men lest they get out of breath while travelling and lose courage in danger. The bear carcass could be brought into the wigwam only through a special door made specifically for that purpose, either in the left or right side of the structure. This ritual was based on the Micmac belief that their women did not "deserve" to enter the wigwam through the same door as the animal. In fact, we are told that childless women actually left the wigwam at the approach of the body and did not return until it had been entirely consumed.[54] By means of such rituals the hunter satisfied the soul-spirit of the slain animal. Of the present-day Mistassini (Montagnais) hunter, Speck writes that "should he fail to observe these formalities an unfavourable reaction would also ensue with his own soul-spirit, his 'great-man' . . . as it is called. In such a case the 'great man' would fail to advise him when and where he would find his game. Incidentally the hunter resorts to drinking bear's grease to nourish his 'great man.' "[55] Perhaps it was for a similar reason that the Micmac customarily forced newborn infants to swallow bear or seal oil before eating anything else.[56]

If taboo was associated with fishing, we have little record of it; the only explicit evidence is a prohibition against the roasting of eels, which, if violated, would prevent the Indians from catching others. From this and from the fact that the Restigouche division of the Micmac wore the figure of a salmon as a totem around their neck, we may surmise that fish, too, shared in the sacred and symbolic world of the Indian.[57]

Control over these supernatural forces and communication with them were the principal functions of the shaman, who served in Micmac society as an intermediary between the spirit realm and the physical. The lives and destinies of the natives were profoundly affected by the ability of the shaman to supplicate, cajole, and otherwise manipulate the magical beings and powers. The seventeenth-century French, who typically labelled the shamans (or *buowin*) frauds and jugglers in league with the devil, were repeatedly amazed at the respect accorded them by the natives.[58] By working himself into a dreamlike state, the shaman would invoke the manitou of his animal helper and so predict future events.[59] He also healed by means of conjuring. The Micmac availed themselves of a rather large pharmacopoeia of roots and herbs and other plant parts, but when these failed they would summon the healing arts of the most noted shaman in the district. The illness was often diagnosed by the *buowin* as a failure on the patient's part to perform a prescribed ritual; hence an offended supernatural power had visited the offender with sickness. At such times the shaman functioned as a psychotherapist, diagnosing the illness and symbolically (at least) removing its immediate cause from the patient's body.[60]

It is important to understand that an ecosystem is holocoenotic in nature: there are no "walls" between the components of the system, for "the ecosystem reacts as a whole."[61] Such was the case in the Micmac ecosystem of pre-contact times, where the spiritual served as a link connecting man with all the various subsystems of the environment. Largely through the mediation of the shaman, these spiritual obligations and restrictions acted as a kind of control device to maintain the ecosystem in a well-balanced condition.[62] Under these circumstances the exploitation of game for subsistence appears to have been regulated by the hunter's respect for the continued welfare of his prey – both living and dead – as is evident from the numerous taboos associated with the proper disposal of animal remains. Violation of taboo desecrated the remains of the slain animal and offended its soul-spirit. The offended spirit would then retaliate in either of several ways, depending on the nature of the broken taboo: it could render the guilty hunter's (or the entire band's) means of hunting ineffective, or it could encourage its living fellows to remove themselves from the vicinity. In both cases the end result was the same – the hunt was rendered unsuccessful – and in both it was mediated by the same power – the spirit of the slain animal. Either of these catastrophes could usually be reversed through the magical arts of the shaman. In the Micmac cosmology, the overkill of wildlife would have been resented by the animal kingdom as an act comparable to genocide and would have been resisted by means of the sanctions outlined above. The threat of retaliation thus had the effect of placing an upper limit on the number of animals slain, while the practical result was the conservation of wildlife.

The injection of European civilization into this balanced system initiated a series of chain reactions which, within a little over a century, resulted in the replacement of the aboriginal ecosystem by another. From at least the beginning of the sixteenth century, and perhaps well before that date, fishing fleets from England, France, and Portugal visited the Grand Banks off Newfoundland every spring for the cod and hunted whale and walrus in the Gulf of St. Lawrence.[63] Year after year, while other, more flamboyant men were advancing the geopolitical ambitions of their emerging dynastic states as they searched for precious minerals or a passage to the Orient, these unassuming fishermen visited Canada's East Coast and made the first effective European contact with the Indians there. For the natives' furs they bartered knives, beads, brass kettles, assorted ship fittings, and the like,[64] thus initiating the subversion and replacement of Micmac material culture by European technology. Far more important, the fishermen unwittingly infected the Indians with European diseases, against which the natives had no immunity. Commenting on what may be called the microbial phase of European conquest, John Witthoft has written:

> All of the microscopic parasites of humans, which had been collected together from all parts of the known world into Europe, were brought to these [American] shores, and new diseases stalked faster than man could walk into the interior of the continent. Typhoid, diphtheria, colds, influenza,

measles, chicken pox, whooping cough, tuberculosis, yellow fever, scarlet fever, and other strep infections, gonorrhea, pox (syphilis), and smallpox were diseases that had never been in the New World before. They were new among populations which had no immunity to them. . . . Great epidemics and pandemics of these diseases are believed to have destroyed whole communities, depopulated whole regions, and vastly decreased the native population everywhere in the yet unexplored interior of the continent. The early pandemics are believed to have run their course prior to 1600 A.D.[65]

Disease did more than decimate the native population; it effectively prepared the way for subsequent phases of European contact by breaking native morale and, perhaps even more significantly, by cracking their spiritual edifice. It is reasonable to suggest that European disease rendered the Indian's (particularly the shaman's) ability to control and otherwise influence the supernatural realm dysfunctional – because his magic and other traditional cures were now ineffective – thereby causing the Indian to apostatize (in effect), which in turn subverted the "retaliation" principle of taboo and opened the way to a corruption of the Indian/land relationship under the influence of the fur trade.

Much of this microbial phase was of course protohistoric, although it continued well into and no doubt beyond the seventeenth century – the time period covered by the earliest French sources. Although tradition has limitations in conveying historical fact, it may nevertheless be instructive to examine a myth concerning the Cross-bearing Micmac of the Miramichi River which, as recorded by Father Chrestien Le Clercq, seems to illustrate the demoralizing effect of disease. According to tradition, there was once a time when these Indians were gravely threatened by a severe sickness; as was their custom, they looked to the sun for help. In their extreme need a "beautiful" man, holding a cross, appeared before several of them in a dream. He instructed them to make similar crosses, for, as he told them, in this symbol lay their protection. For a time thereafter these Indians, who believed in dreams "even to the extent of superstition," were very religious and devoted in their veneration of this symbol. Later, however, they apostatized:

Since the Gaspesian [Micmac] nation of the Cross-bearers has been almost wholly destroyed, as much by the war which they have waged with the Iroquois as by the maladies which have infected this land, and which, in three or four visitations, have caused the deaths of a very great number, these Indians have gradually relapsed from this first devotion of their ancestors. So true is it, that even the holiest and most religious practices, by a certain fatality attending human affairs, suffer always much alteration if they are not animated and conserved by the same spirit which gave them birth. In brief, when I went into their country to commence my mission, I found some persons who had preserved only the shadow of the customs of their ancestors.[66]

Their rituals had failed to save these Indians when threatened by European diseases and intergroup hostilities; hence their old religious practices were abandoned, no doubt because of their ineffectiveness.

Several other observers also commented on the new diseases that afflicted the Micmac. In pre-contact times, declared Denys, "they were not subject to diseases, and knew nothing of fevers."[67] By about 1700, however, Dièreville noted that the Micmac population was in sharp decline.[68] The Indians themselves frequently complained to Father Biard and other Frenchmen that, since contact with the French, they had been dying off in great numbers. "For they assert that, before this association and intercourse [with the French], all their countries were very populous, and they tell how one by one the different coasts, according as they have begun to traffic with us, have been more reduced by disease." The Indians accused the French of trying to poison them or charged that the food supplied by the French was somehow adulterated. Whatever the reasons for the catastrophe, warned Biard, the Indians were very angry about it and "upon the point of breaking with us, and making war upon us."[69]

To the Jesuit fathers, the solution to this sorry state of affairs lay in the civilizing power of the Gospel. To Biard, his mission was clear:

> For, if our Souriquois [Micmac] are few, they may become numerous; if they are savages, it is to domesticate and civilize them that we have come here; if they are rude, that is no reason that we should be idle; if they have until now profited little, it is no wonder, for it would be too much to expect fruit from this grafting, and to demand reason and maturity from a child.

In conclusion, we hope in time to make them susceptible of receiving the doctrines of the faith and of the christian and catholic religion, and later, to penetrate further into the regions beyond.[70]

The message was simple and straightforward: the black-robes would enlighten the Indians by ridiculing their animism and related taboos, discrediting their shamans, and urging them to accept the Christian gospel. But to their chagrin the Indians proved stubborn in their ancient ways, no matter how unsuited to changing circumstances.[71]

Since the advent of European diseases and the consequent disillusionment with native spiritual beliefs and customs, some Indians appear to have repudiated their traditional world view altogether, while others clung desperately to what had become a moribund body of ritual. We would suppose that the Christian message was more readily accepted by the former, while the latter group, which included the shamans and those too old to change, would have fought bitterly against the missionary teachings.[72] But they resisted in vain for, with time, old people died and shamans whose magic was less potent than that of the missionaries were discredited.[73] The missionary was successful only to the degree that his power exceeded that of the shaman. The non-literate Indian, for example, was awed by the magic of handwriting as a means of communication.[74] Even more significant was the fact that Christianity was the religion of the white man, who, with his superior technology and greater success at manipulating life to his advantage, was believed to have recourse to a greater power (manitou) than did the Indian. Material goods, such as the trading articles offered the Indians by the French, were believed by the native to have a spirit within, in accord with their belief that all animate and inanimate objects housed such a spirit or power.[75] Furthermore, there were degrees of power in such objects, which were determined and calibrated in the Indian mind by the degree of functionalism associated with a particular object.[76] For example, the Micmac believed that there was a spirit of his canoe, of his snowshoes, of his bow, and so on. It was for this reason that a man's material goods were either buried with him or burned, so that their spirits would accompany his to the spirit world, where he would have need of them. Just as he had hunted game in this physical world, so his spirit would again hunt the game spirits with the spirits of his weapons in the land of the dead.[77] Denys described an incident which emphasized the fact that even European trading goods had spirits, when he related how the brass kettle was known to have lost its spirit (or died) when it no longer rang when tapped.[78] Thus Christianity, which to the Indians was the ritual harnessing all of this power, was a potent force among them. Nevertheless, the priests who worked among the Indians frequently complained of their relapsing into paganism, largely because the Micmac came to associate Christianity and civilization in general with their numerous misfortunes, together with the fact that they never clearly understood the Christian message anyway, but always saw it in terms of their own cosmology.[79]

As all religious systems reflect their cultural milieux, so did seventeenth-century Christianity. Polygamy was condemned by the French missionaries as immoral, the consultation of shamans was discouraged, the custom of interring material goods was criticized, eat-all feasts were denounced as gluttonous and short-sighted, and the Indians were disabused of many of their so-called superstitions (taboos).[80] The priests attacked the Micmac culture with a marvelous fervour and some success.[81] Although they could not have appreciated it, they were aided in this endeavour by an obsolescent system of taboo and spiritual awareness; Christianity merely delivered the coup de grâce.

The result of this Christian onslaught on a decaying Micmac cosmology was, of course, the despiritualization of the material world. Commenting on the process of despiritualization, Denys (who was a spectator to this transformation in the mid-seventeenth century) remarked that it was accomplished with "much difficulty"; for some of the Indians it was achieved by religious means, while others were influenced by the French customs, but nearly all were affected "by the need for the things which come from us, the use of which has become to them an indispensable necessity. They have abandoned all their own utensils, whether because of the trouble they had as well to make as to use them, or because the facility of obtaining from us, in exchange for skins which cost them almost nothing, the things which seemed to them invaluable, not so much for their novelty as for the convenience they derived therefrom."[82]

In the early years of the fur trade, before the establishment of permanent posts among the natives, trading was done with the coast-wise fishermen from May to early fall.[83] In return for skins of beaver, otter, marten, moose, and other furbearers, the Indians received a variety of fairly cheap commodities, principally tobacco, liquor, powder and shot (in later years), biscuit, peas, beans, flour, assorted clothing, wampum, kettles, and hunting tools.[84] The success of this trade in economic terms must be attributed to pressure exerted on a relatively simple society by a complex civilization and, perhaps even more importantly, by the tremendous pull of this simple social organization on the resources of Europe.[85] To the Micmac, who like other Indians measured the worth of a tool or object by the ease of its construction and use, the technology of Europe became indispensable. But as has already been shown, this was not simply an economic issue for the Indian; the Indian was more than just "economically seduced" by the European's trading goods.[86] One must also consider the metaphysical implications of Indian acceptance of the European material culture.

European technology of the sixteenth and seventeenth centuries was largely incompatible with the spiritual beliefs of the eastern woodland Indians, despite the observation made above that the Micmacs readily invested trading goods with spiritual power akin to that possessed by their own implements. As Denys pointed out, the trade goods which the Micmac so eagerly accepted were accompanied by Christian religious teachings and French custom, both of which gave definition to these alien objects. In accepting the European material culture, the natives were impelled to accept the European abstract culture, especially religion, and so, in effect, their own spiritual beliefs were subverted as they abandoned their implements for those of the white man. Native religion lost not only its practical effectiveness, in part owing to the replacement of the traditional magical and animistic view of nature by the exploitive European view, but it was no longer necessary as a source of definition and theoretical support for the new Europe-derived material culture. Western technology made more "sense" if it was accompanied by Western religion.

Under these circumstances in the early contact period, the Micmac's role within his ecosystem changed radically. No longer was he the sensitive fellow-member of a symbolic world; under pressure from disease, European trade, and Christianity, he had apostatized – he had repudiated his role within the ecosystem. Former attitudes were replaced by a kind of mongrel outlook which combined some native traditions and beliefs with a European rationale and motivation. Our concern here is less to document this transformation than to assess its impact on the

Indian/land relationship. In these terms, then, what effect did the trade have on the Micmac ecosystem?

The most obvious change was the unrestrained slaughter of certain game. Lured by European commodities, equipped with European technology, urged by European traders,[87] deprived of a sense of responsibility and accountability for the land, and no longer inhibited by taboo, the Micmac began to overkill systematically those very wildlife which had now become so profitable and even indispensable to his new way of life. The pathos of this transformation of attitude and behaviour is illustrated by an incident recorded by Le Clercq. The Indians, who still believed that the beaver had "sense" and formed a "separate nation," maintained that they "would cease to make war upon these animals if these would speak, howsoever little, in order that they might learn whether the Beavers are among their friends or their enemies."[88] Unfortunately for the beaver, they never communicated their friendliness. The natural world of the Indian was becoming inarticulate.

It is interesting to note that Dièreville, who observed the Micmac culture at the beginning of the eighteenth century, was the only witness to record the native superstition which compelled them to tear out the eyes of all slain animals. Somehow, perhaps by some sort of symbolic transference, the spirits of surviving animals of the same species were thereby blinded to the irreverent treatment accorded the victim; otherwise, through the mediation of the outraged spirits, the living would no longer have allowed themselves to be taken by the Indians.[89] The failure of the earlier writers to mention this particular superstition suggests that it was of fairly recent origin, a result of the overexploitation of game for the trade. To the Micmac mind, haunted by memories of a former time, the practice may have been intended to hide his guilt and ensure his continued success.

Together with this depletion of wildlife went a reduction of dependency on the resources of the local ecosystem. The use of improved hunting equipment, such as fishing line and hooks, axes, knives, muskets, and iron-tipped arrows, spears, and harpoons,[90] exerted heavier pressure on the resources of the area, while the availability of French foodstuffs shifted the position of the Micmac in the trophic system, somewhat reducing his dependency on local food sources as it placed him partly outside of the system. To be sure, a decreasing native population relieved this pressure to a degree, but, according to evidence cited above, not enough to prevent the abuse of the land.

Other less obvious results of the fur trade were the increased incidence of feuding and the modification of the Micmac settlement patterns to meet the demands of the trade. Liquor, in particular brandy, was a favorite item of the trade – one for which the Indians "would go a long way."[91] Its effects were devastating. Both Jean Saint-Vallier (François Laval's successor as bishop of Quebec) and Biard blamed liquor as a cause for the increased death rate of the natives. Moreover, it was observed that drunkenness resulted in social disintegration as the Indians became debauched and violent among themselves, and, at times, spilled over into the French community which they would rob, ravage, and burn. Drunkenness also provided a legitimate excuse to commit crimes, such as murdering their enemies, for which they would otherwise be held accountable.[92]

European contact should thus be viewed as a trigger factor, that is, something which was not present in the Micmac ecosystem before and which initiated a concatenation of reactions leading to the replacement of the aboriginal ecosystem by another.[93] European disease, Christianity, and the fur trade with its accompanying technology – the three often intermeshed – were responsible for the corruption of the Indian/land relationship, in which the native had merged sympathetically with his environment. By a lockstep process European disease rendered the Indian's control over the supernatural and spiritual realm inoperative, and the disillusioned Micmac apostatized, debilitating taboo and preparing the way for the destruction of wildlife which was soon to occur under the stimulation of the fur trade. For those who believed in it, Christianity furnished a new, dualistic world view, which placed man above nature, as well as spiritual support for the fur trade, and as a result the Micmac became dependent on the European marketplace both spiritually and economically. Within his ecosystem the Indian changed from conservator to exploiter. All of this resulted in the intense exploitation of some game animals and the virtual extermination of others. Unfortunately for the Indian and the land, this grim tale was to be repeated many times along the moving Indian-white frontier. Life for the Micmac had indeed become more convenient, but convenience cost dearly in much material and abstract culture loss or modification.

The historiography of Indian-white relations is rendered more comprehensible when the Indian and the land are considered together: "So intimately is all of Indian life tied up with the land and its utilization that, to think of Indians is to think of land. The two are inseparable."[94] American Indian history can be seen, then, as a type of environmental history, and perhaps it is from this perspective that the early period of Indian-white relations can best be understood.

NOTES

1. Reuben G. Thwaites, ed., *The Jesuit Relations and Allied Documents: Travels and Explorations of the Jesuit Missionaries in New France, 1610-1791* (New York, 1959 [orig. pub. Cleveland, 1896-1901]), VIII, 57.
2. Baron Lahontan, *New Voyages to North America . . . An Account of the Several Nations of that vast Continent . . .*, ed. Reuben G. Thwaites (Chicago, 1905), I, 82.
3. Thwaites, ed., *Jesuit Relations*, V, 25; VI, 297-9; VIII, 57; XL, 151; LXVIII, 47, 109-11; LXIX, 95, 99-113.
4. *Ibid.*, VIII, 41.
5. Nicolas Denys, *The Description and Natural History of the Coasts of North America (Acadia)*, ed. and trans. William F. Ganong, 2 vols. (Toronto, 1908), I, 187, 199, 209, 219-20.
6. *Ibid.*, 432, 450.
7. Peter Farb, *Man's Rise to Civilization as Shown by the Indians of North America from Primeval Times to the Coming of the Industrial State* (New York, 1968), 82-3.
8. See Wilson D. Wallis and Ruth Sawtell Wallis, *The Micmac Indians of Eastern Canada* (Minneapolis, 1955), for a thorough ethnographic study of the Micmac. Jacques and Maryvonne Crevel, *Honguedo ou l'Histoire des Premiers Gaspesiens* (Québec, 1970), give a fairly good general history of the Micmac during the seventeenth century, together with a description of the fishing industry.
9. Julian H. Steward, "The Concept and Method of Cultural Ecology," in his *Theory of Culture Change: The Methodology of Multilinear Evolution* (Urbana, Ill., 1955), 30-42; Andrew P. Vayda and Roy A. Rappaport, "Ecology, Cultural and Non-cultural," in James A. Clifton, ed., *Introduction to Cultural Anthropology: Essays in the Scope and Methods of the Science of Man* (Boston, 1968), 494.
10. W.D. Billings, *Plants, Man, and the Ecosystem*, 2nd ed. (Belmont, Calif., 1970), 4.

11. Roy A. Rappaport, *Pigs for the Ancestors: Ritual in the Ecology of a New Guinea People* (New Haven, 1968).
12. Among the few who have are William Christie MacLeod, "Conservation Among Primitive Hunting Peoples," *Scientific Monthly*, XLIII (1936), 562-6; and Alfred Goldsworthy Bailey in his little-known book, *The Conflict of European and Eastern Algonkian Cultures, 1504-1700*, 2nd ed. (Toronto, 1969).
13. Wilbur R. Jacobs, *Dispossessing the American Indian: Indians and Whites on the Colonial Frontier* (New York, 1972), 25.
14. Billings, *Plants, Man, and the Ecosystem*, 37-8.
15. Sieur de Dièreville, *Relation of the Voyage to Port Royal in Acadia or New France*, trans. Mrs. Clarence Webster, ed. John Clarence Webster (Toronto, 1933), 184. According to the editor (p. 216), the Malecites later replaced the Micmacs living along the St. John, the latter withdrawing to Nova Scotia. See also Diamond Jenness, *The Indians of Canada*, 3rd ed. (Ottawa, 1955), 267.
16. See Rappaport, *Pigs for the Ancestors*, 225-6. If the present essay were intended as a more rigorous analysis of the Micmac ecosystem, we would report on the topography of this region, on the soil types, the hydrological characteristics, the climate, the influence of the ocean, and the effects of fires caused by lightning. But since neither the Micmac nor the first Europeans had any appreciable effect on these physical variables – except perhaps that of water relations – we shall pass over the physical environment and go on to the biological. Suffice it to say that the water of numerous rivers and streams was regulated in its flow by beaver dams throughout much of this region, and Indian beaver hunting and trapping certainly upset this control.
17. For a thorough discussion of Micmac plant and animal use, see Frank G. Speck and Ralph W. Dexter, "Utilization of Animals and Plants by the Micmac Indians of New Brunswick," *Journal of the Washington Academy of Sciences*, XLI (1951), 250-9.
18. Father Chrestien Le Clercq, *New Relation of Gaspesia, with the Customs and Religion of the Gaspesian Indians*, ed. and trans. William F. Ganong (Toronto, 1910), 212-13. Thwaites, ed., *Jesuit Relations*, III, 77; Marc Lescarbot, *The History of New France*, trans. W.L. Grant (Toronto, 1907), III, 93, 194-5. Lescarbot (pp. 252-3) asserts that the Micmac definitely grew tobacco, most likely the so-called wild tobacco (*Nicotiana rustica*).
19. Lescarbot, *History of New France*, II, 323-5; III, 158.
20. Thwaites, ed., *Jesuit Relations*, III, 77-83.
21. *Ibid.*; Denys, *Description of North America*, II, 403; Lescarbot, *History of New France*, III, 80; Le Clercq, *Relation of Gaspesia*, 88-9, 93; Dièreville, *Voyage to Port Royal*, 146.
22. Lescarbot, *History of New France*, III, 219-20; Thwaites, ed., *Jesuit Relations*, III, 77-9.

23. Lescarbot, *History of New France*, III, 222-4. See Horace T. Martin, *Castorologia, or the History and Traditions of the Canadian Beaver* (Montreal, 1892), for a good treatise on the beaver.
24. Le Clercq, *Relation of Gaspesia*, 276-80; Dièreville, *Voyage to Port Royal*, 133-4; Denys, *Description of North America*, II, 429-33; Lescarbot, *History of New France*, III, 222-4.
25. Lescarbot, *History of New France*, III, 220-2; Denys, *Description of North America*, II, 426-9; Le Clercq, *Relation of Gaspesia*, 274-6. Speck and Dexter place caribou before moose in order of importance, but they cite no evidence for such ranking. Speck and Dexter, "Utilization of Animals and Plants," 255.
26. Le Clercq, *Relation of Gaspesia*, 118-19.
27. *Ibid.*, 93-4; Denys, *Description of North America*, II, 412; Lescarbot, *History of New France*, III, 133; Speck and Dexter, "Utilization of Animals and Plants," 255.
28. Speck and Dexter, "Utilization of Animals and Plants," 255.
29. Le Clercq, *Relation of Gaspesia*, 116, 119; Dièreville, *Voyage to Port Royal*, 131; Thwaites, ed., *Jesuit Relations*, III, 107-9.
30. Denys, *Description of North America*, II, 433-4.
31. Thwaites, ed., *Jesuit Relations*, III, 79.
32. *Ibid.*, 81; Speck and Dexter, "Utilization of Animals and Plants," 251-4.
33. Lescarbot, *History of New France*, III, 236-7; Denys, *Description of North America*, II, 436-7.
34. Le Clercq, *Relation of Gaspesia*, 92, 137; Lescarbot, *History of New France*, III, 230-1; Denys, *Description of North America*, II, 435-6.
35. Thwaites, ed., *Jesuit Relations*, III, 83.
36. *Ibid.*
37. Le Clercq, *Relation of Gaspesia*, 109-10, 283; Denys, *Description of North America*, II, 389, 434.
38. Frank G. Speck, "Aboriginal Conservators," *Audubon Magazine*, XL (1938), 260.
39. Denys, *Description of North America*, II, 402-3.
40. *Ibid.*, 426.
41. Speck, "Aboriginal Conservators," 260. Italics in original.
42. Rappaport, *Pigs for the Ancestors*, 237-8; Vayda and Rappaport, "Ecology, Cultural and Noncultural," 491.
43. See, for example, the writings of Speck, especially "Aboriginal Conservators," 258-61; John Witthoft, "The American Indian as Hunter," *Pennsylvania Game News*, XXIX (February-April, 1953); George S. Snyderman, "Concepts of Land Ownership among the Iroquois and their Neighbors," *Bureau of American Ethnology Bulletin 149*, ed. William N. Fenton (Washington, D.C., 1951), 15-34; Robert F. Heizer, "Primitive Man as an Ecological Factor," *Kroeber Anthropological Society, Papers*,

XIII (1955), 1-31. See also William A. Ritchie, "The Indian and His Environment," *Conservationist* (December-January, 1955-56), 23-7; Gordon Day, "The Indian as an Ecological Factor in the Northeastern Forest," *Ecology*, XXIV (1953), 329-46; MacLeod, "Conservation Among Primitive Hunting Peoples," 562-6.

44. Witthoft, "American Indian as Hunter," 17.

45. Murray Wax, "Religion and Magic," in Clifton, ed., *Cultural Anthropology*, 235.

46. See William Jones, "The Algonkin Manitou," *Journal of American Folklore*, XVIII (1905), 183-90; Frederick Johnson, "Notes on Micmac Shamanism," *Primitive Man*, XVI (1943), 58-9.

47. See Stansbury Hagar, "Micmac Magic and Medicine," *Journal of American Folklore*, IX (1896), 170-7; Johnson, "Shamanism," 54, 56-7. Both Hagar and Johnson report that such beliefs in the supernatural and spiritual survive even in modern times, although in suppressed and attenuated form. Le Clercq, *Relation of Gaspesia*, 187, 209, 212-14; Denys, *Description of North America*, II, 117, 442.

48. Witthoft, "American Indian as Hunter," 16.

49. Dièreville, *Voyage to Port Royal*, 139; Le Clercq, *Relation of Gaspesia*, 225-9, 276-7.

50. Le Clercq, *Relation of Gaspesia*, 225-9.

51. *Ibid.*, 226.

52. *Ibid.*, 227-9.

53. Witthoft, "American Indian as Hunter," 16-22; A. Irving Hallowell, "Bear Ceremonialism in the Northern Hemisphere," *American Anthropologist*, XXVIII (1926), 1-175.

54. Le Clercq, *Relation of Gaspesia*, 227.

55. Frank G. Speck, "Mistassini Hunting Territories in the Labrador Peninsula," *American Anthropologist*, XXV (1923), 464. Johnson, "Shamanism," 70-2, distinguishes between the Montagnais, Wabanaki, and Micmac ideas of the "soul."

56. Le Clercq, *Relation of Gaspesia*, 88-9; Dièreville, *Voyage to Port Royal*, 146; Lescarbot, *History of New France*, III, 80.

57. Denys, *Description of North America*, II, 430, 442; Le Clercq, *Relation of Gaspesia*, 192-3.

58. Denys, *Description of North America*, II, 417-18; Le Clercq, *Relation of Gaspesia*, 215-18.

59. Thwaites, ed., *Jesuit Relations* II, 75; Le Clercq, *Relation of Gaspesia*, 215-16; George H. Daugherty, Jr., "Reflections of Environment in North American Indian Literature" (Ph.D. thesis, University of Chicago, 1925), 31; Johnson, "Shamanism," 71-2.

60. Le Clercq, *Relation of Gaspesia*, 215-18, 296-9; Denys, *Description of North America*, II, 415, 417-18; Hagar, "Micmac Magic,"

170-7. Denys (p. 418) observed that most of these ailments were (what we would call today) psychosomatic in origin.

61. Billings, *Plants, Man, and the Ecosystem*, 36.

62. Thwaites, ed., *Jesuit Relations*, II, 75.

63. H.P. Biggar, *The Early Trading Companies of New France: A Contribution to the History of Commerce and Discovery in North America* (New York, 1965 [orig. pub. Toronto, 1901]), 18-37.

64. John Witthoft, "Archaeology as a Key to the Colonial Fur Trade," *Minnesota History*, XL (1966), 204-5.

65. John Witthoft, *Indian Prehistory of Pennsylvania* (Harrisburg, Pa., 1965), 26-9.

66. Le Clercq, *Relation of Gaspesia*, 146-52. The Récollet fathers, especially Father Emanuel Jumeau, were able to cause a renaissance of the old traditional religion by encouraging these people to look to the cross once more for their salvation, although, of course, this time it was the Christian cross. We should bear in mind that the cross was an art motif common among non-Christian people, and of independent origin from that of the Christian cross. Whether the cross mentioned in this particular tradition was of Christian or aboriginal origin should make little difference, for the story still serves to illustrate the process of apostatization.

67. Denys, *Description of North America*, II, 415. Estimates of the aboriginal population of North America at the time of European contact are constantly being revised upward. Henry F. Dobyns, "Estimating Aboriginal American Population: An Appraisal of Techniques with a New Hemispheric Estimate," *Current Anthropology*, VII (1966), 395-416, has placed the figure at a controversial and fantastically high total of 9,800,000 natives.

68. Dièreville, *Voyage to Port Royal*, 116. See Thwaites, ed., *Jesuit Relations*, I, 177-9.

69. Thwaites, ed., *Jesuit Relations*, III, 105-7.

70. *Ibid.*, I, 183.

71. *Ibid.*, II, 75-7; III, 123; Le Clercq, *Relation of Gaspesia*, 103, 220, 224-5, 227, 239, 253. See also Denys, *Description of North America*, II, 117, 439, 442.

72. Notice that when a custom in any society becomes a mere formality and loses its practical meaning, it is easily discarded when challenged by detractors, who may or may not replace it with something more meaningful. See Le Clercq, *Relation of Gaspesia*, 206, 227; Lescarbot, *History of New France*, III, 94-5.

73. Jean Baptiste de la Croix Chevrières de Saint-Vallier, *Estat Présent de l'Eglise et de la Colonie Françoise dans la Nouvelle France, par M. l'Evéque de Québec* (Paris, 1688), 36-7; Thwaites, ed., *Jesuit Relations*, II, 75-7. See Le Clercq, *Relation of Gaspesia*, 220-1, where he speaks of converting a noted shaman to Christianity. Andre Vachon, "L'Eau-de-Vie dans la Société Indienne," Cana-

dian Historical Association, *Report of the Annual Meeting* (1960), 22-32, has observed that the priest replaced the shaman and sorcerer in Indian society by virtue of his superior powers. By discrediting his Indian counterparts (and rivals), the priest became the shaman-sorcerer (i.e., a source of both good and evil power).

74. Lescarbot, *History of New France*, III, 128; Le Clercq, *Relation of Gaspesia*, 133-5.
75. Le Clercq, *Relation of Gaspesia*, 209, 213-14; Bailey, *Conflict of Cultures*, 47.
76. Denys, *Description of North America*, II, 439.
77. Le Clercq, *Relation of Gaspesia*, 187, 209, 212-14, 238-9, 303; Lescarbot, *History of New France*, III, 279, 285; Thwaites, ed., *Jesuit Relations*, I, 169; Denys, *Description of North America*, II, 437-9; Dièreville, *Voyage to Port Royal*, 161.
78. Denys, *Description of North America*, II, 439-41.
79. Le Clercq, *Relation of Gaspesia*, 125, 193; Thwaites, ed., *Jesuit Relations*, I, 165. See *ibid.*, II, 89, where baptism was understood by the Micmac (of Port Royal, at least) "as a sort of sacred pledge of friendship and alliance with the French."
80. Lescarbot, *History of New France*, III, 53-4; Denys, *Description of North America*, II, 117, 430, 442; Le Clercq, *Relation of Gaspesia*, 116; Dièreville, *Voyage to Port Royal*, 161; Thwaites, ed., *Jesuit Relations*, III, 131-5. See *ibid.*, II, 75-7, where the shamans complain of having lost much of their power since the coming of the French.
81. Le Clercq observed that since the introduction of Christianity and especially baptism the manitou had not afflicted them to the degree that he did formerly. See Le Clercq, *Relation of Gaspesia*, 225. See also *ibid.*, 229-33, where cases are recorded of native men and women who seemed to feel a divine call and ordination, representing themselves as priests among their fellows.
82. Denys, *Description of North America*, II, 440-1.
83. Samuel de Champlain, *The Voyages of Sieur de Champlain of Saintonge . . .*, in H.P. Biggar, ed. and trans., *The Works of Samuel de Champlain*, I (Toronto, 1922), *passim*; Thwaites, ed., *Jesuit Relations*, III, 81.
84. Lescarbot, *History of New France*, II, 281-2, 323-4; III, 158, 168, 250; Thwaites, ed., *Jesuit Relations*, III, 75-7; Le Clercq, *Relation of Gaspesia*, 93-4, 109; Dièreville, *Voyage to Port Royal*, 132-3, 139-41.
85. Harold A. Innis, *The Fur Trade in Canada: An Introduction to Canadian Economic History*, rev. ed. (Toronto, 1956), 15-17.
86. Farb, *Man's Rise to Civilization*, 82-3.
87. See Thwaites, ed., *Jesuit Relations*, I, 175-7, and Denys, *Description of North America*, II, 439, for mention of the French lust for furs.

88. Le Clercq, *Relation of Gaspesia*, 276-7. See also Dièreville, *Voyage to Port Royal*, 139.
89. Dièreville, *Voyage to Port Royal*, 161.
90. Lescarbot, *History of New France*, III, 191-2; Denys, *Description of North America*, II, 399, 442-3.
91. Dièreville, *Voyage to Port Royal*, 174; Denys, *Description of North America*, II, 172, 443-52. If we are to believe Craig Mac-Andrew and Robert B. Edgerton, *Drunken Comportment: A Social Explanation* (Chicago, 1969), 111, the Micmac encountered by Jacques Cartier along the shores of Chaleur Bay in 1534 were the first historically documented North American tribe to receive European liquor.
92. Saint-Vallier, *Estat Présent*, 36-7, 42; Thwaites, ed., *Jesuit Relations*, III, 105-9; Denys, *Description of North America*, II, 443-52; Dièreville, *Voyage to Port Royal*, 166; Le Clercq, *Relation of Gaspesia*, 244-5, 254-7. The subject of North American Indian drinking patterns and problems has been the topic of much debate from the seventeenth century to the present. The best current scholarship on the subject, which has by no means been exhausted, is contained in MacAndrew and Edgerton, *Drunken Comportment*; Vachon, "L'Eau-de-Vie," 22-32; Nancy Oestreich Lurie, "The World's Oldest On-Going Protest Demonstration: North American Indian Drinking Patterns," *Pacific Historical Review*, XL (1971), 311-32.
93. Billings, *Plants, Man, and the Ecosystem*, 37-8.
94. See John Collier's report on Indian affairs, 1938, in the *Annual Report of the Secretary of the Interior* (Washington, D.C., 1938), 209-11, as quoted in Wilcomb Washburn, ed., *The Indian and the White Man* (Garden City, N.Y., 1964), 394.

Readings in Canadian Social History

In print in the series:

Volume 1   Economy and Society During the French Regime, to
           1759
Volume 2   Pre-Industrial Canada, 1760-1849
Volume 3   Canada's Age of Industry, 1849-1896
Volume 4   The Consolidation of Capitalism, 1896-1929

Forthcoming:

Volume 5   Modern Canada, 1930-1980's